G

THE GEORGE GUND FOUNDATION
IMPRINT IN AFRICAN AMERICAN STUDIES

The George Gund Foundation has endowed
this imprint to advance understanding of
the history, culture, and current issues
of African Americans.

The publisher gratefully acknowledges the generous support of the African American Studies Endowment Fund of the University of California Press Foundation, which was established by a major gift from the George Gund Foundation.

Jazz Diasporas

MUSIC OF THE AFRICAN DIASPORA

Guthrie P. Ramsey Jr., Editor
Samuel A. Floyd Jr., Editor Emeritus

Jazz Diasporas

*Race, Music, and Migration in
Post–World War II Paris*

RASHIDA K. BRAGGS

University of California Press

University of California Press, one of the most distinguished university presses in the United States, enriches lives around the world by advancing scholarship in the humanities, social sciences, and natural sciences. Its activities are supported by the UC Press Foundation and by philanthropic contributions from individuals and institutions. For more information, visit www.ucpress.edu.

University of California Press
Oakland, California

Library of Congress Cataloging-in-Publication Data

Braggs, Rashida K., 1976–.
 Jazz diasporas : race, music, and migration in post–World War II Paris / Rashida K. Braggs.
  p. cm.—(Music of the African diaspora ; 18)
 Includes bibliographical references and index.
 ISBN 978-0-520-27934-6 (cloth : alk. paper)
 ISBN 978-0-520-27935-3 (pbk. : alk. paper)
 ISBN 978-0-520-96341-2 (ebook)
 1. Jazz musicians—France—Paris—20th century. 2. African American musicians—France—Paris—20th century. 3. Jazz—France—Paris—History and criticism. 4. African American authors—France—Paris—20th century. 5. Paris (France)—Race relations—20th century. I. Title. II. Title: Race, music, and migration in post–World War II Paris. III. Series: Music of the African diaspora ; 18.
 ML3509.F78P36 2016
 781.65089'96073044361—dc23

                                          2015026558

Manufactured in the United States of America
25 24 23 22 21 20 19 18 17 16
10 9 8 7 6 5 4 3 2 1

In keeping with a commitment to support environmentally responsible and sustainable printing practices, UC Press has printed this book on Natures Natural, a fiber that contains 30% post-consumer waste and meets the minimum requirements of ANSI/NISO z39.48–1992 (R 1997) (Permanence of Paper).

For Mom,
who saw great promise in me
and who passed down the strength to fulfill it

Distinctive as it is, U.S. Negro music, like U.S. Negro life, is, after all, or rather first of all, also inseparable from life in the United States at large. Thus, as an art form it is a direct product of the U.S. Negro sensibility, but it is a by-product, so to speak, of all the cultural elements that brought that sensibility into being in the first place.

ALBERT MURRAY

"Encounter on the Seine" underscores the transatlantic structure of the African American Subject, pointing to the ways in which geographic displacement brings to the fore the meanings and meaninglessness of modernity and its civilizing project.

MICHELLE WRIGHT

Contents

Illustrations

Preface

Jazz Diasporas reforms and expands a concept that I first touched on in my dissertation, when I recognized the influence of French jazz critics and musicians on the development and dissemination of jazz. At the time jazz scholarship had for the most part ignored this topic. Years later, and with the outcropping of books that build on the foundation Jeffrey Jackson set with *Making Jazz French: Music and Modern Life in Interwar Paris,* jazz studies is transnational these days. There is no limit to the places that scholars have located and investigated the music. So I no longer feel the impetus to take on this battle, which has largely been fought and gloriously continues.

Jazz Diasporas has taken a different turn but still remembers its dissertation roots. In those early days I felt the danger of conducting research that would ignore the creation of the music in the United States and fail to recognize the contributions of African Americans. The more that I study, the more a potential erasure of jazz's racialized history threatens. This threat has made me question whether this history need remain attached to the music, which was always already hybrid. For, as jazz scholar Burton Peretti argues, jazz is a creolized music: "Jazz holds special importance as a model of créolized culture among once-colonized 'folk'" (Peretti 94). Jazz has always commingled elements of West African, European, and Caribbean instrumentation, rhythm, and harmony. But the power and identity associated with and achieved through jazz have made an impact on individual and collective, racial and national, and musical and cultural politics. These struggles over identity and power exchange have created tensions over who can claim this music. How did French jazz musicians and critics claim the music, and to what ends? How might African American jazz musicians and jazzophiles gain racial and national belonging through this music?[1] Music cannot really belong to anyone. But jazz critics, musicians, and fans have created narratives of belonging throughout jazz history. In answer to these questions *Jazz Diasporas* illustrates tension between states and narratives of belonging. Even the concept of a jazz diaspora assumes a state of tension between "both" and "and," for jazz is both black and white, both American and global.[2]

Acknowledgments

I have written much of this book in transit or while settling into different locales. As I travel, it has occurred to me that movement not only reflects the subject of this book but also the process of its writing. During the years that I have mulled over and teased out ideas, I have moved to and from many new spaces and ways of thinking. With each move forward I have had a great deal of help. While it would take another book to document it all, there are several people and institutions I will take this opportunity to thank.

First and foremost I thank God and my family. My mother, Dorothy F. Garrison-Wade, held my hand throughout this process and continually encouraged me to believe in myself. Her never-ending support has been my bricks and mortar; furthermore, she has reviewed most of this book without complaint. Everlasting thanks go to my dad Earl S. Braggs for consistently giving me a high standard to reach with his own writings and for always encouraging me not to follow but to carve my own path. Also, I am grateful for my dad Anthony Wade; I have stayed on course with the help of his open arms, always listening regard, and consistently sound advice. My grandparents stood by my side the whole way. They unwittingly spurred me to finish by asking the seemingly harmless question, "So when will I get my copy of the book?" I count friends within my family. A stalwart few held me up against obstacles and challenges in completing this book. Many heartfelt thanks go to Tamara Roberts, Ray Gilstrap, Pamela Throop, Jennifer Vargas, Yveline Alexis, and Pia Kohler for their support, which showed itself in multiple forms from listening and offering encouragement to brainstorming ideas and reading my work.

I could easily envisage a cheerleading tour, wherein I shouted out my gratitude for my series editor Guthrie Ramsey and editor Mary Francis.

Guthrie's enthusiasm for my project and methodology and his in-depth knowledge of music of the African diaspora propelled and helped shape this project in so many large and small ways. Mary's attentiveness, accessibility, and experience provided the perfect guidance for this project. A mere "thanks" for their work seems insufficient. I am also grateful for the feedback from the anonymous external readers; their comments helped expand my thinking and offered tough questions to address that strengthened the book.

My dissertation committee propelled and sustained this book in its infant stages. In academia it is not a given to have an adviser who is an excellent mentor and great advocate, so I have always been thankful for E. Patrick Johnson's patience and guidance—more so for its constancy long after the dissertation. Dwight McBride has presented me with multiple opportunities to grow as a scholar; most apparently, he propelled me down the path to explore more of James Baldwin's oeuvre. I also thank my other dissertation and qualifying exam committee members, Margaret Drewal and Jennifer Brody.

I thank several other scholars for exemplifying the type of scholar I aspire to be. For their profound research contributions, their accessible and engaging articulation of knowledge, and, above all, their constant and continual professional guidance and mentorship, I heartily thank Harry Elam, Trica Keaton, Maurice Wallace, Brent Hayes Edwards, Omi Osun Joni L. Jones, and the senior scholars of the Black Performance Theory group.

Many have helped by offering beneficial feedback on my work and writing process. Several groups stand out in this regard: the Paris Critical Theory Dissertation Writing Group; Jean Jamin and Patrick Williams's "Jazz & Anthropology" class at EHESS in Paris; the IHUM writing group; the HCA PhD colloquium; the ATHE and ASTR book proposal workshops; the ASTR "mobility" working group; the National Center for Faculty Development and Diversity; my Williams College writing roundtable and writing date partners; the Oakley Seminar on "migration" and my Africana Studies Colloquium at Williams College; and the CIMMA working group at Université Paris-Est Créteil. I am grateful for several scholars who have been on standby to read and edit works in progress. Of particular note are Jürgen Grandt, Jenny James, Marie Loeffler, Perrine Warmé-Janville, and Paul Merrill.

I also take this opportunity to thank a wealth of other professors and scholars, who through courses or through discussions, conferences, and invited lectures have enriched this project: Michael Borshuk, Donald Clarke, the late Dwight Conquergood, Renee Alexander Craft, Tracy Davis, the late Michel Fabre, Dorothea Fischer-Hornung, Shelley Fisher Fishkin, Fradley

Garner, John Gennari, Jacqueline Goldsby, Stephen Hill, Mischa Honeck, Wolfram Knauer, Anne Legrand, Susan Manning, Jeffrey McCune, Robert O'Meally, Frances Paden, Sandra L. Richards, Jean-Paul Rocchi, Francesca Royster, Margaret Sinclair, Ludovic Tournès, Sam Weber, Tracy Denean Sharpley-Whiting, Tony Whyton, Harvey Young, and Mary Zimmerman.

The process of writing a book is just as much about tracking down leads, following up on suggested contacts, and exploring tidbits of information. So I would like to thank those who connected me with others. Family member Bendt Arendt introduced me to the correspondence of Inez Cavanaugh and bassist Peter Giron, while filmmaker Joanne Burke and writer David Burke first connected me (and continue to do so) with a wonderful community of artists in Paris. I am heartily grateful to the jazz musicians and fans who graciously allowed me to interview them: John Betsch, Jean-Louis Chautemps, Laurent Clarke, Bobby Few, Salim Himidi, Nancy Holloway, Sylvia Howard, Archie Shepp, Hal Singer, Almeta Speaks, René Urtreger, Benny Vasseur, the late Claude Luter, and the late Mike Zwerin.

This book would not have progressed as far or as quickly as it did without the aid of expert staff at the following research institutions: the Northwestern University Library; Special Collections at Northwestern's Deering Library; the Chicago Jazz Archive and Regenstein Library at the University of Chicago; Woodruff Library at Emory University; the Institute of Jazz Studies at Rutgers University; the Schomburg Center for Research in Black Culture; the New York Public Library; the Bibliothèque Nationale de France, Francois Mitterand and Richelieu sites; and the Jazzinstitut Darmstadt.

Throughout this research project I have benefited from financial support from multiple sources. The following departments and fellowships were instrumental in supporting various trips for archival research and conferences: Northwestern University (the department of Performance Studies, the Graduate School, the Center for International and Comparative Studies Conference, the French Interdisciplinary Group, and the Paris Program in Critical Theory); Stanford University (Introduction to Humanities program); Heidelberg Center for American Studies (The Ghaemian Junior Scholar-in-Residence Fellowship); Williams College (the Hellman Faculty Fellowship, Class of 1945 World Fellowship Program, Division I and II Summer Research Program, Writing Roundtable, and supplemental funding for additional research and book subvention).

Last, I wish to thank other family members, friends, colleagues, and faculty who helped in a major way during the journey of writing this book: Tish Anderson, Glenn Baldwin Jr., Jay Bonner, Anya Braggs, Natalie

Strelnikova Braggs, LeRhonda S. Manigault Bryant, Bryan Carter, Katy Chiles, Giridhar Clark, Kathy Coll, Gail Derecho, Stephanie Dunson, Doc Embler, Cynthia Garrison, the late Teddy Gossett, the late Elijah Hansley, Mark Harrison, Ann Holder, Jake Lamar, Bishupal Limbu, Carol Ockman, Emmett G. Price III, Pam Reid, Marilyn Root, Toni Salazar, John Schulz, the late Alan Shefsky, and a wealth of others whose support has been a guiding force.

Introduction

Migrating Jazz People and Identities

At ninety-five years old Hal Singer could still seduce with his saxophone. The measured steps to the raised stage . . . the near misses when sitting on his stool . . . the misheard shout out of the next tune . . . nothing could alter his firm hold on the saxophone. On that fifth day of October in 2014 Singer's saxophone blurted just a bit off sync, though still lilting. But it did not take long for him to mesmerize the audience.

As this master of rock 'n' roll, R&B, and jazz performed, visions of poodle skirt–laden girls flipping and spinning with intricate steps took over my imagination. His music transported me back in time. In 1948 Singer recorded "Cornbread" on the Savoy label. The song quickly hit number one on the R&B charts. Riding the waves of his success, he turned down the opportunity to retain his spot in Duke Ellington's reed section; even though he'd only just secured this esteemed role, Singer had enough recognition then to lead his own band (B. Dahl; Felin).

On that still summery day in October 2014 Hal Singer created a mood of nostalgia and blood memories in the cozy community center of Belleville, Les ateliers du Chaudron (The studios of Chaudron).[1] The lucky ones were sitting upright in chairs against the wall and beside the stage. Most of us were crouched on wooden bleacher-like levels, holding our knees in, sitting on our jackets, and trying not to take up too much space so that everyone could fit in. We were a mixed crowd: Singer's family; Americans long having resided in France; international tourists just passing through; French residents of the tenth arrondissement (neighborhood); and their accompanying friends. We were white, black, and mixed; teens and elders; men and women. Despite the differences, everyone sat in awe as Singer created a bond among us. For he connected us and transported us to times past.

Easing into his flow, Singer led the band with "Freddy Freeloader"—a twelve-bar blues tune that is recognized on one of the best-selling and most well-known albums of all time, Miles Davis's *Kind of Blue*. The 1959 album became a pinnacle point in jazz history, an epic contribution from Columbia Records and its 30th Street studio, and one last spark of bop coolness before free jazz spawned a new avant-garde jazz scene. Based in New York City since 1941, Singer enjoyed plenty of opportunities to collaborate there. He played with saxophonist Don Byas, trumpeter Roy Eldridge, and pianist Wynton Kelly, and that was after he had made his way across the country from his hometown of Tulsa, Oklahoma (B. Dahl). In a 2005 interview he described the intensity of jazz production in postwar New York to me: ". . . the Fats Wallers and Charlie Parkers. They had more musicians working in one block than any other city. New York was the messiah for jazz."

But Hal Singer migrated to Paris in 1965—despite his success, forthcoming job opportunities, and potential for collaboration with so many great jazz musicians working in New York. Having settled in Chatou, a western suburb of Paris, he had resided in Paris for nearly fifty years by the time of his 2014 concert. Marrying a French woman, one of his fans in those early days of playing at clubs like Les Trois Maillets (The three mallets), he raised a family with two girls (Felin). His daughter Stéphanie recognized the sacrifices he had made and his desire for them to have a better life: "In any case, he lived in the United States at a time when it wasn't good to be black; that affected him enormously, I think. And compared to his education, it was like a tiny bit of revenge: 'I couldn't do it, but my girls, they will do it'" (Felin).[2] Singer's perspective was not so different from many a parent's, but he migrated across the ocean to remake his life for himself.

His songs did not hit the pop charts much after his migration, but he kept jazz alive in France—one mentee, band, and audience at a time. He mentored French kids on the bandstand and veterans who became well-known musicians in France, like Steve Potts. On that day in 2014 Steve Potts and The All Stars accompanied Singer. Potts organized this birthday concert, just as he had five years before in celebration of Singer's ninetieth birthday. Potts reminded the audience of the impact of Hal Singer and so many African American jazz musicians who had played in France, the United States, and beyond. For me Singer's vamp that kept going and going and his still urgent vibrato after more than seventy-five years of performing symbolized the enduring journey of jazz and African American jazz musicians in the United States and France.

Hal Singer represented a "critical mass" of African American artists that constituted a recurring artistic presence in Paris from the early 1900s until the present day (Stovall, *Paris Noir* xv). Termed *Paris Noir* (Black Paris), the groups of African Americans residing in Paris were small but influential. Their presence in Paris demonstrated the French desire for African American cultural expression and forged continued connections between their experiences in Paris and the music, literature, art, and politics growing out of U.S. metropolitan hubs like New York City and Chicago. The community of African American artists in the 1920s may be the most well-known. Performers such as Josephine Baker resided in Paris then and created the community that William Shack calls "Harlem in Montmartre" (Shack 10). The group of African American jazz musicians who migrated to Paris after World War II added to this history of Parisian migration. By 1964, more than fifteen hundred African American artists (including other prominent artists like writer Richard Wright and artist/writer Barbara Chase-Riboud) had migrated to Paris (Fabre, "Cultural " 45).

In *Jazz Diasporas* the postwar migrations of vocalist Inez Cavanaugh, saxophonist Sidney Bechet, drummer Kenny Clarke, and the community of artists with whom they collaborated take center stage. This book explores reasons for the migration of African American jazz musicians, strategies they used to thrive in Paris yet maintain relations with the United States, their mentorship of and collaboration with white French musicians, and their transformations in personal identity that paralleled the music's own evolving racial and national identity. In this period jazz helped forward illusions of Paris as color-blind, and some African American musicians willfully but not blindly made use of jazz to achieve success in Paris. Some musicians and jazzophiles subtly used jazz as a tool to critique racialized oppression prevalent in the United States and blur racial boundaries in France.

The 1999 documentary film *Hal Singer: Keep the Music Going,* compared Singer's life in the United States and France. Singer identified differing perceptions and treatment of African Americans as a deciding factor for staying in France:

> I made a good living in America, and I didn't, I wasn't never happy with the system. But when I came here I found that, my life was a little more relaxed. I was given more respect. I found people that had read about this music, knew the history of it, liked it very much. In America, I had not had people that really knew the history of this music and neither were giving the musicians the respect. . . . This is some time the thing that you don't always get being a black musician in America, is respect. (Felin)

Singer's comments reaffirm an oft-asserted narrative that privileges Paris as a place that is more accepting of racialized difference. As we will see, this narrative of Paris as a haven for African Americans builds on exoticized perceptions of and desire for African art, a nostalgic passing down of stories from those who had once lived in Paris, and experiences of African American soldiers stationed in France in World War I and World War II.

The testimonies from musicians touring Europe also portrayed Paris as offering more creative freedom and respect for jazz. Hal Singer described this mystique of European appreciation to me: "A lot of people here read books and knew the life of the people. . . . European fans could recite to you all the records a person had made." In his opinion European fans showed not only appreciation but also intellectual awareness of jazz.[3] The attention French jazz fans paid to his music demonstrated the respect he believed was lacking in the United States. In France Singer felt respected and valued for the contribution he could make to French culture.

Many African American jazz musicians shared Singer's perspective of Paris, but some musicians' feelings of welcome and respect were challenged in the period from 1945 to 1963. Two influential veterans of this period, Sidney Bechet (the French-adopted king of jazz) and writer Richard Wright (the head of the *Paris Noir* community), died in 1959 and 1960 respectively. Mainstream jazz, in many countries, was on its way out—giving way to rock 'n' roll and the newer free jazz genre ushered in by saxophonist Ornette Coleman in 1960. Civil rights tensions exploded in the United States, and the reverberations were felt in France, prompting supportive protests and dialogue, particularly in 1968. Still, the French had their own complexities of race and ethnicity to address. The French republic's universal policy did not recognize difference but purported to include all. A mid-century influx of citizens from French overseas departments in the Caribbean and former African and Asian colonies put this policy to the test.

In response some African Americans returned home, despairing over racial prejudice they saw against French of African descent or motivated by a responsibility to join civil rights protests at home. A steady stream of African Americans flowed through Paris despite it all. The Paris they entered was a much more racially mixed, tense, and threatened city. The opportunities for jazz, and for African American jazz musicians in particular, prevailed for a time in France. By the time Hal Singer migrated in 1965, the perception and the experiences of African American jazz musicians in Paris had begun to take a big turn. Still, traces and hauntings of those post–World War II days remained.

Kenny Clarke had settled down in Paris in 1956 and remained there until his death in 1985. Clarke was one of the key African American jazz veterans who had become too "local" (Zwerin, "Jazz in Europe" 541). He began to tour more outside of France, while French jazz bands increased their performance opportunities, exposure, and confidence in their own land. In fact, I first interviewed Hal Singer to learn more about Kenny Clarke's life and musical production in Paris. Singer and Clarke shared similar reasons for staying, and both fully assimilated into France, raising their families there and never returning to live in the United States.

Listening to Hal Singer in this modern moment, I could hear the blood memories of civil rights injustice and strife he had left behind in the 1960s. While "Freddy Freeloader" ushered in waves of nostalgia for a bygone, jazz-rich era of production in New York, Singer's concluding song spoke of the segregated world of prejudice he'd lived through in the United States. He sat down, held his horn close, and picked up the microphone with his other hand. "Georgia," he spoke-sang out. Even at ninety-five years old, the standard's lyrics came quickly to him. "Georgia on My Mind" was written by Stuart Gorrell (lyrics) and Hoagy Carmichael (music) in 1930, but the interpretation by Ray Charles on his 1960 album *The Genius Hits the Road* is the most popular version. Though it is now the state song of Georgia, "Georgia on My Mind" stood for more than fifteen years as a symbol of Charles's refusal to perform for a white, segregated audience in 1961 Augusta, Georgia (Charles and Ritz 164–65). The state would not apologize to Charles until 1979, when it invited him to perform in honor of naming "Georgia on My Mind" the state song.

I could almost imagine Singer's gravelly yet rich voicings of "Georgia" tracing along grooves and pits of a bumpy journey to equal rights in the mid-twentieth-century United States. He performed jazz to express that condition of life. In *Hal Singer: Keep the Music Going*, he said: "But all of the hardship, but all of the lack of respect that were received, we still kept a positive attitude. We played good and we enjoyed life. And I think that's something that people couldn't understand, you know—how we could get on the bandstand and still make beautiful music" (Felin). As Singer walked off the stage, I recognized jazz as his tool to survive that very existence and to create new opportunities.

"Jazz diasporas" offer just such possibilities. I have conceived this phrase to describe geographically, historically situated cultural spaces that support and spur flexibility, negotiation, and shifting of racial and national identities for migrating African American jazz musicians and communities of jazzophiles with whom they collaborate. There are two types of jazz diasporas: in one sense jazz diasporas involve those who thrive and shape individual identity through musical collaboration outside of their homeland. In the second type of jazz diaspora the music travels and through its interactions alters who performs, represents, and claims the music. I explore both types here. The case studies of Sidney Bechet, with his negotiation of subjectivities as a survival strategy, and Inez Cavanaugh, in her role of nurturing local and global jazz communities, exemplify the first perspective. The relationships between French sidemen like Claude Luter and René Urtreger with African American musicians and my analysis of Kenny Clarke as a connector between perceptions of jazz as "black" and "universal" music illustrate the second type. Chapter 4 represents both types as it puts in dialogue French and African American literature as sites of articulation of African American identity, protest, and liberation through the marriage of music and word.

WHY "JAZZ DIASPORA"? JAZZ AND JAZZ PEOPLE AS TRANSNATIONAL AND HYBRID

Jazz Diasporas commences with two epigraphs that encapsulate the two types of jazz diaspora. Presenting two epigraphs hints at the equal weight and coexistence of both points in the structure, research, and writing of this book. In the first, Albert Murray portrays "black music" as representative of American life and culture and of African American culture within it. He describes African American people as inherently linked to the music. Murray's link claims jazz as black and American music.

With *Blues People: Negro Music in White America* Amiri Baraka, formerly known as Leroi Jones, extended and distinguished this claim on "black music."[4] Fueled by black art and nascent Black Nationalist motivations, Baraka cautioned against the white appropriation of music originated by African Americans and promoted the contributions African Americans have made to U.S. culture. He described the migration of African Americans from south to north, from countryside to urban center, and from underground to mainstream culture. Baraka detailed how the music grew out of struggle, migration, and assimilation. What he ignored, however, was the signal contribution to "black music" by nonblacks and non-Americans.

This is where I intervene. I conceive jazz people as influenced by the transnational and interracial trafficking of music first originated and primarily developed by African Americans. *Jazz Diasporas* extends Amiri Baraka's community of blues people to a jazz people who thrive on cultural interrelation just like jazz's melding of African, Caribbean, and European elements. I do focus primarily on African Americans in this book and discuss jazz as "black music." To me jazz will always be connected to people of African descent and the American land on which it was created. But my position is also founded on an expanded notion of black, American, and jazz cultures.

Jazz is both black and global music. *Jazz Diasporas* demonstrates how this refashioning of jazz's identity (as French and universal) and musicians' identities (as potentially global citizens, transnational negotiators, and exiled rather than American-identified and -situated people) commences and takes shape after World War II. In this way *Jazz Diasporas* continues the work of Paul Gilroy and others who have followed him. The book considers music of the "black Atlantic" as not racially essentialized and pure but rather hybrid and evolving (*The Black Atlantic* 80, 101). Alongside this attention to African American jazz musicians as case studies, *Jazz Diasporas* presents collaborations and relationships forged with non-African Americans; it analyzes how these bonds affected the identities of African Americans and jazz.

In his essay "The Jazz Diaspora" Bruce Johnson tracks the globalization of jazz (33). His essay provides one of the rare uses of the term *jazz diaspora*. By exploring the evolutions and new forms created out of jazz's travels, Johnson's work illustrates the recent turn toward investigations of jazz outside the United States in Anglophone jazz scholarship. Books like Jeffrey Jackson's *Making Jazz French: Music and Modern Life in Interwar Paris,* Colin Nettelbeck's *Dancing with DeBeauvoir: Jazz and the French,* Jeremy Lane's *Jazz and Machine-Age Imperialism: Music, "Race" and Intellectuals in France,* and Tom Perchard's *After Django: Making Jazz in Postwar France* continue to educate the Anglophone jazz public on the participation in and representation of jazz by French musicians and jazzophiles. My focus on jazz diasporas, with emphasis on African Americans and their interracial and international interactions, differs from (but is very much in conversation with) these French jazz texts.

Jazz Diasporas also rests on the premise that jazz and jazz people are inherently transnational. The second epigraph of the book hints at this overarching claim. Michelle Wright analyzes the work of the African American writer James Baldwin, who spent decades living in and in-between France and the United States. Wright argues that James Baldwin and African Americans at large were always already transnational. Her analysis revolutionized my ideas about African American identity. Certainly the journey through the Middle Passage resonated in blood memories, folklore, and African American cultural expressions. But a long line of key African American intellectuals and artists had also migrated to Europe, from writer William Wells Brown in England to activist and sociologist W. E. B. Du Bois in Germany. The impact of their migratory experiences was felt back in the United States. Their travels offered education, artistic experience, and a sense of global consciousness that contributed to African American culture and society.

In the transatlantic journeys of African Americans Paris has been a recurring hot spot. It has served as an intellectual meeting place in which French leaders, writers, and artists of African descent would come and dialogue. As Brent Hayes Edwards has discussed in *The Practice of Diaspora: Literature, Translation, and the Rise of Black Internationalism*, Paris was a site at which campaigns, propaganda, and literary initiatives were built to forward black solidarity. Meetings for proponents of Pan-Africanism in the early twentieth century, African literary journals positing "negritude" in the interwar period, and the International Congress for Black Writers and Artists in 1956—Paris has housed them all. Throughout history Paris remained a site of debate, formation, and articulation of transnational black consciousness.

Yet Paris did not stand alone; rather, it was in dialogue with other key sites of black solidarity. Edwards's consideration of Paris as a unique site of "boundary crossing, conversations, and collaborations" that remains in dialogue with its American counterparts informs my work (*Practice* 4). For jazz in Paris is a site through which cultures and powers are exchanged, performed, and articulated. James Baldwin put it well when he described Paris as a space where he came to reflect on, grapple with, and understand his African American identity better; his reflection and writing led to greater awareness of the possibilities of ethnic identity and the recognition of new limitations in this non-American setting (*Nobody* 137–42). Jazz diasporas create space for just this type of negotiation and questioning of identities. They exemplify Paul Gilroy's notion of the African diaspora: "Diaspora accentuates becoming rather than being and identity conceived diasporically, along these lines, resists reification" ("'. . . To Be Real'" 24). In the nonstatic, growing and "becoming" spaces of a jazz diaspora the identities of jazz musicians, jazzophiles, and jazz itself are always in process while also being tied to national and racial roots. Jazz diasporas support these personal and artistic, collective and individual performances of musical identity. Post–World War II Paris is one of the historically and geographically situated jazz diasporas in which these negotiations of identity proliferated.

JAZZ-AGE SAFE HAVEN

A wealth of scholarship exists on jazz in France during this interwar period. Only recently have scholars begun to showcase the period after World War II. *Jazz Diasporas* contributes to the latter period but also highlights themes, perceptions, and uses of jazz prevalent since the music first traveled abroad. The book also overlaps audiences and fields as it shows jazz in a range of ways, as musical practice, political statement, source of propaganda, tool for community building, site of identity negotiation, and subject of this intellectual project.

Jazz first shocked Paris in 1918. Louis Mitchell and his Jazz Kings played several concerts in Paris to astonished and booing responses, but the all–African American band quickly settled into playing regularly in Parisian clubs such as Casino de Paris (Stovall, *Paris* 37; Shack 24, 77). Concurrently, James Reese Europe led the 369th Infantry Regiment,[5] a segregated African American military band, to tour through France; the French couldn't imagine how to replicate the sounds and even thought the instruments must be engineered differently (Badger 194). In the 1920s, jazz experienced a golden age, primarily in Montmartre, a northeastern quartier in Paris. This development firmly established Montmartre as a trendy jazz hot spot of the era. It seemed that everyone was there. Ada "Bricktop" Smith opened her own eponymous club, where she, the dancer and singer Josephine Baker, and singer Alberta Hunter helped draw in crowds with their spectacular shows (Moody 18–21). Bricktop's club shared the limelight with Le Grand Duc's, where the former pilot and boxer Eugene Bullard was manager. In 1925 Josephine Baker danced in *La revue nègre* (The Black Revue), and she was accompanied by a jazz orchestra that included Sidney Bechet (Shack 35–36).

Baker's success, as well as the period of *l'art nègre* (black art), exemplified French negrophilia (an exoticizing and objectifying desire for African and African-diasporic culture). In *Negrophilia: Avant-Garde Paris and Black Culture in the 1920s*, Petrine Archer-Straw argues that negrophilia advanced the marketing of products and supported resistance against modernity (35–53). In the 1920s and 1930s many art collectors and various artists from Europe and the United States foregrounded a primitivist ideology that portrayed Africans and African Americans as having an exotic and childlike nature. Archer-Straw recounts how this primitivist mentality seeped through various artistic forms, such as the paintings of Henri Matisse and Pablo Picasso, the fabric of Sonia Delaunay, and the art collection of Paul Guillaume. Moreover, artist Guillaume Apollinaire and collector Nancy Cunard sought representations of African bodies, most notably masks (53). They wore these masks to abandon what they considered a staid and complicated Western tradition. African art was a means to easier expression and certain freedoms unavailable elsewhere. Sculptor George Braques relayed that the African masks literally "opened a new horizon" for him and allowed him to "contact more instinctive things" (53).

The French consumption of *l'art nègre* and Baker was motivated by a desire for an exotic "other." Brett Berliner, author of *Ambivalent Desire:*

The Exotic Black Other in Jazz-Age France, defines this term to mean foreign, serving fantasies and acting as a site of escape or fulfillment of cultural dearth; he also links the exotic to the primitive, the savage, and the hypersexual (4–7). Among Baker's most memorable performances was the *danse sauvage* (savage dance) in the *Folies bergère* production of "Un vent de folie" (A wave of madness). Baker wore a skirt of bananas and danced like an animal from the jungle (Martin 313). In this performance French fans perceived her as an exotic figure, noticing her large butt and wild contortions (Dayal 38).

African American jazz musicians were especially prized owing to the French history of negrophilia. In *Le tumulte noir: Modernist Art and Popular Entertainment in Jazz-Age Paris, 1900–1930,* Jody Blake elaborates on what specifically about jazz performance seduced the French public: "Jazz-age entertainment carried the influence of *art nègre* beyond avant-garde galleries. . . . Indeed, the factors that drew the French to popular music halls and nightclubs—their desire for new modes of self-expression and social interaction and their urge to escape from and exult in the pressures and possibilities of the modern world—offer uniquely valuable clues" (8). Blake's statement—like Berliner's—explains one role of jazz and African art in France, as a means for escape. Jazz, especially with its danceable beats, allowed listeners to distance themselves from the stresses, fears, and challenges of modern European life. Jeremy Lane discusses how white French intellectuals, artists, and performance critics perceived jazz as offering a primitive alternative to the modern world. In *Jazz and Machine-Age Imperialism* Lane puts poet and politician Léopold Senghor (who would become the first president of Senegal in 1960) in dialogue with Hugues Panassié, the renowned jazz critic and president of Hot Club of France. Lane argues that, in contrast to other French writers of African descent, Senghor's views of jazz absorbed Panassié's purist, primitivist perception of the music and drew on it to support his own connotations of negritude; for Senghor jazz was a tool for racial solidarity that created divisions between the modern, rational West and the primitive, authentic Africa (122). Lane adds that "for Senghor, as for Panassié, jazz's ability to play this role of antidote to the machine age rested on certain ethnocentric and primitivist assumptions rooted in the ideology and practice of French imperialism" (124).

In *Making Jazz French* Jeffrey Jackson departs from scholarship on jazz in France that primarily emphasizes themes of exoticization, primitivism, and appropriation. Jackson positions jazz not as solely an American export but also as a French import that the French made their own. His book gives credibility to white French jazz production, countering a norm that had portrayed the French as imitators of Americans. He points to the music's assimilation into the very fabric of French culture and identifies several artists that represent a Frenchification of jazz. Describing the process of remaking, Jackson elaborates on the transition from French artists who did not "believe that they could play nearly as well as Americans" to a shift in the 1930s, when musicians such as Andre Ekyan, Stephane Mougin, and Alix Combelle became stars (Jackson 103, 127). Jackson adds that these musicians "had thoroughly imbibed its rhythms in the dance halls and from records," after years of studying American jazz production (127–28).

Though Jackson's argument is intriguing, I do not fully agree. Present-day France has, indeed, incorporated jazz so much into its culture that the festivals, radio programs, and concerts do not seem strange to the French citizen. Yet during the interwar period French critics, fans, and musicians still compared American and French jazz culture, with French jazz production often coming out on bottom. The fact that French artists rarely considered themselves the equals of African American musicians challenges the idea that the French made jazz their own. The strength of *Making Jazz French* is that it reveals an assumption that only American, and primarily African American, jazz musicians are worthy of scholastic attention. Since the publication of *Making Jazz French* in 2003, a wealth of scholars have followed Jackson's lead. They have plunged into studies of French musicianship, as well as French public reception and jazz criticism.

Media-studies scholar Matthew Jordan addresses the role that jazz played in serving French modernity. Jordan traces through jazz criticism and literature ways that jazz shifted from being a foreign threat to being an acceptable part of French culture. In *Le Jazz: Jazz and French Cultural Identity* Jordan argues that "characteristics or qualities initially heard and seen in jazz as markers of otherness against which Frenchness gained coherence went through a historical process of transvaluation, so that those traits once seen and heard as un-French came to be recognized as internal markers or normal, commonsense conceptions of an emerging modern sense of Frenchness" (3). Not until after World War II was there more recognizable assimilation and transculturation of jazz into French culture. After the war, enjoying jazz and even seeing it as part of (rather than foreign to) French culture became the norm (3). Jordan pushes the time line forward a bit from Jackson, who argues that jazz became French in the interwar period. The war was particularly important for French intellectuals like Jean-Paul Sartre, in his disavowal of purists like Hugues Panassié, who would claim that modernist styles like bebop were not actually jazz; Sartre identified Panassié's staunch clinging to New Orleans–style jazz as representative of the fanaticism and realism that thrived during World

War II and from which they had thankfully been liberated (Jordan 236). Sartre's distinction places jazz, in all its evolutions, as representative of France's fight for freedom.

World War II and the postwar period witnessed important events in the acculturation of jazz in France. Whereas Jordan investigates French jazz and cultural criticism as representative agents of change in societal discourse, I hone in on African American jazz musicians' experiences, perspectives, and collaborations to explore changes in the perception and uses of jazz in the postwar era—specifically in the ways jazz performs ideologies of race and nation. One of the most influential and still pervasive ideologies that jazz helped support was the narrative that Paris was a color-blind haven, in which African Americans would be free (or freer than in the United States) from racial prejudice. This narrative has a long genealogy, extending as far back as the first dissemination of jazz abroad.

After World War I, African American soldiers returned to the United States regaling their families with stories of France. These stories were passed down from generation to generation and created an illusion that was absorbed into African American folklore. They were stories of beauty, freedom, and equality. Artists and musicians also shared stories about Paris with friends and family back home. Films like *Paris Blues* furthered this narrative by depicting black musicians as receiving respect and honor as they worked alongside white musicians in Paris. The American-produced film brought African American performers together while also maintaining onscreen the illusion of Paris as a color-blind place for African American musicians. *Paris Blues* also unwittingly foregrounded issues such as racial differences in France, the codependence of France on the United States, and the relationship of jazz musicians to racial politics. The folklore of Paris as color-blind contributed to a broadening perception of racial open-mindedness and liberty in France. But it was an illusion.

COLD WAR JAZZ DIASPORAS

Contemporary scholarship on jazz in France after World War II discounts and demystifies several commonly held myths. In *Paris Blues: African American Music and French Popular Culture, 1920–1960* musicologist Andy Fry works to disprove the myth that the French were more accepting and knowledgeable about jazz than Americans, who often had the reputation of not fully appreciating their native art form. Investigating multiple works of Ernest Ansermet, the Swiss composer credited with writing the first jazz review and with recognizing the brilliance of Sidney Bechet as early as 1919, Fry critiques the privileging of Ansermet as a supporter of jazz and the nostalgic remembering in French jazz history that performs foreknowledge of Bechet's stardom (23, 220–40).

French jazz historians Gérard Régnier and Ludovic Tournès discount another commonly held myth—that jazz was forced out of Europe during World War II. The Nazis forwarded an antijazz regime, positioning it as a "degenerative" music that was produced by an inferior race and threatened Aryan purity (Archer-Straw 114; Tournès 60). They were ultravigilant and tried to stomp out what they perceived as the negative influence of jazz. A 1946 report in *Down Beat* magazine translated a particularly traumatizing moment that Hot Club of France cofounder and *Jazz Hot* magazine founder Charles Delaunay shared: "In October 1943, British soldiers and Hot Club of France personnel, such as Delaunay himself, were arrested and held at Fresnes Prison. Delaunay was questioned for five hours and apparently one of the secretaries was sent to an extermination camp and murdered" (J. Jackson, *Making* 193).[6]

Despite scholarship that claims that live jazz performance was banned under the occupation, Ludovic Tournès notes that it was only in the zones annexed by the Reich—for example, L'Alsace and Lorraine—that jazz was actually banned (60). In fact jazz enjoyed a golden age during the war; even though the Hot Club of France temporarily closed in late 1943, before that time it hosted radio shows out of its bases in Paris and Toulouse (60).

Gérard Régnier augments Tournès's research, demonstrating that it was jazz performed and recorded by Americans that most threatened the Nazis. He discusses ways the French sidestepped the suppression of jazz during the occupation. In some cases the Nazis tweaked their interpretation of the law to bypass exceptional jazz musicians whom they admired, like the Belgian-born French guitarist Django Reinhardt (Régnier 180–81).[7] French fans listened to jazz on radio stations, and there were some festivals organized by the Hot Club, but jazz organizers had to take extra steps to disguise the Americanness of the music and promote French stars and songs instead. American jazz standards were changed to French as they were submitted for approval and authorization from representatives of the Ministry of Culture: "Honeysuckle Rose" was changed to "Rose de miel," and "Tiger Rag" became "La rage du buggle" (Régnier 145). French concert organizers such as Frank Ténot in Bordeaux and Jacques Souplet in Rennes submitted programs before each concert, and they withheld American song names or Jewish artists until approval was confirmed (144).

After years of surreptitious record listening and concertgoing, the French were enthusiastic to catch up with recordings they'd missed out on during the war and the return of touring American musicians—most of whom had escaped Paris in time.[8] In 1946 the Don Redman orchestra, which included Inez Cavanaugh, was the first American big band to tour in Paris after the war. The following years were monumental in the history of jazz in France. In 1947 the Hot Club of France split in two, one side advocating New Orleans–style jazz and the other promoting bebop. Hugues Panassié would espouse the purist former position, and Charles Delaunay would expand attention to bebop, particularly with his record label, *Vogue*. In 1948 Louis Armstrong and his band performed at the first international jazz festival after the war, in Nice. In the same year Dizzy Gillespie toured in Nice and Paris with a seventeen piece big band that included Kenny Clarke and pianist John Lewis among others. The concerts would change the lives of several young French musicians, inspiring them and cementing their plans to play jazz. In 1949 the Paris International Jazz Festival hosted performers from seven countries and brought mega stars from Charlie Parker to Sidney Bechet.

After the festivals, gigs were plentiful. Touring jazz musicians reported more opportunity and pay at concerts abroad. The enthusiasm for jazz was so great that, in several cases, fans protested sellouts and pushed their way in (Ehrlich 94). The Blue Note, Club Saint-Germain, and Vieux Colombier in the Latin Quarter and Saint-Germain-des-Prés headlined visiting stars like Miles Davis and linked young French stars with African American veterans. Pairings included New Orleans–style veteran Sidney Bechet with French clarinetist Claude Luter and bebop-style cofounder Kenny Clarke with French pianist René Urtreger. In contrast to the jazz age, at midcentury the jazz scene moved south of the Seine to the Latin Quarter and Saint-Germain-des-Prés. But just like the interwar period, the jazz scene was rowdy, joyful, interracial, international, and diverse, with intellectuals, artists, and musicians. African Americans again flocked to Paris, and many stayed for a time. Whether prompted by the need to escape racial inequality in the United States, drawn by possibilities of interracial interactions and collaborations, or seduced by more job opportunities in France, the migration of African Americans increased after World War II.

But as we will see, the idea that Paris was a safe haven for these musicians was an illusion. Chapter 3 responds to and deconstructs multiple reasons for migration and strategies for assimilation in Paris. The narrative of Paris as a color-blind haven was and continues to be the most persistent reason. Several factors contributed to this illusion. The narrative persisted because lived experience did not disprove it, and word of mouth did not discount it.

Some African Americans, such as Inez Cavanaugh and Richard Wright, believed there was more equality in Paris. Others, like Sidney Bechet, resonated with the idyllic vision of Paris but only paid it lip service. Still others kept mum to protect their right to live in France. Tyler Stovall, author of *Paris Noir: African Americans in the City of Light,* explains: "Black expatriates were acutely aware of their status as guests of the French. Throughout the twentieth century, the French government had welcomed foreign political exiles on the implicit assumption that they abstain from involvement in French politics" (254). In this cold war period, when a collection of French literati and politicians were protesting the spread of American culture in France, African Americans had enjoyed distinction from anti-Americanism. But by making themselves more present, by pointing out the hypocrisy of the French, they could easily lose that privilege.

Cold war competition between France and the United States further fueled the narrative of Paris as respecting and having greater appreciation for jazz and African American jazz musicians, in particular. As a result of the devastating effects of World War II on the French economy, France's chance for greater power, independence, and modernization hinged on financial aid from the United States (Costigliola 51–54). While the United States loaned $650 million of the $3 billion France requested, the French agreed to encourage free trade in its markets and stand behind the plans of the United States to rebuild Germany (Stovall, *France* 21–22). In this agreement the French were forced to resume importation of U.S. films despite attempts to cut the influence of U.S. imports. They perceived American films as a threat to "'French genius,' cultural independence, and world prestige" (Costigliola 55). Not so with jazz, however. The French government and public might have participated in commercial activities and supported the United States, but French jazz critics and intellectuals emphasized their long-held knowledge of jazz in distinct contrast to what it considered ignorance from the United States.

In this postwar era the U.S. media still marginalized jazz music, particularly African American jazz musicians. In his 1948 history of jazz Sidney Finkelstein detailed how the music had been maligned: "It is called 'primitive,' 'barbaric.' The fact that it was produced mainly by the Negro people of America has been held against it. The fact that it found a home sometimes in brothels or speakeasies, that in its atmosphere and communication it reflects the miserable conditions of life forced upon the Negro people, has also been held against it" (15). *Primitive* connoted interesting, different, and desirable for the French, but in the United States it was base and marginalized. Even though the 1920s and 1930s had introduced swing, and

American audiences embraced jazz musicians such as Benny Goodman and Paul Whiteman, it took some time for integrated bands to find acceptance. Even then, the "straight" music that white audiences favored in concert halls was quite different from the "hot" jazz played in juke joints, primarily for African American patrons (Stearns 124; J. Jackson, *Making* 154–57).

In contrast, French critics had a history of privileging African American musicians over their white American counterparts. In his 1942 revised edition of *The Real Jazz* Hugues Panassié wrote, "I did not realize until some years after the publication of my first book that, from the point of view of jazz, most white musicians were inferior to black musicians" (vii–viii).[9] Moreover, the French scoffed at American practices such as the unequal treatment of African Americans and actually used jazz to protest America, seeing themselves as "confreres" (brothers) of jazz musicians and African Americans (Vihlen 237–39; Lebovics 159). The support of jazz and African American jazz musicians gave French culture an advantage in cold war competition. Jazz critics played their part, throwing up French support of jazz in the face of the U.S. media and public. Jazz critic and musician Boris Vian proclaimed, "France had made more effort than any other country towards the diffusion and comprehension of black American jazz" (quoted in Willett 83).

Next, the acceptance of communism and the space that Paris played in hosting dialogue on different sociopolitical systems and frameworks drew African Americans like singer/actor Paul Robeson and Richard Wright. The censure and censorship of seemingly unpatriotic discourse was very rigid in this period of McCarthyism in the United States: Paul Robeson's passport was seized after the negative response to his activism against colonialism, but particularly after his speech at the Paris Peace Conference in 1949 was misquoted and seen as representative of African Americans' preference for communism (Von Eschen, *Race* 123). African American writer, activist, and sociologist W. E. B. Du Bois was also stripped of his right to travel and could not attend the First International Congress of Black Writers and Artists in 1956 Paris. For African American artists and intellectuals Paris proved a space for articulating dissent, strategizing, and collaborating on how to combat institutionalized injustices against people of African descent, not just in the United States but around the world.

But the illusion of Paris as a color-blind haven would also falter in these years after World War II. Rather than color-blind, France showed itself to be very race conscious after the war. The hypernationalist and color-conscious era of the 1950s and 1960s would complicate experiences of being African American in Paris and perceptions of jazz as a black and American music.

The settling down of key jazz veterans like Bechet in 1951 and Clarke in 1956 offered a foundation of jazz mentors for young French musicians and led to an increased white French jazz scene that began to compete more readily with American jazz musicians. Music journalist Mike Zwerin described the phenomenon as the "local musician"; when an American musician had been around and become familiar, gigs were offered less frequently—the French jazz industry and public seeking the fresher, touring, and therefore temporary musicians instead (Zwerin, "Jazz in Europe" 541). As a result African American jazz musicians were less often afforded a privileged status based on perceptions of exoticism that offered an alternative to French modernity. In the 1960s "local musicians" like Kenny Clarke began to travel more as gigs and wages diminished in Paris.

Though jazz still connoted the primitive, it and its musicians became tools in the cultural and political competition between the United States and France in the Cold War. The use of jazz as a political tool in cold war cultural battles prompted a shift in the perceptions of jazz or, more accurately, the discursive performance of it as a black and American music. In 1956 the State Department introduced the Goodwill Ambassador tours, showcasing famous African American athletes and musicians; initiating the jazz branch, Dizzy Gillespie visited Iran, Beirut, and Pakistan and attracted tremendous crowds in the process (Von Eschen, *Satchmo* 177). With these tours and other activities jazz served as a political tool for the American government, spreading an image of freedom and power to foreign lands (177). As the U.S. government drew on African American jazz musicians to represent democracy to foreign lands, it was accepting jazz and inherently African Americans as iconic of American culture.

While jazz had always been recognized as American music in its travels, it had primarily connoted African American culture. This move branded jazz nationally and not just racially. African American jazz musicians participating in the tours did resist this branding, however. Gillespie spoke out against the racism that continued in America, while Armstrong denied support for Eisenhower and refused to participate in the tours for several years (Von Eschen, *Satchmo* 178–80). But the majority of musicians worked with the government peaceably. Most relevant to the concept of a jazz diaspora is how musicians like Gillespie and Clarke began to collapse American national claims on the music and their personal identities. Gillespie once remarked that he did not want to be limited by only playing in the United States nor playing only American music, since the music, in his opinion, consisted of hybrid elements and had a global appeal (Porter 59). Similarly, Kenny Clarke adjusted his perspective in his time living and performing in

Europe. He began to support the mix of American and European musicians in his Clarke-Boland Big Band, and he suggested that their internationally produced music could compete with the best American music (Hennessey, "Clarke-Boland" 24). I foreground Clarke in chapter 5, exploring how he was an important channel through which perceptions of jazz altered from "black" music to "universal" music.

The word *universal* was particularly important in the mid-twentieth-century moment of widespread French decolonization, for it signified a policy in the French republic of universal humanity, in which all citizens were to be seen in terms of their common French experience rather than (or in addition to) their ethnic differences.[10] The universalist policy of the French was another reason for the breakdown of the illusion of Paris as a space of greater freedoms and racial equality. The editors of *Black France/France Noire*—Trica Keaton, T. Denean Sharpley-Whiting, and Tyler Stovall—explain the modern problem with French universalism:

> On the one hand, there is an evident constitutional and legal discourse of colorblindness in various spheres of French life whereby race has been rejected as a meaningful category, having been discredited as biology and rightly so. Thus, there are, in effect, no French "racial minorities," only French people; nor is there an officially recognized identity discourse as there is, for instance, in the United States or the United Kingdom, where one finds terms such as "Black Americans," "African Americans," and "Black British" to express such differentiation. On the other hand, the lived experience of race—more saliently, anti-blackness—belies the colorblind principle enshrined in the universalist-humanist thought upon which the Republic was forged. (2)

The French government's universalist approach was akin to the U.S. government's hypocrisy in advocating democracy with African American jazz spokespersons while punishing them for free speech abroad and resisting change to racist Jim Crow practices. For while the illusion of Paris as color-blind persisted, the French treatment of its own people of color proved oppressive and deadly in the litany of colonial battles for independence after World War II. The French imperial reach spanned from the Caribbean to Asia. The end of the war and reoccupation of Indochina (now Vietnam) prompted the Vietnamese to fight for independence in 1946, and it was not gained until 1954. The colonies of Martinique and Guadeloupe became overseas departments with deputies representing them in the French National Assembly in 1946. Senegal and Mali gained independence in 1960. Poet and politician Léopold Senghor's sixteen-year stay in Paris as a student, soldier, and teacher would help him rise in the ranks and guide

Senegal's independence with the system of federalism he supported as its first president. In 1962 Algeria wrestled its independence from France, after battling since 1954 and enduring massive deaths. A gory massacre on October 17, 1961, would lead to deaths of Arabs in the streets of Paris and the Seine, demonstrating that violence and prejudice against people of African descent prevailed in France, too. During and after the war Algerian immigration increased. Estimated as 350,000 in 1962, the Algerian population would increase to 470,000 by 1968 (Hamilton, Simon, and Veniard).

In this postwar era of decolonization African Americans became part of a larger wave of immigrants in post–World War II France. Their foreignness had come to represent an ever-threatening migration and acculturation of the other. Covering the Algerian War had altered African American journalist William Gardner Smith's rose-colored perspective of Paris. During the Algerian War he saw the violence and prejudice against Arabs and described it in his 1963 fictional novel account, *The Stone Face*. James Baldwin had never worn rose-colored glasses in his estimation of Paris, but he too learned that one's experience of blackness in Paris depended on relation and ethnic difference. African Americans had a different relationship to the French than French colonists of African descent; he distinguished their needs as different from his own (*Nobody* 141; *No Name* 379). Film and African American cultural studies scholar Terri Francis connects the success of African Americans to this disparate treatment of African Americans and the French of African descent forwarded by universalism and colonialism. In her article on the significations of Josephine Baker, Francis writes:

> France's relationship to Africa and the conflict between its rhetorical humanism and active colonialism drove the phenomenon of black American success in Paris. African-American performers like Baker uniquely permitted the combination of (fantastical) references to ancient Africa and to modern black America—bypassing actual, contemporary Africa. This capacity for a number of readings made Baker and black American jazz compelling to Parisians throughout the twentieth century, but particularly in the 1920s and 1930s, the height of colonial wealth and expansion. True that the waves of immigration that have resulted in the cosmopolitan Paris of today are largely a postwar phenomenon, but France has always had their own *nègres* in a variety of forms and across a number of public and private spheres. (830)

Noting these distinctions, and not willing to support prejudice against other people of African descent, some African Americans were drawn back home. After staying a year in Paris, Maya Angelou had planned to settle there. But she left when her Senegalese friends were discriminated against, while a blind eye was turned to her racial difference (Stovall, "Preface" 305; Angelou 185). The March on Washington led by Martin Luther King Jr. persuaded James Baldwin, who had fled racial prejudice in the United States, to rush back and join the nonviolent campaign for civil rights in 1963.

A good many African American artists also stayed in Paris. Josephine Baker would go on tour to support U.S. civil rights protests, but France had become her permanent home at that point. Such is the sentiment conveyed in her famed song "J'ai deux amours" (I have two loves).[11] Although many African American jazz musicians in Paris remained silent, they used their music to prompt integration through musical collaborations, articulate dissent through performance and interviews, and survive through evolving perceptions, expectations, and experiences of race and nation in the Cold War era.

COMPLEXITIES OF RACE, MUSIC, AND MIGRATION

Since I address different racial classifications in this book, a few notes on terminology may be helpful. I use the term *African American* instead of *black* to address the population of people descended from Africa and born in the United States. When I do use *black*, it is for the particular purpose of discussing the African-descended race in comparison to or in dialogue with American national identity within an African American experience. I also use the phrase *black music*, especially in chapter 5; I draw on this term because it signifies the racialized claims and power struggles that have taken place over the music. The perception of the word *black* or *noir* is different between African Americans and French of African descent; even mentioning the word has different significations and functions. Today, the use of the word *black* is strategic and draws on the resonance and impact of the American civil rights moment, since there was no such movement in France. It can also be politically problematic, assuming solidarity among people of different ethnic experiences (Mudimbe-Boyi 17).[12]

Literature on black culture in France speaks to multiple ethnic experiences, consisting of French from former African colonies and people of African descent in French overseas departments in the Caribbean. For this population I use the phrase *French of African descent*. In the midcentury period with which I am concerned, several terms were used to describe people of African descent. The most common terms for African Americans and French of African descent were *Negro* in English and *nègre* and *noir* in French. But even these terms were stratified owing to class. Gary Wilder reveals a distinction between black experiences undergone by Pan-Africanist intellectuals and writers, such as the founder of the CDRN (Committee for the Defense of the Black Race): "The organization exhorted blacks to overcome racializing distinctions between hommes de couleur (educated blacks), noirs (newly assimilated blacks), and nègres (the poorest and most 'indigenous' colonized blacks)" (240). French of European descent residing in northern Africa were called "Arabs" and "pieds-noirs." When I discuss French jazz musicians and critics, I presume whiteness. This presumption does not further an essentialist perspective but rather recognizes, unfortunately, that the communities of French musicians and critics I discuss are white. When this is not the case, I use other signifiers, such as *French of African descent.*

Next, I have wrestled with what term would best convey migration in this book. In *Jazz Exiles: American Musicians Abroad* Bill Moody describes *exile* as a strategy in which musicians are pushed out of the United States by necessity. In search of jobs and better treatment, migration becomes a ticket to more opportunity and a chance to gain insight about the United States from afar; this migration is often not undertaken for pleasure or because of an uncomplicated choice (Moody xvi). Moody's distinction opens the door for considering migratory experiences of African American musicians not as identity making but as survival prompting. But Moody's definition of *exile* lacks the agency and choice I see at work with many of the case studies I examine; the word *exile* also connotes political violence or asylum, which was not the case for many musicians.

The term *expatriate* is a possibility as well. It suggests purposeful disavowal of one's native country and in some instances newfound citizenship in the receiving country. Some of the African Americans featured in this book left the United States knowing they would likely not return, while others tried living abroad but eventually returned to the States. So expatriation does not accurately convey the wealth of reasons for migration to Paris. Additionally, none of the musicians I explore gave up their American citizenship, even if they gained permanent residency in France. This speaks to their desire to retain some ties and access to the United States.

Immigrant is also not representative, for it suggests a desire to settle into the new culture and assimilate. In my conversations with African Americans in Paris and my archival research, descriptions of their lives suggest resistant immigration. From Hal Singer to Bobby Few, many of these artists held on tenaciously to their American accents. Despite marrying French women, they still socialized with other Americans. Although they lived in Paris for years, all would be hard put to dispense with their American identities. Instead of migrating their national identity, these musicians migrated their bodies, experiences, and jobs. Their hearts, however, often clung to their American nationhood. Since there was a range of possibilities without a comprehensive solution, my answer has been to use the term *migration* and to discuss these figures as "residents" of Paris. For different case studies the language may take on a specific term given the particular experience of migration.

Last, it is also important to clarify what I mean by the term *jazz*. The significations of jazz changed in the post–World War II period and came to encompass varying musical styles. Tenor saxophonist Archie Shepp considers *jazz* a racist term and prefers to use other words, indicating particular artistic genres, to describe his music; in our interview Shepp explained that he prefers not to give further credence to a word that African American musicians didn't even create (Shepp). Several etymology dictionaries and essays connect the early meaning of *jazz* not to music but to sex (Merriam and Garner 19–20; Harper; "Etymology"). From the very beginning *jazz* had multiple etymologies, such that the prevalence of this connotation may be challenged. An etymology dictionary notes the following: "Probably ult. from Creole patois *jass* 'strenuous activity,' especially 'sexual intercourse' but also used of Congo dances, from *jasm* (1860) 'energy, drive,' of African origin (cf. Mandingo *jasi*, Temne *yas*), also the source of slang *jism*" (Harper). Clarence Major's African American slang dictionary links jazz to *jaja*, a Bantu word for dance, while in an alternate definition he traces jazz to a Louisiana slave named Jasper who was nicknamed "Jas" for the exuberant reaction his dancing prompted (255).

There is some consensus on the general type of music that *jazz* describes. British social historian Eric Hobsbawm, African American music and critical race scholar Samuel Floyd, and French composer and musicologist Andre Hodeir differ in approaches to the study of jazz, but they all agree on several elements: jazz first emerged from American and black culture and benefited from international popularity and influences. It is characterized by a strong emphasis on rhythm, particularly offbeat accents and a swing groove. Jazz reflects a combination of musical elements from West Africa and Europe. Other distinctive elements include syncopation, creative variation in pitch and tones with scatting and instrumental play, as well as improvisation, among other key characteristics (Himes, *Jazz* 26–27; Floyd 14–16; Hodeir, *Jazz* 40–42, 210). Although these characteristics do inform my perception of jazz, they provide only a working definition because jazz music resists definition in its ability to combine multiple musics, influences, and forms. Jazz is actually categorized as black music, folk music, American music, and world music.

I use the word *jazz* because it is recognized across the world as identifying a particular type, and often certain eras, of music. While I discuss jazz holistically throughout the text, several chapters focus on important distinctions between blues, New Orleans–style jazz, swing, and bebop. Yet I do recognize the danger of obscuring the diversity and blurring the genres to be found in this music by referring to each as *jazz*. Jazz and cinema scholar Krin Gabbard explains this difficulty: "Jazz is a construct. Nothing can be called jazz simply because of its 'nature.' Musical genres such as the military march, opera and reggae are relatively homogeneous and easy to identify. By contrast, the term *jazz* is routinely applied to musics that have as little in common as an improvisation by Marilyn Crispell and a 1923 recording by King Oliver and his Creole Jazz Band. If today we call something jazz, it has much more to do with the utterances of critics, journalists, record companies and club owners than with the music itself" (*Jazz* 1). Gabbard's distinction between the musical characteristics and the purposes and functions of jazz cautions that the performance and perception of the word have been just as meaningful as the musical production and dissemination. Here, too, I am concerned with how the discourse and experience of jazz perform in post–World War II Paris.

METHODS AND STRUCTURE

In *Jazz Diasporas* I explore the migratory experiences of musicians and their music through case studies of African American jazz musicians (Sidney Bechet, Kenny Clarke, and Inez Cavanaugh) and white French jazz critics and musicians (Boris Vian, Charles Delaunay, René Urtreger, and Claude Luter). I chose these figures because they were all-important in the jazz and African American artistic communities in post–World War II Paris. The African American jazz musicians are reflective of the small, yet influential, group of jazz musicians who lived for five years or more in Paris. These artists help illustrate a heterogeneous narrative. They represent different jazz genres, ages, and genders.

Throughout the text I also analyze aesthetic representations of migration (including songs like "American Rhythm," films such as *Hal Singer: Keep the Music Going*, and literature like *J'irai cracher sur vos tombes*). I take my lead from books like Krin Gabbard's *Jazz among the Discourses*, Colin Nettelbeck's *Dancing with DeBeauvoir*, and Andy Fry's *Paris Blues*, each of which offers insight into the relationship between jazz and popular media and performance like literature, theater, cinema, and dance. My work complements the interdisciplinary foundation these authors have set, combining literature, media, and performance analysis with ethnographic interviews and focusing my attention on African American and white French case studies.

I also draw on theoretical perspectives of critical race theory, performance theory, and postcolonial theory and on correspondence, media clippings, recordings, archived radio and TV programs, and visual and recorded historical documents. My research combines investigation of historical archives and biographies along with performance analysis of musical, cinematic, visual, literary, and cultural texts. But *Jazz Diasporas* is not solely historiography nor solely biography, even though there are elements of both of these methodologies in the book. I discuss the influence of this historical period (with its wars, from World War II to the Cold War to the Algerian War) on the perception and identity of African American jazz musicians. I draw on biographies and autobiographies of artists such as Sidney Bechet and Kenny Clarke, and I contribute to a beginning biographical portrait of Inez Cavanaugh. But *Jazz Diasporas* is not entirely any one of these methodologies but instead exemplifies an interdisciplinary methodology powered by the field of performance studies. I commingle the aforementioned methods with the intent of studying how jazz performs culturally for these musicians, this location, and this time—and why it matters. Performance becomes the lens, theme, and method that holds together all the others. Trained as a performance studies scholar, I am interested in how performance influences and is influenced by society, and I often draw from methodologies such as ethnography, embodied performances, literary and performance analyses, and performance historiography.

Beyond the more obvious examples of musical and film performance, I study a range of performances in *Jazz Diasporas*. I explore social performances, as in the way Sidney Bechet interacts in Parisian society by emphasizing and donning different parts of himself crafted in his hybrid ethnic heritage. Analyzing jazz criticism, interviews with musicians, musical lyrics, and filmic representations of jazz in France, I investigate discursive performances—that is, the way that jazz discourse constructs and forwards particular meanings. The most apparent example of a prominent discursive performance is my consideration of the multiple significations of "universal" jazz in chapter 5. I draw on the lens and language of performance studies to deconstruct cultural performances, such as how blackness is read on Kenny Clarke's body or how Boris Vian performed certain stereotypes of African American experience, even though he never visited the United States.

The impact of performance studies on this book is also apparent in my ethnographic interviews. Though archival research is my primary resource, I have supplemented it with interviews with band members (such as Claude Luter and Nancy Holloway). In these ethnographic interviews the stories of a bygone Paris begin to breathe with new life. My modern-day interactions with musicians from this era has offered another dimension that enhances and at times contests the history I absorbed in the archives.

This strategy takes its prompt from performance studies scholars like Dwight Conquergood, who encourages a shift away from privileging "scriptocentrism" and toward adding embodied knowledge as a valuable way of knowing ("Performance" 146–47). Conquergood writes, "The performance paradigm restores the body as both a source of knowing and a site of ideological inscription and struggle. The performance paradigm insists on face-to-face encounters instead of formal abstractions" ("Rethinking" 187). Performance studies shapes this narrative as it positions embodied knowledge alongside archival knowledge rather than below it.

Embodied knowledge is ever more important given the intangible, visceral, spiritual experience of music making and listening. It is especially important given that jazz, blues, and most "black music" is based on oral storytelling. Music, dance, and poetry are all art forms that have been drawn on by African Americans to express what the written word might ignore or pass over. According to bell hooks, African American performance has the power to attack white hegemony: "All performance practice has, for African-Americans, been central to the process of decolonization in white supremacist capitalist patriarchy. From times of slavery to the present day, the act of claiming [a] voice, of asserting both one's right to speak as well as saying what one wants to say, has been a challenge to those forms of domestic colonization that seek to over-determine the speech of those who are exploited and/or oppressed" (212). Drawing on performance as a key method of researching and articulating the migratory experiences of African American jazz musicians is quite appropriate. This strategy also allows me to "claim" my own voice by weaving in my personal experiences as important "texts" influencing the construction of this narrative.

For my experience of living in modern-day Paris, while researching and writing the book, helps shape this narrative. Each chapter commences with an embodied experience that has connected me with the case study, as is evident with this chapter's description of Hal Singer's performance. A captivated response to an image, a sensorial, emotive description of a song, a memory of walking through modern-day Paris—in these ways I purposefully step into this book's narrative. Such passages not only discuss the topic but also show the impact and feeling of it. This strategy exemplifies how performance studies scholars may perform in word or action that which they investigate. African American performance scholars Omi Osun Joni L. Jones and Sharon Bridgforth do just that in *Experiments in a Jazz Aesthetic: Art, Activism, Academia, and the Austin Project*—which to my knowledge is the only other jazz book driven by performance studies methods. Jones and Bridgforth use jazz and movement as tools for performing and articulating personal and communally shared traumas. Although my own focus is different, I, too, have performed the words of James Baldwin, played the character of Sidney Bechet in an original one-act play, and written and performed a spoken-word piece to articulate what I imagine Kenny Clarke saw, felt, and questioned in his Parisian life.

In this approach there is always a danger of merging oneself with one's study. Where does one end and the other begin? But all research carries with it the biases and experiences of the author, so I want to be open about how my experiences and background influenced the writing of *Jazz Diasporas*. Just as performance studies and African American studies scholar E. Patrick Johnson explains, "I construe my ethnographic [and research and writing] practice as an 'impure' process, as performance" (10). My black, female, American body is an epistemological site, affecting not only how I approach my research but the research itself. The story of Inez Cavanaugh that unfolds in chapter 3 grows out of my own love of vocalists and from my own questions about how to thrive as an African American female residing in Paris. Similarly, my youth in relation to the jazz elders I study has no doubt prompted admiration, respect, and a desire to preserve their perspectives. I am ever aware of the fragility and egocentrism of more traditional jazz histories, which preserve stories of the great musicians while stingily according recognition to the lesser known. Hearing the perspectives of musicians like Claude Luter and Johnny Griffin, who have now passed away, drives me to "keep the music going" and spread the legacy that musicians like Hal Singer have made their life's work. These stories have greatly influenced me in the writing of this book.

Just as I relate to the figures I study, so, too, is this book about relationships rather than just individuals: the relationships of African American jazz musicians with white French jazz musicians, other people of African descent, and other artists who employed jazz music and interacted with these musicians. Chapter 1 examines the later life and career of New Orleans–style clarinetist and saxophonist Sidney Bechet. The 1949 International Jazz Festival in Paris drew Bechet from New York, seducing him to return for more job opportunities. During the final decade of his life (1949–59) Bechet was transformed into a beloved king of jazz in France. Analysis of the 1949 festival, Bechet's memoir, periodical accounts, and the song "American Rhythm" reveals how Bechet constructed his own stardom by performing multiple subjectivities. Shifting among French, American, and African-descended ancestry, he achieved overwhelming success in post–World War II France by way of his ability to play to the racialized expectations and desires of the French. Bechet's life and music come to represent one type of jazz diaspora rooted in ethnic heritage yet wandering from one home to the next.

Chapter 2 illustrates the performance of authenticity in French jazz criticism and the perspectives of French jazz musicians. The chapter takes as its source jazz criticisms, ethnographic and printed interviews, and archival resources on sidemen such as Claude Luter (a saxophonist with Sidney Bechet) and René Urtreger (a pianist with Kenny Clarke and Miles Davis). From the 1930s through the postwar era, French jazz discourse disseminated an authenticating narrative. At the end of World War II Jean Paul Sartre still called French musicians "sad imitators" (Sartre, "I Discovered" 48–49). Sartre and a host of French jazz critics, with Hugues Panassié leading the charge, persisted in harshly critiquing French musicians for not playing "real" jazz. French musicians often internalized these narratives and felt insecure about their playing. However, the confidence and popularity of French musicians began to change through collaborations with African American jazz musicians. By the mid-1950s French musicians continued the legacy of their African American counterparts, creating their own French style and transporting the music beyond American and French borders. This jazz diaspora opens up its racial and national significations to white Europeans but not without much persistent resistance from authenticating narratives.

In chapter 3 Inez Cavanaugh guides us through multiple reasons African American artists migrated to Paris, as well as ways they survived abroad. Archival records, biographies, and ethnographic interviews with jazz musicians uncover Cavanaugh's significant role, particularly as a woman and lesser-known figure, in constructing a post–World War II jazz diaspora. In the winter of 1946 Cavanaugh accompanied Don Redman and his orchestra to Paris, thus performing with the first American jazz band to play in France since before the war (Tournès 119). For five years Cavanaugh entertained and inspired the French literati and was a point person at the heart of Paris Noir. She created a space of sociality in Paris where African Americans could feel at home—eating soul food and swapping news from the United States. Cavanaugh exemplifies the ideas of community and success that Tyler Stovall explicates in his seminal and expansive work *Paris Noir: African Americans in the City of Light.* She also demonstrates the limits and expansion of the communities of Paris Noir and Saint-Germain-des-Prés—revealing those not included in a jazz diaspora (i.e., French of African descent).

Chapter 4 bridges the literature and experiences of white French writer and musician Boris Vian and African American writer James Baldwin. Vian imagines the rage and pain of African Americans from a distance, as he plays alongside jazz musicians in Saint-Germain-des-Prés. He draws on the blues to literally write himself into an African American experience. James Baldwin experiences dislocation from his homeland, yet greater understanding of his African American heritage while residing in Lausanne, Switzerland, and Paris, France. Listening to the blues and staging blues performance in his literature pushes Baldwin and his readers into a confrontation with African American identity. Looking at these two writers in concert with their counterparts in the United States, Ralph Ellison, Albert Murray, and Amiri Baraka, reveals how their blues literature addresses the concerns and struggles of African Americans in the diaspora and expands who may be included in a community of blues people and "black music."

Chapter 5 focuses on bebop cofounder Kenny Clarke, who resided in Paris from 1956 until his death in 1985. This chapter draws on musical collaborations, interviews, biographies, and recordings such as "Rue Chaptal (Royal Roost)" and *Jazz Is Universal* in its analysis. With his migration Kenny Clarke became the cornerstone of the Parisian jazz scene. He was the house drummer for the Blue Note club, the most represented drummer on the *Vogue* record label, and the go-to guy for such groundbreaking projects as *L'ascenseur pour l'échafaud* (Elevator to the gallows) soundtrack. As a highly regarded elder of jazz, he mentored many French drummers, and American musicians flew over to play with him. Through his mentoring, musical collaborations, rhetoric, and travels Kenny Clarke helped transform jazz from "black music" to a "universal" music accessible to, and playable by, those in France and beyond. Clarke represents an unresolved and shifting tension between black pride and authenticity and a desire for universal humanity irrespective of race, which potentially threatens racial erasure. This chapter deconstructs multiple performances of the term *universal* in Clarke's and jazz's journey to assimilation in Europe.

I conclude this study by examining the film *Paris Blues* to foreground several key points expressed in *Jazz Diasporas*. The coda connects the fictional jazz diasporas of *Paris Blues* to the very real lives of present-day African American jazz musicians, as well as my own experiences residing in Paris. Despite a ferocious political revolt by French of African descent in the 2000s, current jazz diasporas still favor African Americans, and there is a separation between the two diasporic communities. But in the end it is relationships rather than differences that make jazz diasporas. The relationships and exchanges of power among African Americans, white Americans, white French, and French of African descent constantly build, collapse, and rebuild to support the survival of jazz and jazz people.

1. Performing Jazz Diaspora with Sidney Bechet

I once stumbled on an amazing photograph of Sidney Bechet (fig. 1). Uncredited, undated, it could easily have gone unnoticed in the Charles Delaunay archives of the Bibliothèque nationale de France. The head-and-shoulders shot features a gray-haired Bechet simultaneously playing a clarinet and soprano saxophone. Lights, as if from a nearby street corner, sparkle through the darkness and caress his shoulders in the black-and-white photo. His shirt is crisscrossed with a pattern of Moravian-reminiscent stars that shine in their own way as well. To me the stars symbolize his success in France. Though his younger self had been dismissed, the veteran Bechet attained national stardom. Staring straight at the camera, Bechet's focused and confident regard dare the viewer not to listen. French jazz critic, promoter, and producer Charles Delaunay once called Bechet "une force de la nature" (*Delaunay's* 187). Even the mediation of this photographic form could not douse Bechet's forceful regard and impact.

Although his gaze intrigued me, the two horns caught my eye the most. They silently hinted at his intent to groove. The clarinet and the saxophone jockey for space between his ballooned jaws and angle outward from his lips. Their conjoined presence is a quick citation of his early start with the clarinet and his addition of the saxophone in his first trip abroad. They also hint at Bechet's accomplishment as the first musician to create a multitrack recording as he played six instruments to be overdubbed in his rendition of "Sheik of Araby."[1] Bechet's fingers grasp both instruments strongly but not tightly. If photos could move, his fingers would skip across the keys. Back and forth, simultaneously, he would play multiplicity—just as he did in his life. By performing multiple subjectivities of Frenchness, Americanness, and African descent, Sidney Bechet played to the racialized expectations of French critics and fans and made a place for himself in

FIGURE 1. Sidney Bechet demonstrates his musical dexterity as he plays two horns simultaneously. Bibliothèque nationale de France.

France. Bechet's life and music created a fluid jazz diaspora, in which he continually shifted between subjectivities to achieve stardom in post–World War II France.

Of all the case studies *Jazz Diasporas* explores, Sidney Bechet is the most discussed in jazz scholarship. From British author John Chilton to French jazz scholar Christian Béthune, Europeans have paid due interest with book-length studies of the star. Before them all, Bechet captured his own story in *Treat It Gentle.* Other scholars have focused on key moments of his work or life, too. African American literature scholar Jürgen Grandt investigated the literary improvisatory aspects of *Treat It Gentle.* Musicologist Andy Fry critiqued the oft-mentioned review and perspective of Ernest Ansermet that acted as proof for Bechet's rise to fame after World War II.

Some authors have stated that Bechet "became" a French star. French studies scholar Colin Nettelbeck writes, "Bechet became a French national treasure. He enjoyed his stardom and cultivated it with good-natured diligence" (69). French historian Tyler Stovall also states, "The French loved Sidney Bechet because to a certain extent he became one of them. His French last name and Créole heritage helped, of course" (*Paris Noir* 174). Stovall notes that Bechet "became" French but only "to a certain extent," suggesting that Bechet was incorporated into French society and culture but not fully. Stovall points to Bechet's actions as the secret to his success rather than falling back on his natural connections to the French (his Creole name, language, and heritage). Stovall underscores how Bechet interacted with the French and positioned jazz music in France. By emphasizing Bechet's actions, Stovall suggests that Bechet actively created his success.

I would add to Stovall's discussion that Bechet did more than "become" French; he "performed" Frenchness by drawing on his Creole heritage. Bechet's attainment of stardom in post–World War II France was not inevitable but rather deliberately achieved through a conscious performance of multiple subjectivities. Like identities, subjectivities are shaped by one's personal experiences and opinions, but they are also influenced by external forces. Bechet played on several: his Creole background connected him to Frenchness, and his autobiography and memories of his ancestry constructed an African (and African-descended) subjectivity. Despite this, however, he never lost attachment to his New Orleans home and music. In this enduring attachment he performed Americanness.

"Becoming" and "performing" differ in several critical ways. *Becoming* suggests a natural, even somewhat passive, transformation. But Bechet's change was not passive but rather deliberately performed. His personality alone suggests that he never unknowingly fell into anything. His own accounts and interviews with bandmates demonstrate how meticulous he was about the quality of music he played and the level of musicianship his band showed.[2] Several French band members were *torturé* by Bechet's rigorous, perfectionist rehearsals (J. Chilton 40; Horricks 1–9; Delaunay, *Delaunay's* 187). So, why would he pay any less consideration to the social roles he performed? *Becoming* also implies that he transformed into something new. But Bechet did not alter his identity. He consistently changed how he portrayed himself instead. This type of performative reading stresses the deconstruction of social roles and cultural interaction rather than accepting them as natural. It positions Bechet as active in the construction of his significations.

In "Remembrance of Jazz Past: Sidney Bechet in France" Andy Fry states that Bechet actively portrays his hybrid heritage through a diverse repertoire. Fry explains that Bechet "achieved a careful balancing act: He was a New Orleans jazzman [spinning the tale of having played with the earliest jazz musicians like Buddy Bolden] but also a Creole who had, in a sense, come 'home' to France and was happy to play a Gallic-inflected repertoire" (316). Fry's analysis pinpoints the ambiguity of Bechet's cultural performances, implying that he shifted his personas and his repertoire to best fit in with his French environment.

Fry's point underscores my own, that Bechet's ambiguous performances were influenced and fueled by his Creole heritage. Postcolonial theorist Édouard Glissant has written about characteristics and experiences of creolization, starting from his own Caribbean background. Though the ethnic experiences differ, Bechet's Creole body and culture similarly weave together various cultures, obfuscating pure essence and clear division between parts in the process. Glissant writes that "the poetics of *métissage* is the poetics of Relation" (*Le discours* 251; my translation). These different interwoven parts, what I have called subjectivities, relate in important ways. For Bechet's distinct subjectivities inevitably tangled together in an ambiguous fashion, leading to an unsettled assimilation into French society. Rather than laying claim to one home, Bechet's restless, mobile subjectivities were part of a jazz diaspora that emphasized individualism while relating to and depending on multiple communities.

Bechet's jazz travels further tested and prompted the instability of the subjectivities he performed. It was not just the hybrid nature of métissage and creolization, but movement to and from subjectivities, which shaped Bechet's (and jazz's) diasporic experience. His movement threatened a potential disavowal of his American roots, his Louisiana heritage. His music and his life disdained (yet also played with) national and racial rootedness.

Bechet's unsettled assimilation in French jazz culture illustrates the kind of "in-betweenness" that Homi Bhabha theorizes in *Location of Culture*. According to Bhabha, the possibilities for identity formation resist an "essential way of being" and promote fluidity. With his concept of the "in-between" Bhabha presents a space for these unfixed identities and privileges "movement back and forth" (3). He writes, "It is in the emergence of the interstices—the overlap and the displacement of domains of difference—that the intersubjective and collective experiences of nationness, community interest, or cultural value are negotiated" (2). Bechet's jazz diaspora is the only space, an interstice if you will, that creates a "fit" and a place of survival. It is a space of "complex, ongoing" negotiation. For just as Bechet played up multiple subjectivities in ongoing negotiations, so did the jazz that traveled with him complicate its reading as singularly African American music.

Paul Gilroy expands this racialized signification of jazz in his seminal work, *The Black Atlantic: Modernity and Double Consciousness*. He describes black music as creolized in its origin, since often it draws on multiple influences (75). Gilroy recognizes the impossibility of a pure black music, since as it is exchanged, disseminated, critiqued, and shaped, black music resists sameness (80). He makes a similar case for people of African descent, one that frames well the subjectivities that Bechet performs: "The history of the black Atlantic yields a course of lessons as to the instability and mutability of racial identities which are always unfinished, always being remade" (Gilroy xi). Gilroy's black Atlantic resists categorizing identities into pure essences such as all black or all white and to recognize that identities are hybrid.

Bechet's subjectivities, rather than states of being, were processes that could be "remade"; they could be performed and functional. Racialized significations, national expectations—these were multiple roles he played rather than an immutable notion of self. Yet Bechet's roles rarely escaped ambiguous signification. Bechet makes the perfect case study to investigate the evolving racial and national identities of jazz in France because both grew out of the hybrid, creolized culture of New Orleans.

Born in 1897 New Orleans, Sidney Joseph Bechet mirrored the birth of jazz in the early twentieth century. New Orleans was a prominent site in the creation and early development of jazz. At the age of six Bechet borrowed his brother's clarinet and rushed out to hear and study the sounds of Buddy Bolden and Bunk Johnson (Bechet, *Sidney Bechet*; J. Chilton 5). He may have grown up playing among legends in the red-light district of Storyville, but like jazz he soon found himself on the road. In 1916 Bechet left New Orleans to play in Texas. He headed all the way to Chicago by 1917, bringing his style of blues and jazz to the North. Jazz historian Ted Gioia discusses the larger phenomenon that Bechet's migration represented:

> Well before the middle of the decade, a large cadre of major New Orleans jazz musicians were making their reputations in other locales—Jelly Roll Morton left New Orleans around 1908; Freddie Keppard departed in 1914 (if not earlier); Sidney Bechet in 1916, Jimmie Noone in 1917, King Oliver in 1918, Kid Ory in 1919, Johnny Dodds around that same time, Baby Dodds in 1921, and Louis Armstrong in 1922. These moves may have begun as brief stints on the road, but in the end proved all but permanent. The vast majority of the New Orleans diaspora never returned to their home state except for brief visits. This exodus was anything but a purely musical phenomenon. Between the years 1916–1919, a half-million African Americans left the South for more tolerant communities in the North, with almost one million more following in their wake in the 1920s. This vast population shift, which has since come to be known as the Great Migration, encompassed the whole range of black society, from doctors and lawyers to musicians and ministers, from teachers and merchants to artisans and manual laborers. (43)

Gioia connects Bechet to others, and not just musicians. He shows how Bechet was not singular in his desire to move but exemplified part of a mass migration. In 1941 New York, African American painter Jacob Lawrence encapsulated the motivations, emotions, and results of these waves of migration of African Americans, most prominently between 1900 and 1930. Lawrence exhibited a series of paintings called *The Migration of the Negro*, consisting of sixty panels accompanied by statements about the experience of migration and assimilation into the northern and western regions of the United States. "His text, which he carefully researched and wrote before he ever made an image, clearly explained why people needed to leave and were still leaving. It described their hopes for something better, depicted the violence and disease they endured, pointed out their strengths and their potential for political power," writes curator Elizabeth Turner in her introduction to the Phillips Collection's catalog of the series (Turner 13). Lawrence's panels vividly illustrate migratory experiences in expressionistic fashion, and his statements clarify multiple reasons for moving: lynching, white supremacy–influenced legislation, unreasonable and unpredictable arrests, unfair treatment of tenant farmers, child labor, and lack of opportunities for education. The hopes and dreams that prompted the Great Migration also influenced migration outside the country. The international migration of jazz musicians like Bechet and the motivations to find more equality in Paris extended the hopes and dreams of the Great Migration.

Considering Sidney Bechet's individual migration, and his music with it, as part of this larger diasporic movement points to the interwoven nature of individual, collective, and musically shared aspects of diasporic experience. In *Blues People: Negro Music in White America,* Amiri Baraka traces the connections among slave songs, blues, jazz, and R&B and links their development and dissemination with the migration of African Americans from South to North, from countryside to urban center, from minority to mainstream culture. But the contributions of nonblacks and non-Americans to "black music" do not fit as well in Baraka's concept of African diaspora. Sidney Bechet's migrations demonstrate the racial and national hybridization of jazz that migration prompted.

Bechet was one of the first musicians to play jazz internationally. He performed with Will Marion Cook's Southern Syncopated Orchestra in England and France in 1919.[3] The band was impressed by the invitation to play for the Prince of Wales in London. Swiss conductor Ernest Ansermet was equally impressed by Bechet, singling him out as "an extraordinary clarinet virtuoso" and "artist of genius" in the first jazz review ever written (Ansermet 177). Bechet was recognized as a groundbreaking soloist in jazz (Teachout). His ability to improvise and his powerful vibrato-led delivery distinguished him from other musicians. *Jazz Hot* critic Maxime Saury found Bechet distinctive from contemporaries like Louis Armstrong, Duke Ellington, and Count Basie because of his pure melodic line, which never faltered, his leadership in guiding the band's improvisational choices, and his force of will that consistently marked the sound as his no matter his accompaniment (22). Ellington himself captured the emotional impact and improvisatory genius of Sidney Bechet: "He had a wonderful clarinet tone—all wood, a sound you don't hear anymore. . . . I consider Bechet the foundation. His things were all soul, all from the inside. It was very, very difficult to find anyone who could really keep up with him" (Ellington and Dance 15). Bechet had a way of strutting into one's heart with his meandering style. His horn tone wavered and wandered in its vibrato. His sound wobbled with a fierce and confident whining as it wandered to the next unexpected phrase—much like he wandered in his life.

In 1925 Bechet journeyed to Europe again, visiting France, Germany, and Russia—to name some of the countries on his itinerary. In Paris he played clarinet in the jazz orchestra of Claude Hopkins's show *La revue nègre.* Trouble soon followed the quick-tempered, gun-toting Bechet. Packing protective weaponry may have been the way to survive in Storyville, but it got him into big trouble again while he was traveling.[4] In 1928 he served nearly a year in a French prison for participating in a shoot-out in Montmartre, Paris. In a disagreement with his drummer, Mike McKendrick, Bechet mistakenly shot a French woman and also wounded two passersby instead of his bandmate; upon his release from jail he was permanently banned from entering France. Luckily, with the help of Charles Delaunay, the ban was temporarily removed in 1949 for the Paris International Jazz Festival and permanently in 1951 (Bechet, *Treat* 152–54; J. Chilton 83–84; Béthune 129).

After the 1949 festival Bechet returned to New York but only until the fall. The festival had increased his job opportunities in France, and he already had gigs lined up starting in October (Béthune 123). He traveled back and forth between the United States and Europe, until his emigration from the United States in 1950. He lived the next nine years in Paris before dying from lung cancer in 1959. During that era he savored the peak of his career under the enthralled glee of French fans, young and old. At Olympia Music Hall in 1955 Bechet celebrated his millionth concert. The fifty-five hundred concertgoers were so enthused they caused a near riot in their attempts to inhabit the fifteen hundred seats (Ehrlich 94, 98). By the time Bechet died, he had sold millions of records and increased the repute of jazz in France. In the process he made a place for himself as France's adopted king of jazz.

FROM NEW ORLEANS TO ORLÉANS: MAKING A PLACE FOR JAZZ

Sidney Bechet was a Louisiana Creole—and proud of it. "He never missed an opportunity to recall his French origins or to speak Creole with Albert Nicholas. And, he insisted that his name be pronounced the French way," wrote Charles Delaunay (*Delaunay's* 188).[5] Bechet's Creole French language was his first tool for fitting into French society. Young French fans found his Louisiana French accent adorable, and even more discerning French jazz critics like Gérard Pochonet called it delightful (Ehrlich 94; Pochonet 16). In his *Esquire* photo spread reporter Blake Ehrlich captured a grinning Bechet hunched over a table as a throng of young French men and women leaned in to hear his next words (Ehrlich 94, 98). Although his pronunciation distinguished him from native French speakers, his Louisiana Creole culture (and the jazz that grew out of it) paved a path for his French stardom and assimilation. Drawing on the language, culture, and music of his Louisiana Creole heritage, Bechet performed Frenchness to fit in with French society. Despite this performed Frenchness, however, Bechet failed to fully assimilate; in multiple ways the French jazz public set him apart as foreign and other.

Bechet's creolized heritage descended from his great-grandmother, a white French woman who married a free African American man. Growing up in a French-speaking, middle-class Creole family in downtown New Orleans, Bechet was exposed to both Creole French and English. His family also valued musical education. In fact, many Creole parents encouraged their children to learn piano and practice classical music. Sidney was the youngest of seven siblings, and all the boys played musical instruments. His father, Omar, even played the flute when he wasn't working as a shoe-maker (J. Chilton 2). His family enjoyed an elite lifestyle until the 1890s introduced codes categorizing them as "Negroes" and imposing segrega-tion. There had historically been a class division between Creoles and African Americans; Creoles were often perceived as a higher class at best and condescending at worst. Musicologist David Ake explains this complex division as reflective of differences in religion, geography, class, language, culture, and skin color. He elaborates on the class status that many Creoles performed:

> The fact that Creole ownership of slaves was not uncommon by the late eighteenth century illustrates quite clearly the emergence of a separate and increasingly prosperous African-diasporic cultural community in the region. . . . The political power and social prestige held by the Louisiana Creole community fluctuated with the changing local governments but generally fell somewhere between the various European-American ethnicities on the one extreme and the English-speaking, African-American population on the other. Even as their economic status began to wane in the nineteenth century, however, Creole society strove to maintain staunchly middle-class values, priding itself on appearing well mannered and well educated (in the European sense) and living within an overall Francocentrism. (*Jazz Cultures* 16–17)

The black codes rubbed against the Creole way of life and produced some tensions. Also, downtown connoted a wealthy status; in contrast, uptown featured the infamous and illicit red-light district of Storyville spread out over two square miles in the middle of the city. Situated below Canal Street and beside the French quarter, Storyville housed legal prostitution for more than twenty years until its closure in 1917 (Barker 99).[6] The style of music matched the locales. Bechet's mother did not like him listening to uptown music or visiting venues there, but the young Bechet dismissed his moth-er's wishes and sneaked out to secure gigs in Storyville (J. Chilton 3–5). He risked his high-class status by performing uptown (Buerkle and Barker 20).

Ake describes Bechet's style, too, as dismissive of classical music training and representative of uptown in comparison to Jelly Roll Morton, another groundbreaking Creole jazz pianist from New Orleans. Morton fashioned himself as a composer, in the tradition of European musical composition, and he had no time for those who could not read music; in contrast, Bechet avoided learning to read music and drew on more Afrocentric characteristics of jazz and blues (Ake, *Jazz Cultures* 25–26). Ake explains, "In fact, Bechet's attitude toward musicking directly opposed European ideals. His playing leaned heavily toward the Uptown, that is to say 'unschooled,' 'low-down,' or 'blacker' styles, and it is precisely these 'rough' techniques that Bechet saw as essential to jazz" (*Jazz Cultures* 26–27). Bechet would later play with Bunk Johnson in the Eagle Band, which performed primarily in Storyville for fans who had wilder and rowdier reputations than the norm (J. Chilton 15). He also played with Freddie Keppard and later did some recordings with Louis Armstrong. Even among these great pioneers of early jazz, the young Bechet was considered a prodigy and quickly mastered the fife, clarinet, and saxophone.

Although New Orleans was segregated, it housed a mix of cultures that were able to successfully coexist. Home to African, European, Caribbean, Creole, and other ethnicities, New Orleans's diverse cultures, languages, and musical styles seeped into the jazz form (Stearns 31–38). Though there were certainly other regions and cities of note in the creation of jazz, the multicultural setting of New Orleans played a key role, wherein jazz combined elements from West African drum rhythms, call-and-response exchanges, and European tonal systems and meters (Stearns 39; Floyd 14–16; J. Chilton 5). New Orleans resembled the "melting pot" that J. Hector St. John de Crèvecœur dubbed America upon seeing many cultures living under one national vision in 1782. The melting pot of New Orleans (just as in jazz) contained a constantly changing number of influences, large and small. In *Jazz: A History of America's Music* Geoffrey Ward and Ken Burns quote British immigrant Benjamin Henry Latrobe: "There are in fact three societies here, 1. The French, 2. The American, and 3. The mixed"; the authors add that Choctaw and Natchez Native Americans, Balkans, Filipinos, Chinese, Malays, German, Irish, and Sicilians migrated to New Orleans, too, and "by 1860, forty percent of the people of New Orleans were foreign-born" (Latrobe quoted in Ward and Burns 6).

This constant influx of people influenced the music. For New Orleans was a place of constant collaboration (and separation) as people of different cultures worked together and segregated themselves according to status. I refer here to the segregation practices of the plantation owners versus the slaves in the antebellum South and, later, the perceived high-society status of Creoles in downtown as compared to African Americans living in uptown.

New Orleans housed these divisions, but it also merged these different cultures and kept changing the mix as new immigrants arrived. The New

Orleans style or Dixieland jazz grew out of this mélange of cultures coexisting in the early twentieth century. Accordingly, it absorbed various musical genres such as waltzes, quadrilles, ragtime, marching songs, funeral dirges, blues, Mardi Gras ceremonial music, religious songs, and European classical music privileged by Creole musicians. New Orleans–style jazz took several forms: smaller combos performing "slow blues and more up-tempo, rag-like stomps and 'honky-tonk numbers,'" brass marching bands, and dance bands that included string instruments and played for everything from waltzes to cakewalks (J. Taylor 49). The instrumentation was wide-ranging, too, featuring everything from brass instruments such as trumpets, cornets, tubas, and trombones to woodwinds such as the clarinet to strings such as the banjo and piano. In most cases New Orleans–style jazz consisted of collective improvisation, polyphonic textures, and heavy use of horns derived from its marching-band influences. The style also introduced some experimentation with tone color and vocal scatting. In the 1940s and 1950s this style was labeled "revivalist," since, for a brief time, young fans demonstrated a renewed interest.

Sidney Bechet romantically recalled the impact of collective improvisation and counterpoint on jazz performance in New Orleans: "In the old days there wasn't no one so anxious to take someone else's run. We were working together. Each person, he was the other person's music: you could feel that really running through the band, making itself up and coming out so new and strong. We played as a group then" (*Treat* 176). Bechet worked within different types of groups in his French career, playing with young musicians such as Claude Luter and collaborating with musicians from different genres such as beboppers Kenny Clarke and Martial Solal. He always rose above the collective aesthetic with his distinctive vibrato, tone, and creative improvisations. Bechet's musical style promoted the collective and the individual just as jazz also layered multiple influences.

Historian Burton Peretti calls this mixed musical heritage the "créolization of jazz": "Jazz holds special importance as a model of créolized culture among once-colonized 'folk'" (94). He later cites examples of creolization in jazz history (the influence of migrants and West Indians, Africans' impact on jazz in 1920s Harlem, and the introduction of Afro-Cuban jazz to America in Dizzy Gillespie's work with Chano Pozo) (96). I would also add such examples as Stan Getz's trip to Brazil in the 1960s and the labeling of bossa nova as a jazz style. With each, jazz was taken in a new direction, and the life and popularity of the music was extended. The collaboration with multiple cultures, creolization, actually ensured the continued growth and success of jazz.

Homi Bhabha presents a way to consider these differences within jazz as nonstatic: "The social articulation of difference, from the minority perspective, is a complex, on-going negotiation that seeks to authorize cultural hybridities that emerge in moments of historical transformation'" (2). Bhabha references Stuart Hall's articulation theory here, which states that combining different cultures into one can alter the interwoven parts. Bhabha adds that historical events help spur these changes. In the example of Bechet's Creole heritage in New Orleans, he encountered many cultures and blended those into his unique experience.

Bechet's Creole language and culture influenced French perceptions of him and his music as well. "I don't know if they remember me in New Orleans, but in old Orléans, they love me!" he exclaimed in 1958 (Ehrlich 97). Bechet felt unappreciated and forgotten by American fans, and the consistent comparison to trumpeter Louis Armstrong did not help. Bechet could never get out from under Armstrong's shadow. He was always compared to Armstrong, and the disparate recognition he received in the United States irked him.

The media often compared the two as well. American reporter Paul Eduard Miller described Bechet in a 1945 *Esquire* article: "The stature and importance of Sidney Bechet is at least the equal of Armstrong, Ellington, Hawkins, Goodman and Hodges, while in the matter of sustained consistency of performance he is their superior" (Miller). Both musicians grew up in New Orleans and excelled at jazz in its birthplace. Yet in the United States Armstrong was the unrivaled king of New Orleans jazz. He had also been developing an international fan base since the 1930s, arriving in London as early as 1932. While French fans were not awed by Armstrong's concert at Salle Pleyel in 1934 Paris (some were actually bored), they still turned out in large numbers to see his show and collaborations in the clubs with French and American players (J. Jackson, "Making" 159).

Bechet's 1920s tours throughout France, Germany, and Russia went without much notice—except, of course, for the gun showdown with McKendrick. Andy Fry investigates the French critics' lack of attention to the younger Bechet. He notes that jazz critic, producer, and Hot Club of France cofounder Hugues Panassié only mentioned Bechet in passing in his 1934 book *Le Jazz Hot*; also, the rave review by Ernest Ansermet in 1919 did little to establish the young genius in France, since it was only republished and introduced to the French in the November/December 1938 issue of the magazine *Jazz Hot* (Fry, *Paris* 231–35). Biographer John Chilton suggests that perhaps Bechet's vibrato was the reason for the early French inattention to him; Chilton adds that "the fierce throbbing that marked his sound touched a nerve within them and they could not listen with pleasure to his music" (293).

Bechet's rise to French fame would finally come with the Paris International Jazz Festival, May 8–15, 1949. *Le monde* devoted a quarter-page spread previewing the festival: "For a week, blacks and whites, seasoned stars and amateurs will take turns performing in this noteworthy event" (Drouin 6; my translation).[7] The festival did not disappoint. *Down Beat* reported: "Paris-Backstage at the Salle Pleyel, an excited crowd shuffled back and forth. Musicians were warming up, stage technicians barked last minute directions, critics and kibitzers chattered excitedly and craned their necks, as 15 minutes late, a French emcee sidled in front of the curtain and announced 'Le Festival Internationale de Jazz est ouvert.' And for a whole week the 25,000 capacity auditorium was jammed" (McPartland).

Jazz musicians from seven countries flocked to perform at the festival. According to *Jazz Hot* and *Down Beat*, the American and Swedish players made the biggest impression, but all countries sent their best musicians (Hodeir, "Le festival" 7; McPartland). Still it was the Americans who stole the show and inspired the most critique. The festival assembled several high-profile American jazz musicians: Charlie "Bird" Parker led a quintet with Kenny Dorham, Al Haig, Tommy Potter, and Max Roach (Vail 57). Sidney Bechet played with different bands, featuring a mix of French and American talent. He played one night with Frenchman Pierre Braslavsky, another with Claude Luter, and yet another night with the American "Hot Lips" Page accompanied by a French rhythm section. The other standout was the Tadd Dameron Quintet, featuring Miles Davis, James Moody, Tadd Dameron, Barney Spieler, and Kenny Clarke. From various fan accounts the festival lived up to the European hype. The young British musician Allan Ganley came all the way from London. After meeting Charlie Parker at Club Saint-Germain and watching Max Roach and "Hot Lips" Page perform multiple nights, Ganley boasted of the memorable experience (Vail 58). A couple of accounts also mention how Parker caused quite a stir when he turned his back to the audience, discounting the same audience rapport Bechet inspired (Hodeir, "Le festival" 7; Vail 59).

The Paris International Jazz Festival was arranged around these two archrivals and genres. By choosing Bechet and Parker, the festival's organizer, Charles Delaunay, agitated two firmly entrenched camps, one promoting New Orleans–style players and the other advocating bebop (Delaunay, *Delaunay's* 187).[8] Bechet represented New Orleans–style jazz, and Parker was an originator of bebop. The festival's promoters consciously addressed the battle between fans of traditional jazz and those who supported the newer bebop style (Zwerin, "Jazz" 542; Stovall, *Paris* 168). Whereas New Orleans–style jazz emphasized collective improvisation, bebop created more space for virtuosic solos often played at a relatively faster tempo. Ingrid Monson adds, "Bebop Combo Jazz improvised style that evolved from big band swing in the 1940s, characterized by exceedingly fast tempos, with improvisational lines based on the harmonic structure rather than the melody. . . . Charlie Parker and Dizzy Gillespie reharmonized and/or wrote new melodies for standard jazz tunes" (Monson, "Jazz" 173–74). Musicians such as Kenny Clarke and Charlie Christian (along with the aforementioned stars) cofounded the bebop style in their experimentations in the concerts and cutting sessions in Minton's Playhouse in 1940s New York City.

But by festival's end, neither Davis nor Parker remained on the lips of French jazz critics and fans. No, it was Bechet. In "Le festival 1949" André Hodeir wrote: "The success story of the Festival was without doubt Sidney Bechet, who with each return to the stage inspired a huge rush of enthusiasm" (7; my translation).[9] French jazz critics claimed Bechet as their own king of jazz. On the cover of the June 1949 issue of *Jazz Hot* he appeared with a crown on his head—the victorious ruler of all who performed in the Paris International Jazz Festival. The cover also foreshadowed Bechet's postwar stardom to come: "In May of 1949 he boarded a plane in New York—together with Charlie Parker, Miles Davis, Lips Page, Tadd Dameron and others—and literally flew towards his years of fame. . . . Between the Sunday and the Tuesday Bechet became a national hero" (Horricks 7).

Bechet's hybrid heritage created this path to stardom. By continually emphasizing the French pronunciation of his name, highlighting his accent, and reminding the French of his own Creole French heritage, Bechet was adapting to his French home. By performing songs like "As-tu le cafard?" and "Petite fleur" in French, he drew on the language of this receiving culture and his Creole heritage to further entrench himself in French culture. He showed his enculturation through his use of the language and his ability to musically comment on the culture. For example, Bechet's original composition "Petite fleur" was generally performed instrumentally, but he wrote French lyrics describing a flower that he would forever guard and love. It was very romantic and made a perfect fit for Paris, a city known for its lovers and romantic trysts. Another original Bechet composition, "As-tu le cafard?" translates as "Have you got the blues?" This song positioned the blues as a music and form of suffering that was at home in the language and culture of French people. Bechet would record countless French and American songs, both covers and originals. He demonstrated that he belonged in France by embracing his new French life and mixing it with his Creole and African American heritage.

Andy Fry adds that Bechet's performance of Frenchness may have been purposefully motivated by Bechet and Delaunay: "What the musician (or perhaps his new manager, Delaunay) had been quick to realize was that it was not only exoticism or 'authenticity' that underlay his appeal but a feigned familiarity, too. As early as October 1949 *Jazz Hot* was reporting that Bechet's renown in the jazz community was crossing over into mainstream success; the general public was falling for him despite their customary disinterest bordering on animosity about jazz" ("Remembrance" 316). Fry's comment expands the audience of Bechet's performances; it was not just the jazz public but also a larger French listening audience that began to accept Bechet.

Not only did the French general public accept Bechet into their fold, but Americans also considered Bechet to be French on occasion, too. An article in the *Toronto Telegraph* states, "New Orleans–born Sidney Bechet who is now the No. 1 American jazzman in Europe likes to tell about the U.S. tourist who approached him after a hectic performance at the Olympia Music Hall here [in Paris] and said: 'You Frenchmen really can play our music. Where do you learn?' The story points up how thoroughly the soprano saxophonist has become a part of the modern French scene. For, if some Americans mistakenly believe him to be French, there are numerous Frenchmen, fooled by his Creole name, who think of him as one of themselves" ("New"). This misidentification of Bechet's nationality points to his great ability to conform and adjust to French society. It also reinforces the multiple significations that his Creole heritage encompassed. Bechet rode the line between two national subjectivities and negotiated what and how he performed. He morphed American cultural expressions into French, thereby manipulating the origin narrative of jazz and his own life. He once commented, "Back in slavery times in Congo Square in New Orleans, them slaves used to gather on a Sunday when they had kind of a day off and they'd dance and sing. The rhythm came from Africa, but the music, the foundation, came from right here in France" (Bechet, *Treat* 194).

Bechet downplayed his and the music's U.S. origins with these words. As a homeland, America was a given. But by omitting it here, Bechet made France prominent in the development of the music. For Bechet playing jazz in France was returning home. His music had French roots, which he had seen in New Orleans and through his Creole background. With his omission Bechet was naming *un relation*, in this case a genealogical and historical relationship between French and American cultural expressions like jazz.

His song selection strengthened *le relation* between the two cultures. Bechet's songs were often versions of old American blues or rags that had been created or performed abroad before arriving in the United States. By performing ragtime, the predecessor of blues and jazz, he promoted a Euro-American genre that already drew on European classical music and syncopated it. Another example was Bechet's tendency to play old New Orleans standards and rename them. For example, his "Panther Dance" was based on "Tiger Rag," a New Orleans favorite. Edgar Jackson makes the connection to France when he writes: "As this is our friend Tiger Rag many may think it a New Orleans product. But in fact it is an old French quadrille, originally known as Praline and said to have been inspired by La Marseilles [*sic*]" (29). This French connection to the quadrille, a march-based musical style, was not discovered by an American but rather a Francophone jazz critic. The Belgian author Robert Goffin identified the number as "the distorted theme of a second tableau of a quadrille I used to hear as a boy, at all the balls of Walloon, Belgium" (Stearns 74). Bechet's performance of quadrilles-turned-rags like "Panther Dance" was affirmation that jazz did indeed have a French heritage too.

Rags like "Panther Dance" were layered with differing renditions and historical significance as they traveled globally. What we hear in the song comes from the layering of the two national versions as they are "remade" into something new yet still retaining their national origins—what Gilroy claims as his version of "the changing same" (Gilroy xi, 101).[10] The relationship between the French and American versions is also important because the two versions cannot be separated. These songs exemplify the creolization of jazz and Bhabha's negotiated articulations of difference. They also show jazz as dependent on *un relation*. In Glissant's poetics of relation, cultures maintain the fact of origin but not of rooted, entrenched identities; Instead their identities shift, collapse and spread according to their relation with other cultures, peoples, and experiences (Glissant, *Poetics* 72). Bechet's repertoire and his creolized heritage demonstrated the importance of interdependence and relation to jazz. By emphasizing the merged French and American contributions of jazz, Bechet created a wider jazz diaspora and identity of jazz. He validated the French contribution while legitimizing the African American contribution by showing the interdependence between France's Old World master musicianship and what was still perceived as low-culture music in the United States. With Bechet jazz was not only black nor only American; it was a music that touched on multiple cultures.

In sum, he would continue to widen his jazz diaspora by playing throughout the French and European countryside and surrounding himself with French musicians in order to blend into French society. Another reason Bechet achieved success in France was his sheer number of performances and tours. Ludovic Tournès confirms this, stating that through the

1950s France hosted many jazz festivals throughout the country, and Bechet had the lion's share of gigs; in smaller regions only the bigger names were known and capable of drawing crowds, so again Bechet profited (Tournès 135–36). In addition he was quite fortunate with the huge success of his recording "Les oignons." According to Tournès, 1.2 million records had sold by 1959 (135). By playing so many gigs throughout all regions of France, Bechet made a home for himself and for his New Orleans style of music in the French jazz industry.

Tournès discusses in more detail how Bechet and other artists spread jazz beyond Paris to other regions of France, thus discounting the perception that jazz was only an urban music mostly found in the cities (134–38). Tournès also notes that Bechet became a part of the music-hall scene; he was billed with such French greats as singer Jacques Brel and even debuted his ballet *La nuit est une sorcière* for President René Coty (286–87). From the late 1800s through the mid-1900s music halls grew in popularity. They were large halls that served as variety theaters, bringing together comedy shows, vaudeville acts, dances featuring nude dancers (as with cancan dancing), and short numbers from some of the most sought-after stars, including the actors and singers Mistinguette and Maurice Chevalier. The common denominator was that music halls were extravagant and considered licentious in terms of French morals (at least in the 1920s and 1930s) (J. Jackson, *Making* 105–8). Along with Bechet, Josephine Baker contributed greatly to the music-hall scene, appearing at the Folies-Bergère, Casino de Paris, and Olympia. So in another way Bechet made a place for himself in the French jazz scene, this time performing among other French musicians of note. Bechet's success in the music-hall scene, and his ability to play alongside white French players of note, distinguished him as a rare performer and further portrayed him as a French mainstay. Even beyond French borders he was a French cultural icon worldwide; in the *Daily Mail* obituary for the star, English reporter Kenneth Alsop described Bechet as at "the level of Chevalier and Piaf, and an institution in the Left Bank caves" (Alsop).[11]

Many French jazz and nonjazz fans alike know the name of Sidney Bechet today. But their pronunciation of his name questions his success at fully signifying as French. Was it pronounced "Besh-ay" or "Besh-ette"? Upon conducting research in Paris, I realized that the French had a different perception of this prominent clarinetist and soprano saxophonist. The biggest clue to this dichotomy was the dual pronunciation of his name. I had heard his name pronounced "Besh-ay" for years, and one contemporaneous article actually spelled it out: "Sidney Bechet (rhymes with say-hey)" (E. Jackson 83). But during my ethnographic interview with Bechet's enduringly respectful former bandmate Claude Luter, I heard "Besh-ette." The 2010 PBS documentary *Harlem in Montmartre* confirmed this disparity. It was recorded in both English and French. The English pronunciation was "Besh-ay." The French, however, said "Besh-ette."

Some students in one of my "Jazz & Anthropology" seminars at École des hautes études en sciences sociales clarified this; our conversation revealed that the French do not pronounce *Bechet* as a French word (Braggs "Sidney"). Ending in -*et* and being of French origin, the name should be pronounced -*ay*. Instead, they pronounce it -*ette*, essentially pronouncing it the way they think Americans would.[12]

But the French are not the only ones to mispronounce it. John Chilton indicated that Louis Armstrong misspelled the name as "Bachet." Chilton adds that American fans retained the pronunciation of "Besh-ay," and he confirmed the "Besh-ette" pronunciation of the French public (21). The correct pronunciation was "Besh-ay." Apparently language had also foiled Bechet's ability to pass as French when he was alive. Pierre Merlin, a trumpeter for Claude Luter's band Le Lorientais, recalled the difficulty of understanding Bechet: "Also, I had difficulty in understanding what he was saying. I think only one of our band spoke English fluently, so it was obvious that Sidney would speak in French, but because of his accent this made things difficult. I suppose he was out of practice, but it wasn't only accent, it was his vocabulary as well" (J. Chilton 216). The difference in vocabulary further signaled Bechet's different cultural experience; it hindered his ability to communicate and collaborate in some ways with his bandmates. This passage also illustrates how Bechet may have been persistent about speaking Creole, but he was just as resistant to more fully conforming to French society by learning French idioms and pronunciations. Given Bechet's stubborn and perfectionist personality, the onus was on his bandmates, not him, to adjust. Bechet's resistance here underscores the tension, ambiguity, and "in-betweenness" of his performance of subjectivities.

His Creole accent not only challenged national assimilation but also connoted his racial difference. "People loved to hear him talk in French, even though it was always Creole. It never changed, or improved, it was what we would call 'petit nègre,'" stated Charles Delaunay (J. Chilton 251). The term *petit nègre* identified people of African descent who lived in French colonies; their French was perceived as more rudimentary than French on the Continent. This label demonstrated how Bechet's pronunciation could perform an ethnic subjectivity different from his own experience. It further distinguished him from his white French colleagues yet linked him to French of African descent—of whom there were very few in attendance at jazz concerts.

Delaunay's comment also hints at the history of primitivism that under-girded French society's desire for African and African-diasporic art forms like jazz. For the term's categorization of Bechet's speech as unsophisticated and rough around the edges parallels early perceptions of jazz as simple, instinctive, and natural music. So Bechet's success depended not only on his ability to perform Frenchness but also on his ability to perform French expectations for and stereotypes of Africans and African Americans. Sidney Bechet would also perform his African diasporic heritage through his writing, performance style, performance choices, and proud defense of the United States.

"AS FAR BACK AS AFRICA":
BECHET'S PRIMITIVE PERFORMANCES

> I was asking myself: "Why am I here?" Well, just as soon as I
> asked the question I knew why. France, it's closer to Africa. I've
> wanted to be as close to it as I could. It's a mood, you'd call it, an
> atmosphere I wanted to put myself into. My grandfather, he was
> Africa. It was like getting back, and I wanted to get back as far as
> I could.
>   It's all true, all that I said about my grandfather. And it's all
> so mixed up with the music. In Paris it's like I can hear all what
> was happening to it when my grandfather was making it, back
> in those days when it had just been brought over from Africa
> and was still finding itself in the South.
>
> SIDNEY BECHET, *Treat It Gentle*

From 1940 to 1951 Sidney Bechet recorded his memoirs; with the help of his secretary Joan Williams and the poet John Ciardi, Bechet's autobiography was finally completed and published posthumously in 1960 (J. Chilton 290–91). *Treat It Gentle* is respected for engaging its audience and making a distinctive contribution to the music autobiography genre. It has also been critiqued as highly performative. For *Treat It Gentle* is a remembering (and sometimes imagining) of Africa that in some ways ignores its midcentury moment of composition and obscures Bechet's real opinions.

In *Treat it Gentle* Bechet claimed a great attachment to his African ancestry, which he imagined through his grandfather Omar. He envisioned Africa as a land from which his slave ancestors were taken and from which black music came. He gloried in his African musical heritage and portrayed the slave, Omar, as his connection to that history. He related jazz, slavery, and his African diasporic heritage to France. By emigrating from the United States, he was closer to his African diasporic heritage and therefore the roots of the music he adored. It was through the United States, and then through France, that he heard the African history of the music.

From his earliest visit to France, Bechet performed Africanness onstage, feeding on primitivist mentalities that surrounded jazz. He returned to France in 1925 to perform in *La revue nègre*. He played clarinet in the jazz orchestra, accompanying the dances of Josephine Baker. During the show Baker was nearly nude as she gyrated and made seemingly animal-like gestures; the French had never seen anything like it (Lemke 87–104). Josephine Baker's *danse sauvage* exemplified primitivism as it translated her black performing body into a jungle animal for the French imagination.

The primitivist ideology pervaded writings on African art by European and American artists and critics of the 1920s and 1930s. Filmic representations of African and African diasporic culture such as *Princess Tam Tam*, featuring Josephine Baker in a rags-to-riches, Pygmalion-like narrative, also realized primitivist perceptions. Primitivism portrayed African and African diasporic culture as exotic, simplistic, instinctive, and an antidote to the complexities and problems of modern society (Blake 3–8).

Much scholarship on Josephine Baker suggests she was compliant with primitivist notions of blackness. But in the new millennium several revisionist studies have demonstrated how she made use of the fetishization of her body, employed parody in performance, and illustrated a mix of white and black signification through her choice of gesture (Martin 313; Dayal 45; Henderson 124–25). Wendy Martin suggests that Baker was aware of the fetishization of her body but that her performances manipulated the responses of her audience. In "'Remembering the Jungle': Josephine Baker and Modernist Parody" she writes, "While Josephine Baker was empowered by the French fascination with her coffee-colored skin and performance as uninhibited savage, there was also a dimension of exploitation in her reification as exotic object. Nevertheless, despite becoming part of the process of commodification, Baker also took advantage of the situation by deliberately manipulating the conventions of primitivism to gain a considerable measure of control over her audience" (313). Martin also contends that while Baker played the sexualized and exoticized object for the audience, she capitalized on performances to promote her career and establish a life of success and freedom that she could not find in the United States (313). Although the objectification and fetishization of her body ignored her individuality and furthered stereotypes, it was also her ticket to success.

In "Josephine Baker and *La Revue Nègre:* From Ethnography to Performance" Mae Henderson extends Martin's work by exploring the ambiguous signification of Baker as a mix of European gesture and black exoticism (125). Situating Baker in relation to contemporary colonial expositions, Henderson illustrates how strangers often identified Baker as African, yet she also represented the very American jazz craze. Moreover, Henderson writes that Baker portrayed herself as overtly sexy and animalistic onstage, yet later in life (with her beauty products and sophisticated dress, for example) she was able to transform herself into a symbol of feminine beauty in French society (117). Henderson's analysis portrays Baker as both a theatrical performer and social actor. Such scholarship reads Josephine Baker as purposefully enacting particular theatrical and cultural roles in order to benefit her life and career. These analyses lend support to my own attempts at investigating Sidney Bechet's performances of multiple subjectivities.

Bechet was viewed with primitivist stereotypes in mind, but he also performed primitivism to his benefit. Although primitivism prevailed as a mentality before World War II, the perception of jazz as a music more connected to a primitive and instinctive nature persisted. Charles Delaunay once wrote, "I appreciated Bechet's simplicity. He was a man of the earth, simultaneously rough around the edges and unpredictably complex" (Delaunay, *Delaunay's* 187; my translation).[13] And it was not a view limited to the French either. In another example American reporter Paul Eduard Miller wrote in 1945: "Lyrically and with simple dignity, he sings out what he feels within himself. Pretense and insincerity are foreign to him—musically he says what he feels, directly, concisely, eloquently—and his background has given him plenty to say" (Miller). Bechet's passionate, emotive style and personality prompted the perception of a nascent simplicity yet emotional depth and fed into primitivist ideologies throughout Europe and the United States.

These perceptions also paralleled the concept of *negritude*, which was first conceived by Aimé Césaire, a Pan-Africanist intellectual who later became mayor of Fort-de-France and deputy of the French National Assembly for Martinique.[14] Césaire first coined *négritude* in the mid-1930s, thereby reclaiming a derogatory term historically used to malign blacks as inferior, dirty, and ungodly. In his 1939 book-length poem *Cahier d'un retour au pays natal* (Notebook of a Return to the Native Land) he wrote:

> My negritude is not a stone, its deafness hurled against the clamor of the
>   day . . .
> it takes root in the red flesh of the soil
> it takes root in the ardent flesh of the sky
> it breaks through opaque prostration with its upright patience.
>
> (Césaire 117; translation by Banoun)

Throughout his works Césaire claimed negritude as a recognition of the contributions of those of African descent—their beauty, intelligence, and strength: "Négritude is the simple recognition of the fact of being black, and the acceptance of this fact, of our destiny as black people, of our history and of our culture" (quoted in Irele 89; translation Irele). Above all, Césaire's concept was a political act. He attempted to identify a collective black consciousness and to empower blacks around the world to build their own institutions, independence, and liberation from oppression, as with the French colonialist forces from his experience as a Martiniquan. Negritude became a philosophy and political movement that differed from the stereotypes and racialized perceptions that primitivist ideologies espoused. However, the concepts shared the characterization of people of African descent as connected to the natural and untutored; the two ideologies represented African diasporic culture as valuable rather than lacking and as contributing worthwhile values and innovations to modern society.

Bechet believed (or more accurately played up to) primitivist perceptions that African diasporic culture was simplistic, natural, and instinctive and also the ideals of negritude that forwarded a shared and valued lineage in African culture. He opened his memoir by offering up a musical lineage. From Africa to Omar to Bechet the music was passed down, he believed: "The black man, he's been learning his way from the beginning. A way of saying something from inside himself, as far back as time, as far back as Africa, in the jungle, and the way the drums talked across the jungle. . . . My story goes a long way back. It goes further back than I had anything to do with. My music is like that. . . . I got it from something inherited, just like the stories my father gave down to me" (*Treat* 4). Bechet characterizes his career and affinity for music as "something inherited" and "as far back as Africa, in the jungle." His emphasis on the primitive in his characterizations of jazz enacts his desire to signify as a progenitor of the roots of jazz and of "black music" vis-à-vis the Middle Passage. Emphasizing connections to slavery, pain, and journeying all positioned Bechet in the origins of jazz as black music. It further embedded him in the French expectations for and imaginings of black performance. Like Baker, Bechet played up stereotypes of African diasporic performance as natural, instinctual, and untamed by civilization.

His attention to Africa, with this romanticized, looking-back lens, also overwrote contemporary issues of Africa. For his descriptions of Africa tied him back to nature and the past, far from the 1950s and the man-made destruction of two world wars. More significantly, it drew attention away from the proliferation of wars of independence and decolonization during the time of the writing of *Treat It Gentle.* While Bechet's sentiments paralleled the romanticization of Africa that Césaire forwarded in his concept of negritude, Bechet sidestepped explicit political support for the protest against colonial oppression that negritude espoused.

From 1950 onward France was Bechet's home base, and he was surrounded by the increased immigration of refugees, politically tense discussions over decolonization, and rampant racism that came with the breaking down of the French Empire. He was not ignorant of his political environment either. He once said, "The French have no call to crow over Americans. I've told 'em so. I've told 'em I've been in Dakar and I've seen what they do to Negroes there, and Frenchmen are no better than anyone else" (Ehrlich 93). Note that Bechet made this comment to an American journalist from *Esquire*, thus not *telling* the French his opinions directly. While Bechet wrote in *Treat It Gentle* that his motivation to be in France was its proximity to Africa, the Africa he portrayed was an imagined past. And, with it, he portrayed an idealistic and blind image of France as in *relation*, rather than in conflict, with the Africa he tried to recall in his music.

Even though Bechet avoided painting the French as oppressors, he still identified violence and pain as part of his African-descended heritage. He located that oppression in the African American slave. No doubt, this was safer than accusing the French of their own racially inspired wrongs. Instead, Bechet used *Treat It Gentle* to locate the origins of jazz in slavery, through Omar's slave performances. He described his grandfather, Omar, as excelling at music and dance and leading other slaves in performances during precious free moments on Sundays in Congo Square ("Along" 83–84). Congo Square was recognized as one of the birthing grounds of early jazz, as it blended West African dances and voodoo rituals with European music and dance styles; for most of the nineteenth century, slaves in New Orleans would come at the end of each week to dance primitive and religious dances (like Bamboula and Calinda) while chanting and pounding on drumlike instruments (Stearns 51).

By calling up the image of Omar, a leader in these slave performances, Bechet linked his passion for performance as a free man with a genealogy of performance under the constraints of slavery. Moreover, given that Congo Square also centralized and preserved some West African customs, Bechet connected himself and jazz to an African ancestry. Jerah Johnson wrote that the square was one of the last places to showcase original African dances (141). Omar represented this past and served as a reminder of "Africanicity," untouched by modernity. Bechet positioned himself as the inheritor of Omar's legacy: "There's so much to remember. There's so much wanting, and there's so much sorrow, and there's so much waiting for the sorrow to end. My people all they want is a place" (Bechet, *Treat* 202–4). Bechet's memoir and performances strove to perform Omar's "remembering song" (202–4).

But after a meticulous archival search John Chilton reveals that Sidney Bechet's real grandfather was Jean Bechet, a free, property-owning carpenter who was documented as "mulatto" in the 1850 census and was bequeathed his freedom through his black mother's death (1). Chilton discusses the reception of the story of Omar and its origin:

> Some critics openly doubted the story of Omar; others felt that the language used was so evocative that truth was irrelevant. Rudi Blesh suggested that Bechet secured his inspiration from one of George Washington Cable's 19th-century tales of old Louisiana. One of Cable's stories, *Bras coupé*, has fleeting similarities to Omar's tale, but much closer in content is the factual story of *Bras coupé* (known both as Squire and Squier, who died in 1837) which was published in 1945 as part of *Gumbo Ya-ya* (a collection of Louisiana folk tales). Sidney may have read that book, or perhaps the Squier's saga had been told to him during childhood. Somehow legend triumphed over reality and became the basis of recollections about his own grandfather. (J. Chilton 291)

So Bechet's literary performance had internalized (knowingly or unknowingly) yet another performance—the legends and tales of Louisiana folklore. In *Kinds of Blue: The Jazz Aesthetic in African-American Narrative* Jürgen Grandt describes Bechet as a literary improviser in *Treat It Gentle*, just as he is a master musical improviser (1–21). Considering Bechet as a literary jazz improviser foregrounds how he creates history, not by playing a straight melody but by riffing on former experiences and influences. Band member Claude Luter's description of Bechet fits Grandt's interpretation of Bechet as a literary improviser, as conscious of how he used words and music to engage his audience. Luter states, "Sidney was positively not a born liar, but when he told a story he always wanted it to be a *good* story" (J. Chilton 292).

The story of *Bras coupé* became a legendary tale of a slave who led a group slave escape and resisted capture for years in mid-1830s New Orleans. By claiming this story as his heritage, Bechet attempted to connect himself to the oppression and fight for liberation of American slave history and music.[15] Nicholas Gebhardt elaborates on the significance of this connection: "Bechet's narrative begins with a fictional account of his enslaved grandfather Omar's death at the hands of a fellow slave. The purpose of this account is to emphasize the fragility of the musical act and affirm the basis of the slaves' collective capacity for psychic survival and creative action. . . . Bechet's description of slavery is critical for his later attempt to articulate the social character of the jazz act, its relation to the musical practices of the slaves, and the significance of emancipation to the formation of black consciousness" (39). Gebhardt's reading of *Treat It Gentle* points to the active ways that Bechet forges a relationship between slavery and jazz; Gebhardt sees *Treat It Gentle* as drawing attention to, and even constructing a continuum among, emancipation, black musical expression, and black identity (8). Of particular note to this discussion is his emphasis on emancipation. For Bechet's ties to emancipation from slavery were tenuous because of his grandfather's experiences as a free man. Bechet's autobiography and music thus forged, rather than remembered, a connection to slavery.

Bechet's performance of an African slave ancestry in *Treat It Gentle* also overwrote the racialized divisions between Creole and African American communities in the New Orleans of his youth. Although he played uptown and privileged jazz over European classical music, the middle-class influence and the impact of his partially white French heritage distinguished not only his ethnic heritage but also his opinions. David Ake deconstructs Bechet's opinions about race: "Indeed, even with someone who often patterned himself after Uptown ways, Bechet could occasionally revert to the virulent racism that characterized Downtown attitudes" (*Jazz Cultures* 25). In support Ake cites an anecdote from saxophonist and Bechet student Bob Wilber: "Creoles like Bechet and Jelly Roll [Morton] did not see themselves as black, yet they were not accepted as white men. This sometimes resulted in strange statements from Sidney, like, 'Them Goddam niggers, doin' this and doin' that, and givin' us all a bad name.' We once sat down in front of the tape recorder while he expounded on the subject, extolling the virtues of the infamous southern racist senator, the notorious Senator [Theodore Gilmore] Bilbo, who had connections with the Ku Klux Klan and all the worst aspects of that business" (Wilber 48). This anecdote is yet more support for the instability of Bechet's performance of African slave inheritance.

Bechet's musical performance of old minstrel songs also challenged his affiliation with an African-descended slave heritage. It was not the free, performative expressions of slaves on Sundays that his interpretation conveyed but, rather, the mockery of slave/master relationships and the ill-conceived romanticization of slave life. For example, one North American reporter raved about Bechet's rendition of "Old Folks at Home," commonly known as "Swanee River." For the reporter Bechet's performance recalled a time past and almost glorified it. It made the reporter miss home, during his stay in France: "What the old man played up there on the stage of the

Olympia Music Hall on the Boulevard des Capucines in Paris was Swanee River, of all things. But when he played it, it wasn't just a traditional air jazzed up; it was a long and loving memory of a lost place. It was real music—homesick music, too" (Ehrlich 94). For French fans "Swanee River" would have created an image of the Old South, as well as memorialized and highlighted that lost era. Playing "Swanee River" in France reaffirmed demeaning representations of African Americans as subservient to white Americans. It reinforced the plantation myth that slaves were actually happy and longed for the American South. Composed by Stephen Foster in 1851, the lyrics feature phrases such as "Sadly I roam / Still longing for the old plantation / And for the old folks at home" (Foster). Foster presented a wandering and free African American haunted not by the tearing away from Africa but by the inability to recover the prewar, plantation-driven American South.

While "Swanee River" seems to romanticize slavery, Ken Emerson draws attention to the multiple and evolving significations of Foster's songs in *Doo-dah! Stephen Foster and the Rise of American Popular Culture.* Emerson discusses how some African Americans did not perceive Foster's songs as misrepresentations of African Americans: "But there is more to 'Old Black Joe' than broad grins and shuffling feet. In *The Souls of Black Folk,* after referring to America, perhaps inadvertently, as the 'foster land,' W. E. B. Du Bois singled out 'Old Folks at Home' and 'Old Black Joe' for praise. Exempting them from 'the debasements and imitations' of 'minstrel' and 'coon' songs, he called them 'songs of white America [that] have been distinctively influenced by the slave songs or have incorporated whole phrases of Negro melody'" (Du Bois 540; Emerson 258). Du Bois and Emerson point to a multilayered perception of this music. For Emerson these songs were not entirely stereotypical, negative, or slanted in their representation of slave culture. For Du Bois they were not purely white; rather, they grew out of interactions between blacks and whites and showed the influence of those interactions on African Americans. Du Bois's perspective is particularly noteworthy, given that with his book *The Souls of Black Folk* he identified spirituals and proclaimed their beauty, cultural value, and representation of not only African American slave culture but also of a racially hybrid black and white American culture. From this perspective Bechet may have performed these racially heightened songs because they were part of an African American slave history with which he wanted to connect. By performing "Swanee River" he paid homage to the music that grew out of slaves' struggles to combat slavery, prejudice, and civil rights injustices. This music somehow expressed, as well as overcame, these struggles—at least in the space of the performance. The fact that Du Bois saw "Swanee River" as representative of slave culture is also significant. Perhaps Bechet, like Du Bois, saw the slaves' sorrowful songs (and other musical genres that imitated, critiqued, and even stereotyped slave culture) as essential to convincing white Americans (and the world) of the enormous value of African American culture.

Or perhaps Bechet performed these songs because they met French desires and expectations, thus securing his success in France. Andy Fry makes a similar argument, though it concerns Bechet's French repertoire. Fry analyzes not only how Bechet relates American slavery to jazz, jazz to Africa, and Africa to France but also adds Creole popular songs to his "remembering song" repertoire. Later in his description of France as "nearer to Africa," Bechet writes that "being there is nearer to all my family and brings back something I remember of Omar and my father, too. So I started to record some lovely Creole tunes that I remembered from when I was young and some I made myself out of the same remembering" (*Treat* 194–95). Fry insightfully reads Bechet's choice of Creole songs as possibly a commercial decision but even more possibly "as attempts to play—or play back—into being a self-consciously creolized identity, one that by this time had much more to do with Paris than it did with New Orleans" ("Remembrance" 323). Using this logic, Bechet could align himself with a fictionalized slave ancestry in his memoirs, as well as perform racially sensitive songs like "Swanee River." He could relate both American-centered performances to the French public. For a French audience these two seemingly contradictory acts performed similarly. They both portrayed African Americans as victims of an oppressive American culture. Even in this post–World War II era, nearly a century after slavery had ended, events like these burned into French cultural imagination the image of African Americans as a people fighting for freedom against American injustice.

The French had already linked jazz and black music to triumph over oppression for many years. French cultural historian Jeffrey Jackson translates and elaborates on the perspective of René Dumesnil, a popular French critic of the interwar era: "Born out of oppression, as Dumesnil put it, black American songs 'are examples to vanquish the oppressor or reasons to hope for liberation.' Playing jazz, observers like Dumesnil noted, offered a form of emotional freedom from the lives that blacks led in the United States" (J. Jackson, *Making* 87). So French jazz critics and fans perceived African Americans as using music to express, relieve, and even counteract their torment. Songs like "American Rhythm (Klook Klux Klan)" reified this perspective.

INTRODUCING SIDNEY BECHET, INTRODUCING "AMERICAN RHYTHM"

"American Rhythm" was Bechet's leitmotif, his chosen theme song. At the beginning of most performances he walked in on dramatic drum spatters, as he played the melody to "American Rhythm." Though the title literally describes the rhythm (in this case jazz rhythms) as American, the song expresses Bechet's African and American journey, while situated in France. It demonstrates a jazz diaspora as it moves among African, American, and French characteristics and offers a temporary musical home to the participants and jazz itself. The song's recording home was Paris, France, where Bechet was enticed by Charles Delaunay to record for his label, Vogue. Bechet culled mostly visiting American jazz musicians with the lone French bass player, Pierre Michelot, to record on October 20, 1949 (J. Chilton 221).

Bechet's All-Star Band consisted primarily of African Americans who already lived in France or migrated soon thereafter, such as trumpeter Bill Coleman and drummer Kenny Clarke.[16] This project represented a moment of community for the musicians; it was a time for catching up on events from home, collaborating with friends, and, in some instances, prompting new collaborations. The American players and American-styled music helped them create some familiarity and establish a home away from home, if only while the music was playing.

For the French this gathering (and many afterward) would help promote jazz in France. The Swing label, later renamed Vogue, was the first jazz-only label in France; Charles Delaunay founded the label in 1937, two years before Blue Note (Tournès 52). Recording U.S. musicians in France meant less negotiating and waiting for new U.S. releases to come across the water. In sum, both the American and French musicians were resituating themselves through these recording sessions, trying to find another space for themselves.

"American Rhythm" commences with drummer Kenny Clarke, who sets a duple meter alongside a spatter of accents. The low timbre of the drum created by the prominent use of tom-tom beats, and the interlocking rhythms of the drums and sax that follow, recall the singing and dancing of Omar and his slave community. Fabrice Zammarchi elaborates: "Shortly after he took up residence in France in 1949, Bechet recorded an amazing tune, 'American Rhythm,' which revealed his preoccupation with his African-American ancestry. The recording was a soprano-drums duet with Kenny Clarke, in which Bechet improvised with witty eloquence and verve on the diminished chord, while Clarke lit 'the powder keg' on his drums in what must have been an imaginative attempt to recapture the legendary drumming and singing at Congo Square in antebellum New Orleans" ("An African American" 9). In this musical reimagining of Congo Square the song serves as a site of cultural memory that recalls the racialized oppression of slavery, the Sunday performances as liberatory acts of momentary expression and resistance, and the creation of a space of cultural diversity and innovation through performance. For example, along with the music, the slave dances put in dialogue multiple cultural styles; early nineteenth-century dances would feature black dancers performing the African bamboula alongside the French contre-danse (J. Johnson 145). The tables were turned in the creation of "American Rhythm" as a similar musical creolization occurred—but this time on the other side of the ocean, in Paris.

As the song continues, Clarke settles into a syncopated drum pattern after a few measures, and Bechet enters on soprano saxophone. Clarke plays on the downbeat, as Bechet commences a syncopated melody. At times Bechet spurts out notes. At other times he glides over the rhythms Clarke lays down. Although Bechet's line is the most prominent, distinguished by its volume, tone, and setting of the melody, Clarke's drumbeats are never lost under the expressive intoning of the saxophone. They stab into the listener's consciousness with continuous jazz riffs and a constantly changing rhythm.

In midsong Clarke changes from a steady accent to a drumroll, asserting layers of beats that flow into each other. His dramatic drum play insists on never forgetting and always intoning the African roots of the music. In these moments it is as if Clarke plays out Bechet's descriptions in his autobiography, where he weaves tales about the music's roots from "as far back as Africa, in the jungle." With the interlocking rhythms, tension between sax and drums, rhythmic changes, and offbeat accents that respond to Bechet's call, Clarke seems to riff on a variety of African drumming styles (Chernoff 95, 113–14). Clarke's performance here connotes an African past while also connecting to the modern experience of African Americans.

Clarke's playing also touches on the vexed history of African Americans. Indeed, the song's parenthetical title, "American Rhythm (Klook Klux Klan)," draws a connection between past injustices and the contemporary racism these musicians endured. The title not only signals the importance of rhythm in jazz vis-à-vis its African past but also functions as a critique of the United States and how the predominant creators of the music, African Americans, have been oppressed.

"Klook" (Clarke's nickname) makes a play on words and also situates the band personally in this struggle. "Klook" serves to mangle the full phrase by replacing the "Ku." This wordplay makes fun of, and dismantles the power of, the Ku Klux Klan (KKK). In the best way they know how, these musicians are throwing a wrench in the signification and force of the KKK. Here jazz literally disrupts the clandestine organization's meaning and power. Rather than physical violence, the musicians use rhythm to hit back at racism in the United States. More importantly, they lay claim to what is "American."

Bechet's horn illustrates the story of American rhythm—from Africa to the United States to France to everywhere. He commences on the steady, swinging beat of Clarke. Bechet's horn sets the theme and then embarks on variations. He seems to wander in one melodic direction, while Clarke's drumming is dramatically present throughout the song. He continually changes the types of accents he adds and creates an unpredictable path as well. The two still manage to dialogue, particularly when Bechet launches into his distinctive vibrato and Clarke supports with accented hits that mimic Bechet's pitch wavering and brash tone color.

In his review Edgar Jackson calls the album unsuccessful because of the two differing styles that Bechet and Clarke represent: "The main clash is between Bechet and Kenny Clarke. The latter's almost boppish drumming is a none the less disconcerting contrast to Bechet's New Orleans mode because there is so much of it" (29). Yet I think that "American Rhythm" succeeds because of the layers of difference; it is propulsive in multiple areas, and it makes the ear focus in one direction and then the next. For this reason the song is forever engaging and unpredictable. The song also extends geographically, settling for a while in one place only to move to the next. Each nation becomes home but only until the next journey: France is literally the birthplace of this song. The drumming style unquestionably signifies African rhythms and suggests Africa is the homeland of the music, while the song title brands the music as an American rhythm yet highlights the breaks in that national rhythm with its mention of the KKK. However, the different homes that the song visits actually come together and rub against the grain in a way that actually draws the listener in.

The two musicians' play brings the three nations into *un relation* as they, at times, parallel each other, riff off of each other, and depart from one another while always remaining related. The song merges all of these nations under the banner of American rhythm. Yet French and African influences are evident in the multiple subjectivities of Bechet and in the musical creolization of jazz production. The song makes a case for multiple ethnic influences and multiple migrations of jazz—departing from the common claim of jazz as native to the United States.

By returning to this song in each concert, Bechet not only uses it to introduce himself; he also has a say in reintroducing American rhythm—in shaping the diaspora of jazz. Bechet's meandering saxophone tugs and pulls between multiple cultural influences, as he plays his life story in "American Rhythm." In the convergence of elements (with Clarke's tom-tom beats, the American signification in the title, and the production setting in France), "American Rhythm" becomes a space in which Bechet draws together multiple subjectivities gained through a diasporic experience. Bechet's jazz diaspora merges multiple models of hybridity, as he shifts "in-between" ethnic subjectivities in a space that "remakes" itself only "in relation" to the other.

Music is the only space where these relationships could occur. For Bechet music is the one space that continually claimed his heart and situated him. At the end of his autobiography he writes, "What I'd be feeling is 'the music, it has a home.' As long as I got a heart to be filled by it, the music has a place that's natural to it. I could sit there and listen, and I'd smile" (Bechet, *Treat* 219).

2. Jazz at Home in France

French Jazz Musicians on the Warpath to "Authentic" Jazz

> Is jazz at home in France? Certainly, it has always been at ease here, as if our country was its second home, where it came sometimes for refuge but also to develop and awaken itself. France is one of the places where numerous events marking the history of this music took place without restriction: during the two wars around Pigalle, after the liberation in Saint-Germain-des-Prés . . .
>
> YVAN AMAR[1]

"Why do you study jazz in *France?*" Upon hearing the topic of my research, people inevitably ask this question. My answer: Parisian culture has absorbed jazz to such an extent that it's hard to imagine when it was ever new and foreign. For example, Paris boasts a year-round attention to jazz via radio stations like TSF Jazz, which broadcasts under the tagline, "la seule radio 100% JAZZ" (the only 100 percent jazz radio station in France).[2] Such privileging of jazz is rare even in the United States; luckily, the station is available from afar through its website.

Whenever I have the pleasure of returning to Paris, I am surrounded by myriad jazz options; the lilting sounds have often awakened me from my slumber on Saturday and Sunday mornings. On the corner of Rue Mouffetard in the Latin Quarter, my apartment faced the street musicians amid the bustling marché that daily overtook the street. Over shouts from vendors advertising bargain prices, the strains of their New Orleans–style and *Manouche* jazz (gypsy jazz in the style of Django Reinhardt) enticed tourists to stroll and sample the surrounding goods. In my waking hours I too have joined in this jazz bustle—wandering down streets, glancing at artwork of Josephine Baker sold along the Seine, and browsing through cheap CD collections of Sidney Bechet and Louis Armstrong. While these cultural artifacts symbolize a bygone era of jazz, they are still celebrated as part of contemporary Parisian culture. Rather than foreign, they have become a part of the idyllic Paris one sees in photos and films.

The summers offer one of my favorite pastimes: attending outdoor jazz festivals. Loaded down with blanket, cheese, baguette, fruit, wine, and a healthy appetite for live music, I have happily braved the long lines and low five-euro entrance fee at festivals like the Paris Jazz Festival at the Parc Florale. From Cameroonian saxophonist Manu Dibango to African American saxophonist Joshua Redman, I gorged on jazz most recently in the summer of 2014. It was by no means a standout year, as there are always plenty of jazz festivals in Paris: the Festival jazz à Saint-Germain-des-Prés, Le festival Banlieues Bleues, the touring JVC jazz festival, and smaller festivals at key jazz clubs like "Le jazz de Demain" at Le Baiser Salé (The Salty Kiss) and "Jazz sur Seine" featuring 120 performances in twenty clubs.

I remember rushing across the Seine on one summer day to the Paris jazz club Duc des Lombards (Duke of the Lombards). The club has locked a spot on the jazz-centered street, Rue des Lombards, for more than thirty years now. Duc des Lombards was an appropriate place to meet the Madagascar-born Paris transplant Salim Himidi, who had been a young African undergraduate student at the Sorbonne in the mid-1960s. The jazz scene was still so prolific in 1964 that rather than a distraction from his study, it was a way of life—especially for youth culture. Himidi gleefully shared his jazz experiences with me as we skipped across streets, peeked around corners, stopped, started, and asked for directions in search of a poetry event ensconced in an underground cave not too dissimilar from the venues of the era he described. In the words of performance studies scholar Shannon Jackson, I felt like I could "enter the performance of history" (32). As I walked through modern-day Paris, I was aware that the buildings differed from those of the midcentury moment; still, though, time seemed to fold over on itself. I felt the history of jazz in Paris as my body interacted with the city, and Himidi's words painted a past Parisian path to walk along.

"Wow, all these people were here!" I exclaimed as Himidi rattled off a long list of jazz stars: American players Sonny Rollins, Don Cherry, Errol Garner, Kenny Clarke, Jimmy Gourley, Dexter Gordon, Nathan Davis, Roland Hayes, Willie Dixon, Memphis Slim and French players René Urtreger, Martial Solal, and Sacha Distel would all come together to play at Jazzland, Les Trois Maillets (The three mallets), Le Chat Qui Pêche (The fishing cat), and the Blue Note. The Blue Note in particular was a jazz institution in 1950s and 1960s Paris; it was located on 27 Rue d'Artois in the eighth arrondissement, near the Champs Elysees.

Himidi recalled:

> This was the meeting place. This was the place where people would meet after hours. They had jam sessions; usually Fridays and Saturdays drew bigger and bigger crowds," he advised. "Blue note was the one

place where you had a permanent group that was permanently playing there. . . . Those were the days when jazz was very very popular and attracted a lot of artists here. And, usually the big performers who were here for jazz, for concerts, knew that after their concerts they could always meet at Blue Note because that's where they belonged. It was like a community. And the musicians there were established names. These are people who, who you know, who grew up in the wake of Charlie Parker. Dexter Gordon played with Charlie Parker. Kenny Clarke played with Charlie Parker. So, this was a kind of, their base, where they would meet now. What is interesting is that they would usually come at 1 o'clock, 2 o'clock in the morning, at the time when most of the customers, their usual customers would have already left. So the place would be almost empty and they came in and they just met there and they got into what they called jam sessions, improvisations you know, and that was the time when the best music was played. And I enjoyed that very much. (Himidi)

Himidi's modern-day remembrance showcases three points of import: the acculturation of jazz in France depended very much on a sense of community and the building of relationships between touring and residing African Americans and French jazz musicians. Jazz festivals and clubs like the Blue Note became not only centers for African American artists but also centers of learning for young French musicians like pianist René Urtreger. In the two decades after war's end there were many jazz gigs and touring musicians flocking to Paris to perform. This jazz era has become memorialized as a watershed moment in French jazz history and memory.

This post–World War II and still war-inflected period nurtured an important transition in African American and French musical collaboration because of the increased opportunities for mentorship with the migration of African American musicians. While war in its many forms would further define French jazz musicianship, it was not the dissension and conflict that was characteristic of war but rather the opportunities to relate, identify, and collaborate that increased the confidence of French musicians. A French jazz identity, rather than being something separate from jazz as an African American music, was created in relation to it.

The analysis of jazz in the post–World War II era departs a bit from much pre-millennium jazz scholarship. There are several extensive studies on the acculturation of jazz in France: Ludovic Tournès's *New Orleans sur Seine*, William Shack's *Harlem in Montmartre*, Larry Ross's *African American Jazz Musicians in the Diaspora*, Jeffrey Jackson's *Making Jazz French*, and, most recently, volume 1 of Laurent Cugny's *Une histoire du jazz en France: Du milieu du XIXe siècle a 1929.* These books either investigate the interwar era or provide a historical survey across the twentieth century.

This chapter's focus on the evolved musical experience and discursive perception of French jazz musicians after World War II distinguishes it from the aforementioned scholarship. Another distinction is that I do not investigate them alone but in relation to their African American musician mentors, exploring French musicians such as clarinetist Claude Luter and pianists René Urtreger and Martial Solal and their collaborations with saxophonist Sidney Bechet and drummer Kenny Clarke. This chapter represents a model of musical collaboration that has sustained the second type of jazz diaspora—that is, a space of shifting identities for the music itself. The discourse among French jazz critics and musicians in the 1940s and 1950s was racially and nationally focused and exclusive, yet, underneath, the identity of jazz was in flux. This shifting, not just in French cultural perception but also in recognition and repute of French musicians, did not begin to alter until World War II and the postwar era.

Jazz scholarship has turned the tide with its post-millennium attention to the post–World War II era as well. In 2004 Colin Nettelbeck offered the first prominent study of the post–World War II era of jazz in France, arguing that it was the fifteen years after the war that spawned the love affair between jazz and France that I now take for granted (65). With *Le Jazz: Jazz and French Cultural Identity* Matthew Jordan also identifies the post–World War II era as the moment in which jazz changed from a threat to a French cultural tool: "While these and many other examples [such as the monument of Sidney Bechet in Juan-les-Pins that Jordan references] bear witness to the French love of jazz, what one does *not* find in contemporary media discourse are critics who label jazz a threat to their notion of French culture. I read this discursive absence, one that did not appear until after the German occupation, as a sign that jazz is now an assimilated or naturalized part of French culture" (3). Jordan uses this discursive absence of jazz as the foreign other to ponder how "true" French identity incorporated and fed on jazz. Nettelbeck also explores the impact of jazz on a changing French cultural identity, via intellectual criticism and cinema. I investigate how the postwar period significantly shaped a French jazz identity through the persistent performance of authenticating narratives, wherein French critics and musicians highlighted racial authenticity and essentialism. Throughout the 1940s and 1950s, the transition and growth of French jazz production also fed off the concept of war—hence the organization of this chapter around multiple wars.

WORLD WAR II AND THE LIBERATION OF AFRICAN AMERICAN—OCCUPIED JAZZ?

On December 9, 1935, a German radio broadcast proclaimed that the Nazis would "eradicate every trace of putrefying elements that remained in our light" (Bergmeier and Lotz 138–39). The Nazis tried to wipe out jazz, seeing it as a threat to a pure Aryan society. Jazz symbolized the primal, degenerate, and inferior, and African American jazz musicians were perceived as impure and base right alongside Jewish performers, who were also well known for their contributions to the jazz industry. Plans had been in the works since March, when Hitler assigned Reich Minister of Propaganda Joseph Goebbels to contain the threat that jazz presented. In *Harlem in Montmartre: A Paris Jazz Story* William Shack summarizes the Nazis' early strategies to quell the popularity and effect of jazz on occupied Europe: "German authorities banished jazz from all radio programs on the grounds that it was a form of musical decadence. The German Broadcasting Company (RRG) informed the press that 'the Berlin programme is banning all the dubious dance styles that healthy public opinion calls "Nigger music" in which provocative rhythms predominate and melody is violently abused'" (118). Ironically, just as Germany attempted to contain the spread of jazz in Europe, jazz was enjoying a golden age in France. From the mid-1930s through war's end, French jazz critics and promoters made a great impact on the dissemination and appreciation of jazz throughout the world.

In 1934 Hugues Panassié wrote *Le jazz hot,* arguably the second book solely about jazz. (The Belgian Francophone Robert Goffin wrote the first book, *Aux frontières du jazz* [1932].) Many French historians and jazz scholars claim *Le jazz hot* was the first book to validate jazz as worthy of study and not as inferior to European music; more than that, *Le jazz hot* shared a passion and enthusiasm for the music as beautiful and recognized the brilliance early on as well as spurred the success of some up-and-coming stars (Gioia 25; Tournès 12; Stovall, *Paris Noir* 94–95; Lane, "Jazz" 41; Balliet 1–2). Charles Delaunay founded the magazine *Jazz Hot* in 1935, which became the premiere journal for French jazz fans, musicians, and critics.[3] It was second only to *Down Beat* by a matter of months. (*Down Beat,* now recognizably the best resource for fans to find jazz events, recordings, and reviews, was first published in 1934 Chicago.) In 1936 Charles Delaunay penned the first full jazz discography ever. With the label Swing, Delaunay and Panassié commenced the first jazz-only record label in 1937. Goffin, Panassié, and Delaunay became the French jazz critics of note. They securely placed France on the map as a country interested in and knowledgeable about jazz.

During this interwar era, argues historian Jeffrey Jackson, French jazz musicians distinguished themselves from American performers. Although many perceived jazz as a threat to the French chanson style, some musicians performed chansons in a jazzy style, attempting to incorporate the new trend, writes Jackson (*Making* 8). The music had always symbolized *art nègre* and all the primitive connotations that went with it. But Jackson claims that white French musicians embraced, innovated, and Frenchified jazz in this interwar period. He pinpoints the shift in discourse and performance from jazz as something foreign to an acceptable form of French entertainment:

> Throughout the 1920s, many listeners often dismissed French players as second-rate jazzmen who simply could not perform as well as the Americans. But beginning in the late 1920s and the early 1930s, French musicians, who had seen American bands in the nightclubs of Montmartre and Montparnasse, and who had listened to jazz records imported from the United States, began to play jazz with both serious commercial and critical success. . . . During the 1920s, critics had charged that jazz was an alien sound. But when performed by Ventura, Grégor, Grappelli, or Reinhardt, jazz no longer seemed to be "Americanizing" or "Africanizing" French music. Instead, these players offered jazz as a music that audiences could now accept as an integral part of French entertainment. ("Making" 151)

However, aside from the world-renowned guitarist Django Reinhardt,[4] the French jazz musicians of the interwar era were not well known outside of France and did not change worldwide perception or desire for jazz outside of France.

Additionally, French musicians of the 1930s (and beyond actually) suffered from what William H. Kenney III terms "a French inferiority complex in jazz" (13), which challenged their mastery of and confidence in jazz performance: saxophonist and clarinetist André Ekyan believed even after intense study of records that his technique was "insufficient" and orchestration "poor," while pianist Stéphane Mougin bemoaned the fact that there was no "simple formula," and despite a jazzlike arrangement of notes at the end of the day early jazz records were not comparable to American efforts (Kenney 14). In "The Assimilation of American Jazz in France, 1917–1940," Kenney encapsulates the core deficiencies of French jazz musicianship, noting that French jazz musicians lacked swing in their jazz rhythms and demonstrated disjointed play and a lack of facility with chord changes (12–13).

The Frenchification of jazz, at least in terms of French musicianship, would thus take much longer and require other signal moments in the relationship between French modern culture and any claim on or innovation of the music. Even contemporary French critics like Hugues Panassié disagreed that French jazz musicians had made the music in some way their own by wartime. Their works performed authenticating narratives that privileged African American jazz production as "authentic." After the publication of *Le jazz hot* Panassié's criticisms more prominently linked racial makeup rather than musical skill to "authentic" jazz.[5] Panassié's work forwarded a racially essentialist mind-set in favor of African American jazz musicians—except for Jewish American clarinetist Mezz Mezzrow and select white and Jewish musicians whom he believed played with a certain African American sensibility. "He admitted that he had enjoyed the records of the McKenzie-Condon Chicagoans at first but, once apprized of the error of his taste, apologized and devoted the rest of his life to the promotion of Black American jazzmen" (Kenney 16). In his 1942 book *The Real Jazz,* which was first published in English and not translated into French until 1946, Panassié depicted jazz as an expression of one group of people, as authentic only when played by them, and saw people of African descent as best qualified to play jazz and naturally equipped to perform it. He wrote: "While the Negro masses among themselves have an instinctive feeling for this music, white people approach it with resistance and assimilate it slowly" (21).

This authenticating narrative performed by spreading and creating a particular essentialist discourse that other critics and performers drew on and augmented; Panassié's advocacy of real jazz as African American jazz performed beyond the page; it functioned by actually opening some doors for African American jazz musicians. Author of *Blowin' Hot and Cool: Jazz and Its Critics,* John Gennari explains well the stakes and impact of this authenticating narrative for the French jazz public: "The most enduring legacy of this purist jazz discourse was its attention to musicians—especially black musicians—whose body of work and reputations might otherwise have been overlooked or shunted to the margins in the more commercially focused fan magazines" (94). Likewise, William Kenney III and Eric Hobsbawm (then known as Francis Newton) note that Panassié's approach led to many performance invitations and the production and distribution of records by African American jazz musicians; this meant that the French jazz public's perception of jazz was primarily of African American musicianship (Kenney 16; Newton 243–45).

Interestingly, French of African descent did not rise to French expectations of jazz performance. In a January 1944 Hot Club of France circular, an article described a contest hosted by École normale de musique that showcased French jazz students of African descent. The participants were judged as demonstrating the qualities of their race but lacking in skill; they were ranked below even the most average white European jazz musicians ("Musique nègre"). The study supported a hierarchy of white French players over black French players, and it further bolstered the French need for African Americans to build a home for jazz there.

The essentialist perspective of Panassié and *Jazz Hot* (as the representative media face of the Hot Club of France) would be critiqued by renowned British music journalist and author Leonard Feather for their unswerving and one-sided promotion of African American jazz musicians: "Mr. Leonard Feather is always stunned by European jazz magazines, notably *Jazz Hot*, that devote nearly all of their pages to black musicians. This is why he challenged us to undo this bias in an article characteristic of an American review" (Derens 8; my translation).[6] In response *Jazz Hot* mimicked the American critique style and in its June 1952 issue set about advocating a more *objective* history of jazz criticism.

The American music magazine *Metronome*, among many other publications, also called out Panassié's essentialist perspective, though jazz scholars John Gennari and Andy Fry note respectively that *Metronome* discounted the white and Jewish musicians like Jack Teagarden and Mezz Mezzrow that Panassié had also showcased. Fry notes, however, that although Panassié had harshly criticized French jazz musicians, he had on occasion also consciously decided not to compare them with American musicians (Gennari 95–96; Fry 106).

William H. Kenney III elaborates on the reaction of French jazz musicians to these negative judgments from the French jazz press:

> He [Hugues Panassié] and Robert Goffin discovered passion, emotion, spontaneity, freedom and anguish in Black jazz, but order, melody, form, poise and detachment in white jazz. Panassié complained about how difficult he found French jazz musicians, and they, in turn, must have found his message discouraging. The musicians approached jazz as a set of musical principles which could be learned from the Black masters by those who possessed the gift of improvisation. The result would never sound exactly like Black American jazz but the fundamentals of jazz could be assimilated into a sort of cultural synthesis . . . what Charles Delaunay called "l'école française" of jazz. This synthesis was achieved by each of the French musicians who persevered with jazz, steadily perfecting his understanding and mastery, but the pinnacle of this cultural process was to be occupied by two exceptionally talented musicians: Stéphane Grappelly and Django Reinhardt. (16)

War would birth *l'école française*, the French school of jazz that Delaunay foresaw. But the distance and isolation from live jazz and mentorship by

American players continued to fuel this French inferiority complex. During World War II, jazz in France would be tested. If jazz by African Americans was usually the most "authentic" jazz, World War II threatened to wipe out the development of Paris as a home for jazz.

But jazz managed to survive during the war—amid some precautions, close calls, and exceptions. In *Jazz et société sous l'Occupation* Gérard Régnier meticulously investigates the dangers and opportunities for jazz to survive during the Vichy regime. In one example he shares Delaunay's fears and the precautions he took in November 1940, despite the advice of the jazz "purists" who saw the precautions as an inconvenience to restarting the Hot Club of France (HCF) after the war. Delaunay advises his HCF secretary to discontinue speaking of the HCF and *Jazz Hot* and to get rid of the records, magazines, and all documentation at the offices on Rue Chantal—so that these jazz institutions and materials would appear to be defunct (Régnier 7–8).[7]

Additionally, Hugues Panassié had broadcast a short-lived jazz show in 1942 that was later prohibited by the Vichy (Perchard, *After Django* 6). As I mentioned in my introduction, French jazz promoters had to change American song titles to French ones, play up unique French styling as Hot Club of France star Django Reinhardt did with his *Manouche* style, and perform and frequent jazz concerts in secret. But for the most part the Nazis did not so much ban jazz in France as they condemned *American* jazz. The survival of jazz during the Nazi occupation depended on a discursive shift and a national claiming of jazz, at least in name. The moniker of *French* jazz kept the music alive.

Jazz came not only to survive through its Frenchification but also became a source of survival, something for fans to cling to during the war. Perceptions of jazz as black music and of African Americans as oppressed during slavery and in the contemporary U.S. practices of segregation and racism made it a symbol of freedom. The desire for freedom one day soon, despite Nazi occupation, helped French jazz fans relate to jazz and to bond. Not only did jazz become even more Frenchified; it became a universal representation of freedom.

In a report translated for a 1940 issue of *Down Beat* Charles Delaunay described jazz, just as the French commenced a four-year occupation under the Nazis that could potentially douse the fiery French connection to jazz: "And jazz is not white, nor black, nor Jewish, nor Aryan, nor Chinese, nor American! . . . Jazz is much more than an American music—it is the first universal music. It may be termed international because, instead of addressing itself solely *to the mind* (which is dependent on national tradition and culture), it speaks directly *to the hearts* of men (who, when the fictions of 'education,' 'tradition,' and 'nation' are ignored, are very similar, just as the Lord intended them to be)" ("Delaunay" 6). Delaunay's "international" discursive performance was a political weapon that connected French jazz fans and European jazz fans and painted a picture of jazz as the same no matter from where it hailed.[8] He was alluding to a global jazz community; in the lingo of this book it was a jazz diaspora that had collapsed its national, racial, and cultural identities to be universally accessible. By sending the report to the American magazine *Down Beat*, Delaunay hoped to build a bridge between jazzophiles in the United States and France especially, attempting to privilege the French as prominent members of this global jazz community.

While the war made connection between jazz communities tough, thanks to the interwar efforts of the Hot Club of France, with its reissues of American records and the introduction of the Swing label, jazz fans could still secretly listen to, study, and perform jazz. Such was the case for French clarinetist Claude Luter. Born in 1927 Paris, Luter came of jazz age during the war by listening to just such recordings. Originally inspired by the Martiniquan musician Stellio, who popularized the beguine musical genre and who apparently reminded him of clarinetist and saxophonist Johnny Dodds, Luter soon began playing clarinet in 1941 after having been taught piano by his father (Zammarchi, *Claude* 25, 27). As with all French jazz musicians in the early and mid-twentieth century, recordings were crucial to their development. They would create the path to Luter's heart and entry into jazz: "I think it was 1941, at the beginning of the Occupation, that I fell for the recordings that Panassié produced on Swing" (Luter, interview with Adler). Luter was actually impressed with Bechet even before they met: "People used to automatically say that our early band was styled on King Oliver's Creole Jazz Band, but there was a time before that when we had been influenced by the 1938 recordings that Sidney made with Mezzrow and Tommy Ladnier. . . . But we were very familiar with Bechet's music, so naturally we were greatly honored to work with him" (quoted in J. Chilton 220).

Despite the jazz-unfriendly wartime era, Luter performed with what would evolve into the band the Lorientais. Luter's biographer, Fabrice Zammarchi, shares the memories of bandmate Pierre Merlin on how the band got more playing experience: They particularly liked to listen to records at a place in Chanteclerc and play at a bistro called Pam-Pam on the corner of Rue Saint-Michel and Rue Monsieur le Prince in the Latin Quarter; though the band members fluctuated, they would meet up and play at surprise parties during the war (Zammarchi, *Claude* 28, 36–37).

During the occupation and postwar period jazz stood for freedom. In claiming, protecting, and performing jazz despite potential risk, French jazz fans were manifesting their freedoms. They could also identify more with this music that they saw as an articulation of African American identity and experience. With their lives and livelihood restrained, threatened, and even taken under Nazi occupation, French fans identified in a new way with jazz, as survivors. In *Blues People: Negro Music in White America*, Amiri Baraka elaborates on survival, which he sees as inherent in the music of African Americans: "That there was a body of music that came to exist from a people who were brought to this side as slaves and that throughout the music's development, it had had to survive, expand, reorganize, continue and express itself as the fragile property of a powerless and oppressed people" (*Blues People* ix). Listening to jazz under German occupation was acknowledgment of oppression and a signal that one could survive and continue on, for jazz performed the ideology of liberation.

When the war finally ended, reconnecting with the thriving jazz scene in the United States was another form of liberation. Isolated by water but also from the lack of American musicians still in France during the war, Luter and other French musicians and fans had missed out on new recordings and tours from the biggest American stars. "The popularity of jazz had been swelled by the removal of the Nazi embargo on black American culture. 'Le swing' had secretly been enjoyed during the occupation in cellar bars, and as the need for secrecy vanished, the appetite grew," writes Jean-Paul Sartre's biographer Roland Hayman (258).

While the end of the war drew the French jazz public's attention to the United States again, it also created a new, distinct image of jazz in France. The underground cellar clubs, called *caves*, were the meeting places of youth excited about their return to freedom. The Saint-Germain-des-Prés crowd of zazous, existentialists, French filmmakers, and American tourists and residents thrived in the caves.

Zammarchi describes well this marriage of liberation and jazz entrenched in the caves of Saint-Germain-des-Prés: "From 1945 to 1950 a new world was born in the caves of Saint-Germain, where Sartre's existentialist doctrine happily mixed with the revolutionary music from the U.S. . . . An emblematic figure of Saint-Germain-des-Prés, the jazz clarinetist Claude Luter launched the New Orleans style in France after the war and he remained the soul of this music" (*Claude* 18, jacket cover; my translation).[9] Luter would become a symbol of this liberation. His performances in these underground caves defied the Nazi crackdown on playing and performing American jazz songs and styles during the occupation. With the openings of the Lorientais[10] in

1946 and the Tabou in 1947 (which became the Club Saint-Germain in 1948), he became a regular performer at the first caves to open up in Saint-Germain-des-Prés after the war. Before bebop swept through the French jazz public, cutting it in two with its unique sound and revolutionary, anticonformist ideology, New Orleans–style jazz was still considered revolutionary. For it was performed primarily by African American artists and racially distinguished from the similar Dixieland style in jazz criticism and marketing. Notably, Luter became the French face of New Orleans–style jazz, not Dixieland—so much so that even French critics supported him: he was already friends with Boris Vian, whom he'd heard play trumpet during the war with the Claude Abadie Orchestra; Vian and Luter tried to start a band before the Lorientais called the New Orleans Club, but it was blocked by the Nazi police (Zammarchi, *Claude* 33–36). After seeing Luter perform at the Lorientais, French jazz critic Frank Ténot wrote, "The jazz of the Liberation was rather symphonic. The music of Claude was super classic. The cult of origins. More New Orleans even than hits from New Orleans" (*Frankly* 48; my translation).[11]

In 1947 Luter was even featured in *Jazz 47*, a special edition of a journal entitled *America* that advertised French jazz clubs like Vian's new club Tabou and key French stars like Luter while also presenting essays on significant American jazz figures, important characteristics of jazz, as well as jazz inspired art. In the essay "Basin Street à Paris," Hergé ends by saying, "Claude Luter and his friends vigorously retook the fallen flame from the hands of Buddy Bolden and King Oliver" (71). Yet the promise of young French stars to take the mantle from Americans was shot down by Jean-Paul Sartre's opening essay of the journal, "I Discovered Jazz in America." Ralph de Toledano contextualizes the existentialist intellectual's trip to Nick's bar in Greenwich Village, noting that Sartre "listened to the wide-open Dixieland jazz for which the place is noted" (de Toledano 64). In comparison to the jazz he witnessed in New York, Sartre situates French musicians as having "plenty of recordings" but being "sad imitators" (Sartre, "I Discovered" 48).

A year later, in 1948, Boris Vian called out white musicians for holding back African American musicianship. Though his essay entitled "Should White Jazz Musicians Be Executed?" was satirical and witty, the essentialist heart of it rang true to Vian's beliefs. Vian wrote in the April 4, 1948, edition of *Combat* magazine: "The problem is the following: black music is increasingly encumbered by sometimes harmonious but always superfluous and usually avoidable white elements. Should we continue to congratulate and encourage the whites in question, should we criticize them or simply tell them to go take their suspenders and hang themselves?" (Vian and Zwerin, *Round* 46). Though Vian's essay was hyperbolic and intentionally controversial, the essentialist and reverse racism prevalent in Panassié's 1930s criticism was alive and well not only in his postwar commentary but in the perspective of Boris Vian, who was more progressive and open to new jazz styles than Panassié.

Given this racially and nationally authenticating discourse that was so critical of their efforts, white French musicians demonstrated an inferiority complex that was still very prominent at the end of the 1940s. Their insecurities were not unfounded. While the French excelled and set the standard for classical music composition, "the idea of improvising was what really caught the musician," noted music journalist Mike Zwerin, adding that they were "never instructed in rhythm" (Zwerin interview). The response of many French musicians was to learn, and not change the status quo, but replicate it. Ludovic Tournès writes that in the 1940s American musicians were still very much the model for French jazz musicians; he shows the similarity of French compositions from 1947 and 1948 compared to American bebop songs, stating that French musicians rarely composed personal themes for fear of a backlash and negative publicity (241–42).

During the 1949 Paris International Jazz Festival Sidney Bechet played with several French musicians, including Claude Luter. Bechet remarked that the young musicians didn't ask when they could play for him but rather when he would play for them (Vian, "Orgueil" 346). This comment suggests a lack of confidence when practicing. Claude Luter's impressions of his frequent bandleader, Sidney Bechet, exemplify this mentality. When I interviewed Luter in 2005, I mentioned that I'd like to interview him because he'd worked with Bechet. Luter answered that he didn't "play" with Bechet, that it was more like he "watched" him (implying that he was learning more than contributing). He was firm about this. Despite all he'd learned from Bechet, Luter emphasized a difference in skill level between the two—suggesting he could never reach the same level since Bechet had an innate calling and honed talent for performing soulful and expressive jazz.

In 1949 Luter was just twenty-one years old when he first played with Bechet at the festival.[12] Though Bechet was much older and set in his ways, he taught Luter much about musical interpretation. Bechet was certainly not an easy taskmaster; he had very high expectations and would work the band until the song was just perfect. French jazz radio host Alain Gerber characterized it as a scrupulousness that fueled Bechet's obsessive search for pure jazz; for Gerber, "Dear Old South Land" was particularly illustrative of Bechet's rigid standards ("Sidney Bechet"). Bechet's high expecta-

FIGURE 2.   Claude Luter and Sidney Bechet perform together in post–World War II Paris. Photo by Philippe Le Tellier / Paris Match / Getty Images.

tions of work ethic, timeliness, and production further shaped the relationship between him and Luter as more akin to teacher and student. Teacher Bechet would pass on his expectations and experiences, helping Luter develop into the New Orleans–style jazz icon he remains today. "Passing it on" is a process of learning from veteran musicians. Paul Berliner describes this approach in *Thinking in Jazz: The Infinite Art of Improvisation* as an essential part of jazz culture and a key to advancing as a jazz musician (489). He argues that success in jazz performance involves everything from "total immersion in the music's language" and "constant experimentation" to cultural exchange or "passing it on" (486–500). This is just the process Luter underwent. From 1949 onward Bechet recorded and performed with Luter quite a bit (fig. 2); however, after five years he switched to playing with other young players like André Rewéliotty. Though Luter was still in contact with his mentor and they would sometimes perform together, Luter returned to establishing his name and reputation apart from Bechet. His career peaked after Bechet's death. It was as if Bechet had passed on his legacy to Luter. Along with Claude Bolling and a few others, Luter kept New Orleans–style jazz alive. Until his death in 2006 he had a regular gig twice a month at Le Petit Journal on Rue Saint-Michel in the heart of the Latin Quarter in the fifth arrondissement. He drew crowds of older fans, reminiscing about the good old days in this cave, which was so similar to the 1950s jazz caves. He represented New Orleans–style jazz in France.

Yet despite his success and iconicity, Luter still categorized himself in 2005 as more of a student than a collaborator—as a "sad imitator" of the master, in Sartre's words. Luter's continued admiration and reverence for Bechet points to the persistent hierarchy after the war between not just American but African American jazz musicians and French musicians.[13] Granted the music had been created on American soil, so it was reasonable to expect different perspectives of the two. But for a long time African Americans in particular (because of perceptions of primitivism, exoticism, and more exposure) were sought after, while French jazz musicians were perceived as incomparable. Martial Solal suggested that "there was some prejudice" and that "if you were a medium or bad [playing] visiting American jazz musician, you automatically got an audience" (quoted in Culshaw). René Urtreger asserted the same point: "Sometimes even a medium black American musician, when he arrived in France he had more chance to work, and to be engaged, to play because he was a black American" (Urtreger). If Jeffrey Jackson's argument about Frenchification of jazz in the interwar period is true, then this divide between African American and French jazz musicians would certainly have collapsed by this era—thirty years and counting after the entry of jazz in France. However, French jazz musicians continued to deal with their own insecurities about skill and the perceptions of the critics, fans, and American musicians. The aforementioned examples of authentic seals of approval matched by doubts of French proficiency demonstrate an ambivalence in perceptions of French jazz as authentic—both by critics and fans, as well as musicians. In his investigations of jazz in Japan, Taylor Atkins compares the similar journey of Japanese musicians in pursuit of a unique jazz style to the earlier development of jazz in France: "The model I present here for understanding jazz in Japan is rooted in the most salient characteristic of that country's jazz community, a consistent ambivalence about the authenticity of its own jazz expressions (an ambivalence similar in nature to that [with] which several generations of white

American and European jazz musicians have grappled). Based on racialist conceptualizations of authenticity, this ambivalence motivated some prominent jazz artists to develop what I call 'strategies of authentication' to legitimate jazz performed by Japanese" (*Blue Nippon* 12). In the case of jazz in France Charles Delaunay played a key role in performing similar "strategies of authentication." The changes in discourse connecting jazz in France to jazz around the world was one such strategy; another would be to remedy the skill gap. Attempting to rectify this gap, Delaunay offered constant invitations to play and stay, which led to more live concerts and performances with visiting musicians. Charles Delaunay, Sidney Bechet, and Kenny Clarke would accede; the 1948 and 1949 jazz festivals were monumental moments that contributed to their decisions to migrate to France.

A JAZZ WAR: MOLDY FIGS VS. SOUR GRAPES

The violent, fanatical ideologies of World War II and the emotional liberation at war's end modeled key themes in a cultural conflict between traditional styles like New Orleans or Dixieland and the World War II–born style of bebop. During the war jazz fans missed out on bebop. The music had progressed significantly since its inception by Kenny Clarke, Dizzy Gillespie, Charlie Parker, and Charlie Christian at Minton's Playhouse in 1942 New York City. French fans had built up quite a desire to hear these recordings for themselves. "Salt Peanuts," composed by Gillespie and Clarke in 1945 New York, was the first bebop recording heard in France, but it wasn't exported until 1947. When French fans listened, the response was so intense it instigated some fistfights at jazz clubs (Gillespie and Fraser 331–32). The Hot Club of France commenced a debate over whether bebop was really jazz; the argument was so serious that terms like *le schisme*, *la scission*, and *la guerre* (schism, split, war) were all applied to this battle over the authenticity of jazz. In 1947 the Hot Club of France split, dividing French jazz fans into two camps. This divide put the cofounder of the Hot Club of France, Hugues Panassié, on the side of older styles. French jazz critics and fans perceived this music as traditional and called its practitioners "moldy figs." The other cofounder, Delaunay, put his energy and funds behind the fledgling bebop genre. He supported the group that was perceived as modern and progressive. Jazz media nicknamed bebop musicians "sour grapes."

Panassié had actually excluded bebop from the jazz category altogether. His influence was so significant that in 1949 bebop fans were considered traitors to the jazz tradition (Tournès 175). Since Panassié still had tremendous support and expressed dire statements about bebop, Delaunay was working against a significant tide of negative opinion.[14] This debate reached epic proportions in France, and the reaction to bebop was similar for a time in the United States. Amiri Baraka describes it as an uproar, claiming that critics (mostly white) were in a "fanatical fury" over the music: "From the stodgy Panassié calling it 'heresy' to *Down Beat* giving unthinkingly harsh reviews that they later had to redo, the early reception of bebop was unkind worldwide" (Baraka, *Blues People* 188–89).

Perhaps the reaction was so strong because bebop was one of the most revolutionary jazz genres. In contrast to swing it rubbed against the grain of the U.S. political fabric. The most notable difference was that the music could never be labeled simply "dance" music. It was too reflective, layered, and rebellious for that. Also, beboppers wanted to move past the stereotypical, all-smiles and amenable images symbolized by performers like Louis Armstrong (Guthrie, *Race* 106). The genre challenged racial conflict, asserted a desire for nonconformity, and was initially considered avantgarde music. Even worse, the bebop genre was perceived as "a subterranean 'cult' of drugs and subversive extravagance" (Guthrie, *Amazing* 189).

Charles Delaunay became an early proponent of bebop. He visited the United States in 1946, recorded "Rue Chaptal (Royal Roost)" with musicians like Kenny Clarke, and purchased new bebop recordings to ship back to France. When asked by Panassié to send some to Panassié's base in Nice, Delaunay exclaimed, "Man, you should come here and find out what is happening. Because if I get rid of these records, the place would be burned in half an hour with all the musicians who are coming anytime of the day and the night to listen to these records" (quoted in Gillespie and Fraser 331).

This distance between their feelings about the worth of bebop prompted the Hot Club of France split. In his autobiography Delaunay also attributed the split between himself and Panassié to jealousy. Panassié felt left behind, in terms of getting to know and appreciate these recordings and artists (Delaunay, *Delaunay's* 160; Gillespie and Fraser 331). Instead, Panassié remained a staunch supporter of traditional jazz and held the helm of president of the Hot Club of France, while Delaunay increased his participation in festival promotions and recordings. The 1948 Nice jazz festival and Dizzy Gillespie's seventeen-piece big band tour, directly after Panassié's jazz festival, accentuated this cultural war.

From February 22 to February 28, 1948, Hugues Panassié organized the Nice jazz festival around Louis Armstrong's All Stars, who represented a more traditional jazz style. Although Armstrong did not disappoint, young French jazz bands like Claude Luter's Lorientais performed amid doubts about their skill as jazz amateurs. Luter commented that "the older musicians hated us. They believed they'd always be kings, but we the young musicians disrupted that. They thought we played horrible music, when we tried to model ourselves on New Orleans orchestras like King Oliver's [Creole Jazz Band]" (Luter, *Jazz Hot* 7; my translation).[15] Actually, the festival would bring more repute and acclaim to his band. Louis Armstrong followed the festival with gigs in Paris. He joined the band at its eponymous club, Le Lorientais, on March 1, 1948. Photos and comments illustrate Armstrong's respect for their sound.

In his biography on Luter, Fabrice Zammarchi tracks down several commendations from Armstrong, Panassié, and others that contributed to a shift in the perception of young French jazz musicians like Luter.[16] In one such passage Armstrong praises Luter and the Lorientais: "Marvelous, these youngsters are formidable. . . . I heard Claude Luter in Nice for the festival. When I heard him play the first chorus, I thought I was in the presence of Johnny Dodds. . . . And his tone! You know the tone of Dodds? Broad and rough. . . . If I was free, I would play with them" (Daubresse 3). Whereas at the beginning of the festivals Luter and his Lorientais were considered interloping novices, by the end of the festival and resulting gigs in Paris they had changed some opinions on the skill level of French jazz musicians. It would be a long road. After the Paris International Jazz Festival in the following year, French critic and musician Andre Hodeir shot down the accompanying band of Sidney Bechet: "Luter's band was as we've known it to be: brutal, primitive, hot without swinging. . . . When will the Lorientais decide to work on their accuracy?" (*Jazz Hot* 7–9; my translation).[17] Luter and other young French musicians like Pierre Braslavsky and André Rewéliotty were still failing from lack of skill. But with festivals like these and the increased time it bought to accompany and jam with touring African American musicians, they began to improve their craft and exposure.

Delaunay also used festivals, concerts, and the eventual migration of African American jazz musicians to boost French jazz, for Delaunay recognized a "weak link" in French playing. He told interviewer Phil Nurenburg that "it remained that way until the war—that the rhythm was the 'weak link' in French jazz musicianship. We always tried to ask the visiting musicians how to play it [rhythm]. But they couldn't. . . . They hardly could make explanations about it" (Delaunay, "Preliminary"). The 1948 Jazz Festival offered them the opportunity to interact with the best in the business.

Gillespie's tours and Clarke's concerts introduced the French to even more rhythmically adventurous playing against a steady beat. Soloists had to have a strong understanding of time-keeping in order to depart from it.

Though the French showed interest in and appreciation for the music, they were still not as practiced in jazz, particularly the newer bebop style. Jazz had reigned for a couple of decades before the war. But during the war French jazz fans had lost touch with the new styles and, more significantly, with visiting musicians whom they could learn from.

With some luck and insight, in 1948 Charles Delaunay was able to organize concerts in Nice and Paris that would serve as an introduction to the modern style; for many French jazz fans it would be their introduction to live bebop. He rescued Gillespie's big band when their manager ran into financial difficulty; having withdrawn from promoting the band originally because of a lack of money, now Delaunay could deal directly with the group: "He could ask a band with no money to share the risk of the enterprise with him. He underwrote the travel costs and organized a series of concerts, plus a lightning (and extremely effective) publicity campaign" (Shipton 205–6).

The concerts of Dizzy Gillespie's big band that followed were like a surprise counterattack, stunning in the audience reactions they received and impressive even to the nonmusic press. "The war of jazz erupts in France" was emblazoned on a quarter-page spread of the French daily newspaper *Liberation;* the newspaper featured a detailed visual and literary breakdown of "figues moisies contre raisins aigres" (moldy figs versus sour grapes) ("La guerre des jazz éclate"; my translation). "Bebop provokes a new battle of Hernani at Salle Pleyel," exclaimed the February 22, 1948, issue of *France Soir* (Schiller 3; my translation). On the same day, *Figaro* featured an article on "the jazz war . . . with Dizzy Gillespie's bebop offensive" ("La guerre des jazz"; my translation).[18] "The War of Jazz Conquers France" also boldly appeared in the headlines of *France Soir* (Schiller 3).

The 1948 concert was the first live encounter with bebop for many French fans. French musicians rushed to listen to the most recent bebop recordings and learn how to play. The first bebop recording by the French had been produced by Swing on July 4, 1947 (Tournès 240). The band called itself the Bebop Minstrels and included Americans Allan Jeffreys (trumpet) and Jack Carmen (trombone) and Frenchmen André Persiany (piano), Benny Bennet (drums), Emmanuel Soudieux (bass), and Hubert Fol (alto sax). But most fans and musicians still credited the U.S. production of jazz with being more authentic and seasoned than French versions. The reaction to Gillespie's concerts had many fans rooting for the traditionalists and booing the modernists. Schiller writes in the *France Soir* review of the concerts: "The audience was mostly bobby soxers and when the Luter band followed, they dubbed it Brigade Luter" (3). By then Luter was a well-known amateur, whereas Gillespie was still a little-known name in France—despite having toured in France and England with Teddy Hill's band in the spring and summer of 1937.

Gillespie's 1948 jazz festival was a sure stunner for other fans. By the end of a concert in Nice the audience was so awed by the performance that an eerie silence followed, to the astonishment of Delaunay (Delaunay, *Delaunay's* 171). French bassist Pierre Michelot saw the concert at Salle Pleyel in Paris; he had never seen anything like it and was stunned by how "fabuleux" (fabulous) the band was (Hennessey, *Klook* 72). Dizzy Gillespie discussed the fascination with the music he observed during this tour: "The most impressive aspect of the tour was the way our music had taken hold among European musicians. All the young European musicians copied my records with Charlie Parker note for note. They'd paid five and ten dollars a copy for those records, and the reception we enjoyed in Europe exceeded in warmth and enthusiasm anything we'd ever experienced in the United States" (Gillespie and Fraser 335).

The concert had an impact on its players as well. Kenny Clarke admitted it was one of the factors that persuaded him to migrate to Paris in 1956 (Broschke-Davis 50). He would play with Pierre Michelot, Martial Solal, René Urtreger, and others, taking on Delaunay's call to improve "the weak link" in rhythm. As a pianist, René Urtreger was a core member of the jazz rhythm section (which usually consists of a pianist, drummer, and bassist and sometimes a guitarist). Relationships like that between René Urtreger and Kenny Clarke kept jazz alive amid the threat of rock 'n' roll's takeover. The bond between Urtreger and Clarke would also further shape France as a home for jazz and French musicians as go-to and ready-to-go collaborators rather than mentees.

COLD WAR COLLABORATION AND STARDOM: "PASSING IT ON"—CLARKE, URTREGER, AND SOLAL

"Should French jazz be buried?" asked the bold block-lettered title of Charles Delaunay's essay in the May 1949 issue of *Jazz Hot* (Delaunay, "Faut"). The essay questions whether French should even be used as a prefix for jazz, instead of judging jazz as either good or bad rather than attaching other qualifiers. Yet the essay is also visually framed by headshots of key French figures from guitarist Django Reinhardt and saxophonist André Ekyan to clarinetist and saxophonist Hubert Rostaing and Claude Luter's band, the Lorientais. Delaunay then goes on to list some of the top French musicians, holding them up with pride against European jazz musicians: "Everyone knows that this music is black music, because it was not only created by them but time and again they have showed themselves as the uncontested masters. . . . I believe I can say with all impartiality that among all the groups of musicians from the countries that took heed of the message of blacks, before the war the French took a place of honor with individuals like Django Reinhardt, Stéphane Grappelly, André Ekyan, Philippe Brun or Alix Combelle" ("Faut" 18).[19]

This essay is an authenticating narrative that performs French authority in jazz. It portrays Delaunay as a gatekeeper who best knows the national hierarchy of authentic musicianship, and it shows Delaunay's belief in the potential of French jazz musicians to develop as "authentic" players. Given Delaunay's promotion and knowledge of French talent like Reinhardt, it is curious that he would also ask if French jazz should be buried. Delaunay's question suggests that French jazz is dead or so bad that it isn't worth reviving. Throughout the essay Delaunay flip-flops between chiding French jazz musicians for not talking to or developing more of a rapport with visiting American musicians, while also noting instances in which American musicians have praised the French musicians they have watched perform ("Faut" 18–19).

Delaunay's flip-flopping between praise and chiding offered both the carrot and the stick to up-and-coming French jazz musicians. Published in the same month as the 1949 Paris Jazz Festival, the essay may have been an admonishing prompt for French jazz musicians to rise to the occasion and take advantage of the opportunities for accompaniment, socializing, and mentoring that the festival offered.[20] The festival did just that, setting the foundation for Claude Luter and Sidney Bechet's fruitful future collaborations and prompting Bechet to return to Paris for permanent residence.

Pianist René Urtreger would also benefit from Americans, like Kenny Clarke, who stayed. Urtreger first met Clarke in the winter of 1944. Clarke had been shipped to Paris and was leading a military band and had even switched to trombone (Hennessey 56). He was actually stationed with another fellow 1948 big-band mate, John Lewis, on whom Paris would have a lasting impact as well. At the time, Urtreger was just a youngster. (Born in 1934 Paris, he was a classically trained pianist and became enamored with jazz after listening to recordings.) At his first sight of Clarke, Urtreger was in awe. Actually, he was a bit afraid of him, intimidated by Clarke's brilliance. Yet Urtreger noted that Clarke's personality and skill impressed him and everyone actually; moreover, Clarke demonstrated an openness that encouraged him: "He just loved to play good music with good musicians. That was his only goal. . . . He didn't care who was playing with him, young, old, French . . ." (Urtreger). Clearly, Clarke recognized potential in Urtreger.

FIGURE 3. René Urtreger plays piano for a Lester Young recording session for Verve in 1959. Lester Young (tenor sax), Jimmy Gourly (guitar), Jamil Nasser (bass), and Kenny Clarke (drums) are also featured in this Barclay Studio session. © Herman Leonard Photography LLC / CTS Images.

Being young and having not grown up among a great deal of live jazz or mentorship opportunities, Urtreger was looking for multiple ways— through jam sessions and playing with visiting musicians—to improve (fig. 3). He recalled how Clarke supported his growth: "Kenny always trusted me like a son. When I was in trouble in an orchestra with a musician who said why did you take that young guy . . . he'd always take my defense. He'd say no, René, he is okay, no, no, no" (Urtreger). The youth and passion of figures like Urtreger contributed to making France a home for jazz. But the relationships shared between the novices and masters also prompted this transformation. Clarke mentored Urtreger by freely *passing on* his knowledge of the jazz industry and offering Urtreger confidence, support, and opportunity. "Passing it on" is essential to jazz culture: A young musician earns the right to learn from a mentor. What follows are jam sessions where mentees must demonstrate their skills in pressured environments. There is also constant daily practice and integration of the music into life (P. Berliner 486). Practice and mentorship are key to this approach. Also, young musicians must keep trying despite failure; they must maintain their confidence and love of the music. For in this postwar era jazz performance proficiency did not yet come from taking classes at a university. It came from studying with mentors, entering cutting contests, practicing profusely, and making the most of gigs. This jazz performance practice is what musicians like Clarke and Sims shared with Urtreger and other young French musicians.

Hearing Urtreger talk about Clarke, I began to understand that the relationship was more than mentor and mentee. The words *father* and *son* come to mind: there was the age difference; at twenty years his senior, Clarke had much life and musical experience to share. Clarke had also vouched for Urtreger when other musicians doubted his talent. Urtreger had discussed some of his struggle with drugs, his decade away from jazz, and playing in show business; all of these things had taken him away from the concentrated practice and frequent performances required of a top jazz pianist. Clarke was there for him when he reentered the industry. They were like family; in fact, I learned that their sons used to play together. In sum, Clarke became Urtreger's guide, backup, and confidante.

As Urtreger's skill grew, he gained opportunities through this friendship with Clarke. It was through their connection that he met Miles Davis. In 1956 he toured throughout Europe from France and Germany to Switzerland and Scandinavia with several top-notch American bebop players: Miles Davis, saxophonist Lester Young, and the Modern Jazz Quartet. The band's rhythm section was all French, with Urtreger, bassist Pierre Michelot, and drummer Christian Garros.

In 1957 Clarke invited Urtreger to record with Miles Davis, Clarke, and French jazzmen Pierre Michelot on bass and Barney Wilen on tenor sax. At Le Poste Parisien Studio in Paris on December 4–5 Urtreger performed on the now-famed soundtrack for *Ascenseur pour l'échafaud* (Elevator to the gallows), directed by Louis Malle. At only twenty-three years of age, and still shuttling back and forth between stints of his required French military service, Urtreger participated in the first-ever improvised jazz score and got to play with Davis—only two years before Davis's pivotal album *Kind of Blue*. The soundtrack for *Ascenseur pour l'échafaud* was the first-ever film soundtrack to be improvised, thus not based on any set script. Bandmate Pierre Michelot recounted the process: "It worked well. Miles had already seen the film. We had some idea of the harmonic structure but very little, in fact. We could do absolutely what we wanted" (quoted in Clarke, "Kenny Clarke"). Urtreger's playing skill counters what Mike Zwerin has indicated was one of the primary challenges to French jazz performance, improvisation (Zwerin interview). For Urtreger could improvise comfortably with one of the masters of improvisation and innovation at the top of his game in the late 1950s. Urtreger's nightly playing and introductions to multiple American stars and opportunities improved his skills quickly.

From Club Saint-Germain to the Club du Vieux Colombier Urtreger played at many of the top-notch clubs in the heart of Saint-Germain-des-Prés. These days he fondly remembers his time playing at the cave Le Chat Qui Pêche, which opened in the mid-1950s on Rue de la Huchette in the Latin Quarter. He was a part of the Donald Byrd Quintet, playing piano, with Byrd on trumpet, Bobby Jaspar on tenor saxophone, pianist Walter Davis Jr., Art Taylor on drums, and Doug Watkins on bass guitar.[21] In the mid-1950s and 1960s Claude Luter played in Kenny Clarke's famed house band for Blue Note in Paris. The band shuffled between the following personnel over the years: Clarke on drums, French bassists Pierre Michelot or Jean-Marie Ingrand, white American (and permanent French resident) Jimmy Gourley on guitar, and René Urtreger or African American Bud Powell on piano. In our conversation Urtreger noted that he was a part of Clarke's quartet until 1964 (Urtreger). To hold the same seat as Bud Powell was impressive, given Powell's brilliance at spare and speedy melodic interpretations with dissonant chord play. To share the seat, Urtreger had to have musical chops. In his biography on saxophonist Stan Getz, Dave Gelly describes Urtreger's high-level of play during Getz's 1959 performances at the Blue Note: "Urtreger had, by this time, played piano for virtually every major soloist visiting the French capital. He was therefore more experienced than many of his U.S. peers and, rather like Al Haig, he was able to sum up a soloist's needs in an instant" (103). For Urtreger had finally left the nest, and he was respected as a good musician. He recalled to me that "a few years later, I was able to play with Sonny Rollins or people like that, or Miles or Stan Getz, J.J. [Johnson], the greatest guys" (Urtreger).

Today, René Urtreger has become a part of the legacy of bebop, particularly of the postwar Saint-Germain-des-Prés jazz scene. Even at the age of eighty (at the time of this writing), Urtreger was still hailed for his contribution to *Ascenseur pour l'échafaud*. But he didn't start off as an icon; he started off young, impassioned, and ready to put in the time to learn. The 1950s through mid-1960s offered a plethora of opportunities to, in Delaunay's words, take "heed of the message of blacks," in his journey to more confidence and experience with live jazz performance. While Urtreger highlighted African American musicians that inspired and mentored him, the role of mentor was not limited to or characteristic of all African Americans.

French saxophonist Jean-Louis Chautemps was a contemporary of René Urtreger and played with him often. In our 2008 interview Chautemps admitted that African American saxophonist and Parisian resident Don Byas liked to get together musicians and jam regularly in the afternoons. Byas would never let French novices participate, as they were just too bad. At the time Chautemps recalled that he did not yet play very well. He finally got the opportunity to improve, by learning from white American saxophonist Zoot Sims. Sims helped him by providing multiple opportunities for them to play together. From the Americans who stayed, these opportunities to learn were even more prevalent. Chautemps would also play with Kenny Clarke in the Jacques Hélian band when Clarke first migrated to Paris in 1956. This opportunity led to many future collaborations between the two (Chautemps).

I purposefully distinguish the mentorship and collaboration with African American musicians like Kenny Clarke because René Urtreger's coming of jazz age in this era exemplifies a marriage between the French and African Americans in the Parisian jazz scene. This is important because the jazz scene in this period was still very much influenced by the essentialism that Panassié so strongly asserted in the 1930s. Even in the aforementioned essay Charles Delaunay reproduced an authenticating narrative that promoted jazz as a music created and mastered by African Americans; this performance of authenticity still persisted fifteen years after Panassié's *Hot Jazz*. The perception that African Americans could play better than their French counterparts was absorbed in several ways, such as the increased attention to and identification of African Americans in particular for tours and festivals. Urtreger himself noted that concert programs and tour lists would all boast the names of predominantly African American artists. When these artists arrived, Urtreger added, "they were received. They were already very known. Their records made them famous and when they arrived, they were treated like heroes."

The 1950s era was not only the second golden age of jazz; it also produced an increase of African Americans migrating to France—some returning, some taking advantage of the G.I. Bill, some following the myth of a color-blind Paris. The rise in African American immigration and jazz popularity did not coincidentally coexist in the 1950s but rather fed off of each other. The need and desire for an autonomous *French* jazz grew out of the post–World War II era and fed off political tensions during the Cold War thereafter. The relationship between African American jazz musicians and the development of jazz by French critics and musicians helped with French cold war competition and cultural independence from the United States.

During the Cold War, France preferred to stay neutral in the conflict between the United States and the Soviet Union since it felt loyalty to both sides. But it was also increasingly worried about its identity as a country and its authority worldwide. Charles de Gaulle had plans of his own to build a stronger, more independent France after World War II and wanted to take France into the modern age (Costigliola 51–54). As a result France desperately needed funds to rebuild. Similarly, the U.S. government needed support from France "in order to build a strong non-communist Western Europe" (Costigliola 45). In the end France promoted several U.S. political and economic policies that, while boosting the French economy, seemed to infringe on its independence. Part of the U.S. plan for reconstructing France, and Europe overall, was to export U.S. products, support European economies, and increase U.S. economic power; as the United States invested in European technologies such as telecommunications and semiconductors, it also exported cars, food, appliances, film, clothes, and music (Pells; Kuisel; Vihlen; Winock; Stovall, *France*). Richard Pells states that in the 1950s, U.S. investments in Europe approached $2 million. France's first major import had started directly after the war vis-à-vis the Blum Byrnes Agreement in 1946. In accepting a $650 million loan from the United States, the French had to encourage free trade in its markets and stand behind the plans of the United States to rebuild Germany (Stovall, *France* 21–22).

The first major concession that came out of this agreement involved film. France was required to import U.S. films despite attempts by the French to cut the influence of American imports. In Costigliola's opinion both sides were aware of the power that film could have on France's economy and culture. He argues that the U.S. mission to increase film exports to Europe was a highly strategic form of propaganda. The words of the president of Paramount Pictures confirmed this intent: to teach "people in foreign lands about the things that have made America a great country . . . to put across the message of our democracy" (55). The French had long held a position of excellence in high culture, and France desired a return to its former stature. The war had not only torn its lands but also torn into its cultural dominance (76). By disseminating American film, the French were putting their own film industry at even more risk.

Whereas the French perceived film, Coca-Cola, and other U.S. products as threats to their core values, there was not much fuss over jazz in France— at least not in this late era. For jazz was arguably assimilated into French culture as early as the 1930s. Jazz was just as prevalent as U.S. film and had entered France at nearly the same time, yet the French public flocked to it.

Jazz became even more at home in France during the Cold War because the music helped the French cultural image and competition with the United States by inviting African American musicians to Paris. Showcasing them in tours furthered the myth of Paris as a color-blind haven (and the image of France as accepting of all races). This image of France opposed media images that featured protests, marches, and violent confrontations of the U.S. civil rights movement in the 1950s and 1960s. Despite its attempts at propaganda, the United States found it could not hide its unjust treatment of African Americans from the world. Scott Gac sheds even more light on the negative reputation of the United States at the time: "Of course, with pictures of tortured black bodies and Josephine Baker decrying a new slavery in the South, communist media accessed a seemingly endless stream of material to present to their readers. . . . There it was, not only in communist sponsored publications but in the popular presses in India, Mexico, Greece, Haiti, and Great Britain; the United States was being characterized worldwide through racial conflict." In sum, representations of U.S. actions against its own citizens were a great detriment to a nation advocating its democratic ideals in contrast to communism. Critics that praised African American musicians (like Panassié), national media that featured jazz debates as serious journalistic news (like the *Figaro*), and continued word of mouth and invitations among African Americans about France as a welcoming place tended to destabilize the U.S. government's attempts at Cold War propaganda.

Jazz also served as a tool of soft power, helping the French to raise their cultural status during the Cold War. Highlighting Claude Luter and his band's visit to Russia in 1962, French studies scholar Elizabeth Vihlen notes that the French "saw themselves as cultural ambassadors, bridging the gap between East and West" (274). Luter transported jazz to places that white Americans were often blocked from entering during the Cold War era. In 1962 Russia Luter's music was respected as highly representative of jazz. Luter professed that for the Soviets jazz was not just music of the United States but also Western music: "Jazz is synonymous with freedom. . . . For a Soviet, jazz represents before all else the West and is equated with the absence of intellectual constraints" (quoted in Vihlen 274). Jazz, in the hands of French musicians, became a source of soft power. As Luter performed jazz in Russia, he also promoted cultural values like freedom and Western democracy. It is also significant that the Russians considered these performances good jazz, not good *French* jazz. This distinction demonstrates the full transformation from insecurity and imitation to adoption and dissemination. In this moment Luter's jazz was perceived as authentic.

French jazz production was also tied in with a burgeoning French film style called *Nouvelle Vague* (New Wave), which was one way the French began to culturally distinguish themselves once again. Though the French had to host American films, the late 1950s would also witness the birth of their own tradition-busting style, which often featured lesser-known actors in French cityscapes, quotidian dialogue, naturalistic acting, real-life conflict, and innovation in montage such as jump cuts (Neupert vi–xxix). French New Wave cinema made realism cool and differentiated itself from the predictable plot lines, happy endings, shot sequences, and formulaic nature of American cinema at the time. Some elements of *Ascenseur pour l'échafaud* offered a precursor to the style. But three years later, in 1960, Jean-Luc Godard made a huge impact with the elements of the New Wave style he showcased in *À bout de souffle* (*Breathless*); Godard remains famous for this film and its innovations. As with *Ascenseur*, one part of the cultlike legacy of this film was its jazz soundtrack performed (and composed) by pianist Martial Solal. Solal would go on to compose a great many film soundtracks, taking commissions from such stars as French writer and filmmaker Jean Cocteau to American actor and director Orson Welles (Culshaw).

Born in 1927 Algeria, Solal began playing the piano at six years old. As an adolescent he started to train under the saxophonist and bandleader Lucky Starway and practiced by learning to accompany recordings of such jazz stars as Louis Armstrong, Fats Waller, and Benny Goodman (Prévost). Solal moved to Paris in 1950 and became one of the French standouts, performing with the revolving circle of touring and residing American jazz stars prevalent in midcentury Paris. Solal built his reputation, similarly to Urtreger, by accompanying the best. He also played at the Blue Note, recording most often with Kenny Clarke, and he even produced two commendable recording sessions with Sidney Bechet. In 1957 Bechet joined with Solal's quartet (one session included Kenny Clarke as well); these recordings illustrated Solal's versatility, that even as a primarily bebop pianist he could jam with the New Orleans–style old guard as well.[22] As house pianist at Club Saint-Germain he played with everyone it seems, from French mainstays like Django Reinhardt and André Hodeir to

American stars like Lucky Thompson and Lee Konitz. Apart from Reinhardt he is one of the most internationally recognized and popular French jazz musicians. "By the early 60s he was becoming fairly well known in the States, and his classic 'At Newport '63' album sported the legend 'Europe's Greatest Jazz Musician,' and had laudatory sleeve notes not just from Ellington but Dizzy Gillespie," reported the *Toronto Telegraph* (Culshaw).

Solal's great esteem in the United States and his prolific career particularly in French film soundtracks served to put French jazz musicians on the map, not as imitators but as innovators. 1n 1963 Solal performed at the Newport Jazz Festival and throughout New York. His fifty-five days in the States were phenomenal. He remembered thinking Americans found his music to be bad, when really it was just a mistranslation—bad was good, magnificent actually (Solal 77–82). Imagine performing in the land of jazz and to be impressive there, particularly in the jazz hotspot of New York. Solal succeeded. Given Solal's continued legacy, recognition, and high repute, the question of why I would study jazz in France is easier to answer.

After World War II, jazz settled further into Paris, making a home and name for itself through the standout musicianship of performers like Claude Luter, René Urtreger, and Martial Solal. Their travels illustrated that the community of musicians disseminating jazz globally had become more diverse: Luter performed jazz in Russia and was able to get through the Iron Curtain when white Americans could not; Urtreger represented the New York jazz club Birdland, named after American bebop icon Charlie "Bird" Parker; playing in a mixed band of Americans and French on-tour, Urtreger helped disseminate those tunes far beyond New York to Scandinavia and Switzerland; Solal performed and was a hit in New York City; the major metropolitan site of jazz in the United States was interested in his French take on the music. As they traveled, these musicians were changing the perception of just what was "authentic" jazz. Though arguably still not recognized in an Americancentric jazz canon, they widened the recognition of jazz in France beyond just Django Reinhardt. This shifting face of jazz, to what I discuss as universal jazz in chapter 5, occurred through multiple types of exchange, from imitation, to passing it on, to innovation.

Today there is less questioning of whether jazz in France is "authentic" or even if there is a *French* versus *American* jazz. In our discussion in 2005 Mike Zwerin said the tide had shifted. Zwerin was a white American reporter who had once played his trombone in Miles Davis's band in 1948 (a year prior to the first *Birth of the Cool* recordings) before settling in Paris in 1969. He reviewed popular music, particularly the European jazz scene, for the *International Herald Tribune* for twenty-one years. In Zwerin's opinion American players were no longer required for a thriving jazz scene in Paris; they weren't as "cool" and they were getting older. Their music was no longer as distinctive or cutting-edge as the period with which we are concerned. Despite that, Zwerin said that the Americans were still the stars in France.

The opinions of some American residents in Paris seem to support that claim. On rounding up American friends to go to a concert in Paris, I find that the inevitable question is always, first, my opinion on whether the music is good and, second, whether the musician is American. Permanent American residents in Paris still draw a distinction. Chapter 3 reveals the comments of African American jazz vocalist Sylvia Howard, who still can see a difference, a lack of rhythm, from French musicians today (Howard). And in my 2005 interview with John Betsch, the African American drummer echoed Zwerin's observation about the French musicians' continued attention to composition and lack of ease with improvisation.

Even in our 2008 interview French saxophonist Jean-Louis Chautemps still distinguished between European and American jazz. He located the beginning of European jazz with Joseph Goebbels, who, Chautemps noted, liked jazz but detested what he perceived to be a Jewish music performed by African Americans. Chautemps added that the Nazis pushed for Europeans to create a distinctive European jazz, and they modeled it on the work of Cole Porter, whose music they saw as quite different from Jewish and African American jazz (Chautemps).

Chautemps's comment encapsulates several of the key issues this chapter has addressed: the impact of war, the search for authenticity, and the role of relationships in French jazz musicianship. The First World War introduced jazz to France at its end. In the interwar period Paris housed African American jazz musicians, creating a *Harlem sur Montmartre,* as William Shack's book title indicates. In this period French musicians studied records, played alongside Americans, and through the creation of the Hot Club of France and Swing records began to imitate American jazz, as well as to change French public perception of it as foreign. But World War II and the two decades thereafter highlighted the political connotations of this music, attaching a national claim on the music for its very survival during the war and later for its assimilation by French jazz musicians. The difference between American and French playing would continue to be noted, except for standouts like Reinhardt; then in this postwar period there would be more like Luter, Urtreger, and Solal who would make that distinction less necessary. Like Chautemps, who performed with and befriended Kenny Clarke from the mid-1950s onward, they looked to the visiting and residing

African Americans for their inspiration and mentorship. It was primarily African American jazz production that these French jazz musicians built on and continued the legacy of, while also making a name for their own French perspective and experiences. While some may still look for the actual African American contribution within the label of *French* jazz, it is not easy to distinguish where Bechet ended and Luter continued or to separate the contributions of Urtreger from the collective French/English/American collaboration that was *Ascenseur pour l'échafaud*. And few try to, anyway, for jazz has become at home in Paris; it has been absorbed. That means, for better or worse, that American-born music and musicians have become interwoven in jazz in France, too.

3. Inez Cavanaugh

Creating and Complicating Jazz Community

Her voice haunted me. At first I could only imagine it. On the pages of *Le manuel de Saint-Germain-des-Prés* Inez Cavanaugh stood—her torso tilted back, her eyes raised upward, her hands spread to the sky while her mouth widened as if singing a full vibrato. As trumpeters backed her and fans smiled, she caused "un petit spectacle" at the Club du Vieux Colombier (Vian, *Le manuel* 173).

For a long time I couldn't hear her for myself. Each library held tightly to its rare materials, and I had yet to find a remastered recording for sale with some of her recordings. Finally, I heard her sing "Every Time I Feel the Spirit." Her voice punched through my stereo speaker, giving a little taste of that long-ago moment. But I felt loss. Had I passed Hotel Cristal without much notice as I hurried daily to study French at the nearby Sorbonne? The building had whispered nothing of her famed apartment parties. Had I unknowingly passed the Club du Vieux Colombier amid modern-day clubs like Le Baiser Salé? Where was it located, and did echoes of her vibrato still pervade its aura? In this city of light, where so many African American men owned the spotlight, I wondered about the migratory experiences of Cavanaugh and others who contributed to, but fell off, the pages of French jazz history. Perusing biographies, autobiographies, Parisian guidebooks, reviews, discographies, photos, and correspondences, I have pieced together parts. But many gaps remain of Inez Cavanaugh's life in Paris.

Singing with French saxophonist Claude Luter, collaborating with writer Richard Wright, opening a jazz club, and showcasing artists in her home, Cavanaugh carved a niche in the jazz community on the Left Bank in those post–World War II years (fig. 4). This is not phenomenal in and of itself. There were plenty of African Americans in the heart of this scene: Don Byas, Sidney Bechet, Kenny Clarke, and Bud Powell, among others. The

FIGURE 4.   Inez Cavanaugh performs at the Club du Vieux Colombier with a band featuring Claude Luter (clarinet) and Christian Azzi (piano). © Jacques Rouchon / Roger-Viollet / The Image Works.

significance of Cavanaugh is that she was a woman, an African American woman. So her experiences abroad were not common.[1] By traveling, negotiating, and managing her job opportunities, Cavanaugh resisted traditional middle-class white female roles in homemaking and marriage, and she eschewed stereotypes of the strong, black matriarch holding her family together. Also, when African American women did tour and front bands in Paris, such as Billie Holiday's 1954 and 1958 tours, most did not stay. Apart from Josephine Baker's continued success in this era, not much has been written or discovered about figures like Inez Cavanaugh and pianist and singer Hazel Scott, for example, who stayed for more than five years in Paris.[2] Cavanaugh exhibited rare prominence and authority as a female African American vocalist and journalist in the male-dominated jazz scene of post–World War II Paris. She embodied various reasons for African

American migrations, exemplified their survival strategies, and nurtured as well as negotiated her way in an ethnically mixed jazz community.

This chapter begins to excavate the life story of a woman about whom little is known in jazz scholarship but whose contributions were significant to the creation and maintenance of a jazz diaspora in post–World War II Paris. But this chapter is about more than just one person. Cavanaugh introduces other stories, thus opening this narrative to a series of collaborations and migratory experiences for both African American men and women living in Paris. Her home, club, and friends were fully integrated into the jazz scene of the late 1940s and 1950s. Her life and work illuminate reasons why so many African American jazz musicians made Paris their home, key experiences and issues in living abroad in Paris, and their prompts for leaving or staying. The case of Inez Cavanaugh also introduces the concurrent possibilities of local community and global movement encompassed in a jazz diaspora.

Born in 1909 Chicago, Cavanaugh made her way to New York City to begin a multilayered career in jazz as a publicist, journalist, singer, and club manager. A passion for jazz led her to her lifelong companion, Danish duke Timme Rosenkrantz, who was poor in funds but rich in knowledge and public relations talent. The two worked diligently to promote artists. Rosenkrantz is credited with discovering pianist Errol Garner and being the first to record saxophonist Don Redman. Cavanaugh was the secretary for poet Langston Hughes (D. Clarke, *Donald Clarke's*). She was also the manager or publicity agent for Duke Ellington—reportedly writing a one-hundred-page text to accompany his album *Black, Brown and Beige* (Fabre and Williams, *Way* 35; L. Dahl 169; D. Clarke, *Donald Clarke's*). Writing liner notes for *Ellingtonia* as well, her early days promoting Ellington turned into a lifelong friendship. In 1973, as Ellington convalesced at home after a hospital visit prompted by his battle with lung cancer, he gave special instructions to his staff: "[Inez] was a very dear and important person to him. . . . Duke asked me to feed her, give her money and bring her to my house, and make sure nothing bad happened to her" (Patricia Willard quoted in D. Clarke, *Donald Clarke's*).

Beyond liner notes Cavanaugh wrote jazz reviews for *Metronome* and *New York Amsterdam News* (Fabre, *From Harlem* 166; Griffin, *If You* 206). While *New York Amsterdam News* was an African American–run newspaper, her work with *Metronome* and *Esquire* demonstrated her insider status with mainstream jazz journalism as well. For example, she reviewed Fats Waller for *Crisis* (the journal of the NAACP), and she was the only woman to sit on the jazz jury for *The Esquire Jazz Book*.

Cavanaugh gained clout as a jazz journalist, a very rare position for an African American woman in the 1930s. Most jazz critics were male and white, but Cavanaugh stepped around these obstacles. When Rosenkrantz realized that jazz had gone dormant in his home of Denmark and throughout Europe during the war, he called on Don Redman to put together a band to tour Europe, starting in Copenhagen and then traveling to Paris (Olav Harsløf quoted in Büttner). He picked Cavanaugh to be the band's vocalist.

When she arrived in Paris, it was conceivable that jazz fans would be sparse after the negative perceptions held by the Nazis and attempts at restricting American jazz during the Nazi occupation; but although live jazz may have been harder to come by, underground concerts and private listening persisted, and even radio shows featured jazz—organizers simply withheld Jewish and American artists' names until the radio program was affirmed (Fabre, *From Harlem* 165; Régnier 144).

On December 15, 1946, Cavanaugh accompanied the Don Redman Orchestra and presented the French with a sample of postwar American jazz. The music had changed considerably during the war with the creation of the bebop genre. Amateur fans were thrilled with the concert and celebrated the return of American players. No African American jazz band had toured since 1939, except for military units. The Redman Orchestra finally brought American jazz musicians back to France after the war; its concert in Salle Pleyel spurred an enthusiastic return of jazz musicians to Paris, particularly in the 1948 and 1949 French jazz festivals (Shack 113–14; Tournès 119).[3]

Saxophonist Don Byas, pianists Aaron Bridgers and Art Simmons, saxophonist/clarinetist Sidney Bechet, drummer Kenny Clarke, pianists Bud Powell and Mary Lou Williams, and vocalist Inez Cavanaugh all arrived in the mid-1940s and early 1950s and nurtured the Parisian jazz scene. Meanwhile, Louis Armstrong and Duke Ellington—and boppers Charlie Parker and Miles Davis—intrigued the French crowds on their tours, leaving much wonder and a lot of emulation in their wake. Well known today for his producing, composing, and arranging, Quincy Jones lived in Paris several times throughout his career, once as A&R (Artists and Repertoire) director of the *Disques Barclay* recording house, where he sought Kenny Clarke out as often as he could for recordings (Hennessey, "Clarke-Boland" 127, 132). Between 1950 and 1964, the population of African American artists in Paris tripled from five hundred to more than fifteen hundred (Baldwin quoted in Stovall, *Paris* 232; Fabre, "Cultural" 45). African American musicians like saxophonists Nathan Davis and Johnny Griffin, trumpeters Donald Byrd and Don Cherry, drummer Art Taylor, and pianists Kenny Drew and Errol Garner were just a few of the artists who migrated to Paris from 1962 to 1965.[4]

There were several reasons for this continual stream. The American military proved an instrumental tool for the migration of African American artists: "The G.I. Bill gave World War II veterans full educational benefits, paying the tuition and living expenses of those who chose to go to college after demobilization. Millions took advantage of these benefits" (Stovall, *Paris* 141). Artist Herbert Gentry was one of many African American soldiers who moved to France on the G.I. Bill. Gentry returned to once again experience the beauty and good life he had previously enjoyed: "I first saw Paris when I was in the army. After serving with the 369 Anti-aircraft outfit, I joined the special services unit because they were stationed just 60 miles outside of Paris. I just loved that city. I used to go there every night just to walk around. . . . I promised that I would return to Paris and I did" (Gentry 9). With his wife he would later open an art-infused jazz club, Chez Honey, where clients could discuss art and relax over music and food (Stovall, *Paris* 149).

While the American military presented opportunities for Gentry and other African American soldiers to see life abroad and study later on the G.I. Bill, military service during the war also put into high relief the racism and limitations with which they had been dealing for so long in the United States. Saxophonist Johnny Griffin migrated to Paris because of the greater respect and better treatment he had received during his tours: "The way people treated black musicians—or jazz musicians in general—was comparable to the respect they accord to classical artists. Coming back to New York, I ran into the same old hassles; . . . I'd enjoyed a period of relaxation and felt I could have a more dignified life in Europe, so I took off in the summer of 1963" (quoted in Moody 63). For Griffin, Paris afforded a life where blacks were treated with decency and respect—in sum, with humanity.

Also, while World War II had provided a source of comparison and an expediency for departure, the Cold War and the battles over civil rights in this era just as much spurred migration. These two cultural wars were often linked, as Mary Dudziak's enlightening book attests in its title, *Cold War Civil Rights: Race and the Image of American Democracy.* Communism played a key role in either keeping African Americans in Europe or pushing them there. Paul Robeson made a speech at the Paris Peace Conference sponsored by the Soviet Union in 1949 Paris. What he said while touring in that last week of April would change his life and career forever, even though it was immediately misrepresented by the Associated Press and later by the House Committee on Un-American Activities.[5] A French translation of the speech is housed in Robeson's archive at Howard University and reports the following. Though Robeson's remarks were improvised and the text is translated, it is one of the closest representations of what was said that day: "We in America do not forget that it is on the backs of the poor whites of Europe . . . and on the backs of millions of black people that the wealth of America has been acquired—And we are resolved that it shall be distributed in an equitable manner among all of our children and we don't want any hysterical stupidity about our participating in a war against anybody no matter whom. We are determined to fight for Peace. [Applause]. We do not wish to fight the Soviet Union. [Applause]" (Robeson). The response was explosive, with the NAACP quickly saying that Robeson did not speak for all African Americans and Jackie Robinson publicly taking a stance against the comment (Thomas 23–36). Robeson's passport was revoked in 1950, and his rights to travel were only reinstated in 1958—too late, after his career and health were in decline.

The renowned intellectual and writer on race relations and proponent of Pan-Africanism W. E. B. Du Bois had also been stripped of his right to travel. So he could not speak at the First International Congress of Black Writers and Artists, which was headed by Senegalese writer Alioune Diop and his journal *Présence Africaine* in 1956 Paris. Responding to the invitation, Du Bois sent a cable including the following statement: "I am not present at your meeting today because the United States government will not grant me a passport for travel abroad. Any Negro-American who travels abroad today must either not discuss race conditions in the United States or say the sort of thing which our State Department wishes the world to believe. The government especially objects to me because I am a socialist and because I believe in peace with communist states like the Soviet Union" ("Après la congrès"). Du Bois encouraged participants not to be stymied by the prohibitive forces of colonization and imperialism that would keep minorities silent. In her biography of pianist Hazel Scott, Karen Chilton meticulously illustrates how Scott's tireless commitment to civil rights for African Americans, women, and artists drew attention from the House Un-American Activities Committee and was a prominent factor in her near decade-long self-exile in Paris starting in the late 1950s (137–72).

Beyond political differences, some African American artists believed there was a more positive reception of African American art and music in France. They were seduced by the prospects of greater creative opportunities and more respect. Saxophonist Hal Singer, who has lived in the Paris suburb of Nanterre for nearly fifty years, described this to me: "A lot of people here read books and knew the life of the people. . . . European fans could recite to you all the records a person had made" (Singer). So in his opinion it was not just appreciation but rather intellectual awareness that European fans demonstrated.

In contrast Miles Davis once argued that European audiences and recordings were less cutting-edge because Europe was removed from the heart of jazz creation and innovation found in the United States (Davis and Troupe 218; Stovall, *Paris* 180). Writer Richard Wright affirmed this sentiment when he made the following observation of the Tabou club in 1947: "Then the music was bad and loud and an imitation of the American New Orleans style and the French boys and girls who were trying to dance and act like Americans made a self-conscious job of it" (Fabre and Williams, *Way* 42).

Other African American artists came to Paris and stayed because they relished the artistic freedom they found while visiting there, particularly the experimentation and collaborations. Artist Ollie Harrington wrote that the artistic community in Paris was a totally open one that encouraged an "atmosphere of camaraderie, a sharing of ideas, techniques, and often soup, all of which seem indispensable in the making of the artist. I never even remotely experienced anything like that at 'home' except perhaps in Harlem" (quoted in Stovall, *Paris* 148). Harrington pointed to the uniqueness of Paris in presenting this type of artistic freedom.

In addition to artistic freedom, collaborations in the intimate Parisian jazz community were at times groundbreaking. There was bebop's controversial showdown at Salle Pleyel in 1948 (made possible by jazz promoter Charles Delaunay and Dizzy Gillespie) and the first-ever improvised jazz score in *Ascenseur pour l'échafaud* (prompted by Boris Vian's introduction of Miles Davis to Louis Malle). The second jazz-only record label, Disques Vogue, was initiated by Charles Delaunay in 1947 and fortified by Sidney Bechet and Kenny Clarke's recordings. All of these events positioned Paris as a center of collaboration. Paris also enacted collaborations between African Americans, for example bringing together Hal Singer and Kenny Clarke to record for the first time.

There were artists who used Paris as a stepping-stone. Don Byas stayed in France for a bit but then settled in Holland. The same was true of saxophonist Dexter Gordon, who migrated to Denmark. Trumpeter Don Cherry lived in Paris from 1965 to 1967 but then left for Sweden and explorations throughout Asia. His stay was brief, but the image of his "thumb trumpet" poised from ballooned lips as he captivated crowds in Le Chat Qui Pêche still makes the then-student-now-retiree Salim Himidi smile in memory (Himidi).

Others like Kenny Clarke used Paris as a home base to return to after tours throughout Europe and Asia. In the 1960s Clarke cofounded the

Clarke-Boland Big Band, a multinational band that recorded in Cologne, Germany, but toured in England, Switzerland, and throughout Europe. Paris's proximity by train and plane to many prominent European cities made it a good location for touring and travel. While the aforementioned reasons helped attract African American artists, the perceived history of racial equality and job opportunities ranked highest as reasons for migration.

WHY PARIS? JOBS AND RACIAL EQUALITY AWAIT

Paris had jobs! At least that's what Inez Cavanaugh thought. She came to Paris because she perceived it as having promising job opportunities. In this post–World War II era jazz jobs were hard to come by. From 1942 to 1944 the labor union of the American Federation of Music (AFM) instituted a recording ban that restricted union musicians from recording at all. The AFM and Britain's Musician's Union had already joined up to ban foreign musicians from doing live performances in the respective countries from 1935 to 1955.[6] Add to that the difference in pay and rampant appropriation of copyright and royalties that some African American musicians experienced, and Paris seemed to offer the opposite. Paris beckoned with more job opportunities and a desire for African American musicianship. Pianist and composer Michel Legrand offered Kenny Clarke a job in 1956. Though it later fell through, Clarke quickly found more engagements (Hennessey, *Klook* 124). Mary Lou Williams had worked in London and France; she was enthused to extend her stay in Paris for two years, as there were no French union restrictions in comparison with her experiences in Britain ("Europe"). As for Cavanaugh, she had heard of job opportunities and couldn't see why anyone would stay in the United States considering it all.

Before moving to Paris, Cavanaugh had paved a path of success, not as a high-profile singer but rather in several behind-the-scenes roles as a journalist and secretary. She decided to try her luck abroad despite her access to these top-notch positions. Writing to her friend and jazz pianist Mary Lou Williams in 1947, she revealed, "That's why I wanted to get everybody I could out of America last year. I felt this coming. It always does after a war. . . . The labor lock-out is on. . . . I can't understand why everyone was so hard to convince . . . and to think of those guys going *back* when we got the news" (1).

Sidney Bechet also wrote about the difficulty of finding work in the United States: "All the damn jockeys on the radios was playing Jazz numbers, answering all kinds of requests, making all kinds of expert explanations all wrong. Everybody was excited, but no Jazz musicianer had a job except to make records" (*Treat* 192). In 1930s New York he once gave up performing to make ends meet with a laundry and tailoring service (J. Chilton 96). In France, Bechet became a king of jazz; he never again had to fear unemployment. With his movie roles, steady club gigs, and opportunity to write a musical ballet, Bechet's opportunities in France were a world apart from his lowest moments in the United States.

In the mid-twentieth century Paris appeared to live up to its reputation as a place where jobs for musicians and other artists were plentiful. French festivals were a big draw for jazz musicians. They offered gigs and continuity (since they occurred each year). After making connections there, one could start to count on that work each year. By the time the Newport Jazz Festival (the first annual jazz-only festival in the United States) commenced in 1954, France boasted several big festival venues in Paris and Nice. Though they were often one-time events, the 1948 and 1949 festivals featured Dizzy Gillespie and Charlie Parker among others, and they were monumental moments in the history of jazz in France.[7]

There were also increased job opportunities in clubs. Club Saint-Germain headlined visiting stars like Miles Davis. The Blue Note linked young French stars and African American veterans, such as bebop jazz drummer Kenny Clarke with French pianist René Urtreger. Some clubs also highlighted more French players and bands. Le Tabou started off slow in 1947 but became a hot spot for Dixieland jazz as it featured key French artists as well as jazz critic and trumpeter Boris Vian's house band, the Claude Abadie Band (Fabre and Williams, *Way* 64; Stovall, *Paris* 165).

Several new clubs opened after World War II; Club Du Vieux Colombier led the charge. Cavanaugh regularly accompanied Claude Luter's band. "The V.C. is packed every nite and I'm really going over this time," she excitedly wrote to Rosenkrantz in May 1949 (Cavanaugh, Letter to Timme, May). However, vocalist and writer Maya Angelou gave her much competition, singing at La Rose Rouge (Fabre, *From Harlem* 64). The Blue Note, Le Chat Qui Pêche, Mars Club, and Jazzland also provided competition on the Left Bank.

Job opportunities were certainly a big pull for many African American musicians settling in Paris, but the perception of Paris as color-blind had long been a prominent motivating factor. Soldiers' experiences in both world wars went a long way in solidifying the illusion of Paris as color-blind. African American cultural critic Amiri Baraka has suggested that World War II opened the world up to African Americans, making them aware of foreign culture and society and emphasizing the discrepant treatment they received in America: "The sense of participation and responsibility in so major a phenomenon as the World War was heightened for Negroes by the relatively high salaries they got for working. . . . But this only served to increase the sense of resentment Negroes felt at the social inequities American life continued to impose upon them" (*Blues People* 178).

African American soldiers had returned home after World War 1 and regaled their families with stories of France. In his book *Harlem in Montmartre* William Shack details how these soldiers had glimpsed beautiful France juxtaposed with the destruction of battle. They told their families that they dreamed of returning. Shack also reveals a personal account of his own father's experiences. During World War I his father had "made sharp comparisons with the racial hostility they experienced in the company of white American soldiers. [He learned that] a 'colored man' in America had to travel and study in France or England to be recognized as 'equal' to a white man" (xiii). For Shack's father France was a land of more freedoms. The war had not only been a fight for world freedom; it had also opened the door to ethnic freedoms for African Americans fighting against U.S. injustices.

These soldiers' stories were passed down from generation to generation and created an illusion that was absorbed into African American folklore. This illusion was underlined by a long line of writers and artists who moved to Paris. Valerie Mercer notes that African American artists had arrived in France as early as the 1830s, and Michel Fabre adds that even before painter Henry Ossawa Tanner came to Paris in 1891, there were several others who studied at the Beaux-Arts school (Mercer 38; Fabre, "Cultural" 33). The 1920s represented a peak in the migration of African American artists to Paris. One such example was the brief sojourn of Langston Hughes, which is well noted in his autobiography, *The Big Sea*.[8] Hughes had dreamed of France ever since he read the poems of Guy de Maupassant; Fabre further reveals, "In Hughes's mind the image of France early evoked literary accomplishment and absence of racial prejudice" (*From Harlem* 63). Hughes finally made it to France but with only seven dollars to his name. Still the dream was alive, and as soon as he set foot in Paris, he rejoiced: "I was in France. La Frontière. La France. The train to Paris. A dream come true" (Hughes and Rampersad 147).

Henry Crowder, an African American jazz pianist, had stayed for years in interwar Paris while having an infamous seven-year affair with the white British writer and political activist Nancy Cunard, who had been in Paris since 1920. Crowder recounted his dreams of Paris on his 1928 ship voyage: "A chance to live as every other man lived regardless of his color" (quoted in Shack 44). Given the choice between a foreign locale and a history of oppression and segregation in the United States, many artists dreamed of Paris as a haven that furthered liberal-minded thinking about race. As these artists fled the racism of the United States in the 1920s, they contributed to a broadening perception of open-mindedness and liberty in France.

The dream had only solidified decades later. Driven overseas by American racism, especially practices of segregation, another wave of African American artists sought a haven in Paris after World War II. Living in Paris for ten years, Nathan Davis recounted: "I ran into little or no prejudice there. It is hard to separate it from the music. We were looked at as special. I would advise anybody to go and live in a foreign culture, especially in one so rich as France" (quoted in Moody 132). Davis's positive experience further contributed to the illusion of Paris as color-blind.

American popular culture didn't help either. Famous songs like "La vie en rose," which means "a life in pink," further popularized and disseminated this illusion. In 1947 Louis Armstrong first recorded the song Edith Piaf had first performed in 1946. In fact, his version is arguably as popular and enduring as hers. But Armstrong did more than cover the song; he translated, rewrote, and transformed it. Whereas Piaf's is a passionate torch song of a remembered love, Armstrong hypnotizes the listener into a fantastical love affair with Paris. His musical interpretation begins its seduction with a soft tumbling across the high register of piano keys. The high tones descend, waterfall-like, repeating and mesmerizing with a whispering effect. The rhythm section emphasizes the backbeat. A walking bass, percussion, and guitar sustain a repeated vamp. Four measures later, Armstrong's signature trumpet enters and layers on a raspy tone with a lilting, lazy pace. The music sets the mood for the lyrics he intones in the next verse.

> Hold me close and hold me fast
> The magic spell you cast
> This is la vie en rose . . .

Armstrong substantially reworked the meaning of the song, transforming it from a tortured memory to a present and future vision of idyllic love. The fact that his version is the most well-known by many, at least among the English-speaking public, is important. In this recording Armstrong became a representative of France, or at least the American vision of France, as "romance incarnate." This song has become a tried-and-true symbol of France in many films, *Wall-E* being a contemporary example. This symbol connotes a city replete with outdoor cafés, sophisticated fashions, delectable pastries, and love-struck couples embracing on bridges overlooking the Seine. It's significant that Armstrong is also identified with France in this song, because it links African Americans to France, suggesting that African Americans have access to "la vie en rose"—but specifically in France. These media examples also demonstrate that Americans, often African Americans, prominently performed this rose-colored narrative of Paris as a color-blind place of social and professional opportunity.

The media's role in disseminating this narrative became especially clear when I spoke with pianist and vocalist Almeta Speaks. Speaks grew up and came of age in 1940s North Carolina. She first visited Paris in the mid-1950s and decided to split her home between Paris and Toronto in 1999. Speaks's interest in Paris first came from African American periodicals:

> She [Aunt Edna] used to have subscriptions to magazines, good magazines, cause you know *Ebony* and all those were good magazines, *Life Magazine, Look,* all of those really good magazines. And she had the subscriptions to the newspapers, black newspapers, there was one in the *Pittsburgh Courier,* there was the *Amsterdam News,* there was *The Chicago Defender. . . .* What you got out of white newspapers was who went to jail, who robbed somebody, who got killed. All of the negative, everything that was negative that went on in the community, you could get it in the white newspapers, it was like a vow not to uplift the black community so they didn't get above themselves. But the black newspaper told us about Hazel Scott, Adam Clayton Powell. . . . It told us about movements, it told us about teachers who were making strides. It told us about black people who were making strides in the armed services. It told us about black classical performers. . . . And we learned that they lived in places like France and Germany and Russia. The thing that always struck me, and ahhhhh, I loved reading the ones who lived in London and who lived in Paris. So my eyes were filled with all these people. I knew there was something beyond Reidsville North Carolina. (Speaks)

Speaks's memory was strong enough to propel her to visit. She fashioned images of financial success, stardom, political activism, and artistic freedom that proliferated when African Americans traveled outside the States. In his seminal study of African Americans in Paris, *Paris Noir: African-Americans in the City of Light,* Tyler Stovall also posits a political function for the success of African Americans in Paris. Stovall's expansive lens portrays a "critical mass" of African Americans that constituted a real artistic presence in Paris from the early 1900s until present day (xv). He uses their success in France to critique an American public that has long ignored the achievement of African Americans (xvi). Jazz becomes one of many activities that illustrate the success of African Americans in Paris.

Looking at the "critical mass" of African Americans created in Paris in the mid-twentieth century (and before, in the 1920s, and inevitably after, in the 1960s), I notice a continuum—a recurring example of African American "community" and "success" abroad, in Stovall's terms. Pointing this out in handed-down stories, in film, and through African American media outlets advertised that success and provided proof and detail for those living in the United States. Those were the reasons for migration; those were the benefits. But, as I discuss later in this chapter, the narrative of Paris as color-blind proved more illusion than reality the longer one stayed and the later in the twentieth century it became.

CAVANAUGH'S COMMUNITY AWAY FROM HOME

> As members of a community of their own within Parisian culture—the French called them Am-Am—black Americans had established social centers, cafes like Chez Honey, . . . where expatriates met one another as well as visitors from the States.
>
> DAVID HAJDU

Life magazine proclaimed it "the most popular *chez* in Paris"; African American journalist William Gardner Smith described it as "a Left Bank institution"; and Chez Inez soon overtook the space of Perroquet, a nightclub featuring Guadeloupian singer Moune de Rivel's popular Caribbean songs (Carson 107; W. Smith, "It's Six" n. p.). Opening its doors in 1949, Chez Inez was a jazz restaurant located on Rue Champollion just behind the Sorbonne in the fifth arrondissement (Fabre and Williams, *Way* 35). Chez Inez housed an ethnically mixed Parisian jazz scene and supported connections among African Americans during the three years of its existence. James Baldwin described its importance as a space of congregation and networking: "It is at Chez Inez that many an unknown first performs in public, going on thereafter, if not always to greater triumphs, at least to other night clubs, and possibly landing a contract to tour the Riviera during the spring and summer" (Baldwin, *Notes* 85).

Always smiling in her pictures, whether with Sidney Bechet or fellow singer Billie Holiday, Inez Cavanaugh drew people in and was known for her ability to uplift the mood, especially in her own club (D. Clarke, *Billie* 148; Rosenkrantz, *Harlem* 44). The good spirits of the owner and the convivial club atmosphere were played up. The sign on the entrance proclaimed: "Aperitifs, music, dinner, happiness. This Is It." Cavanaugh's song lyrics advertised, "Someday he'll come along, the man I need, and he'll be big and strong, the man I feed" (Carson 107). At Chez Inez, Cavanaugh would play games and always try to do something new and exciting to keep her patrons relaxed and enjoying themselves (Letter to Timme Rosenkrantz, May; Letter to Timme Rosenkrantz, June).

An assortment of people mixed at Chez Inez, so the restaurant took on an important networking role in Paris. Rosenkrantz described Chez Inez as "a place where Eartha Kitt and the entire Katherine Dunham troup [*sic*] could be found . . . after the party was over . . . on the Eve of Christmas or New Year's . . . peeling potatoes, making pies for the next day's festivities!" (Rosenkrantz, "Liner Notes"). In addition, photos and articles place Cavanaugh with top stars like Billie Holiday, Louis Armstrong, and Sidney Bechet, among others (D. Clarke, *Billie* 148; Rosenkrantz, *Harlem* 44; Carson 107; Bechet, *Sidney Bechet*).

Inez Cavanaugh forged connections between the jazz scene and community of African Americans living in Paris; she also identified ways for herself and her compatriots to thrive in this jazz diaspora. Although a large jazz scene had existed in 1920s France, Tyler Stovall argues that the 1950s represented an even more popular period (*Paris* 167). Performers had firmly established Montmartre as a world-famous jazz center in the 1920s. But after the war everyone headed to the Left Bank (the half of Paris that lies south of the Seine) and sought out jazz in the neighboring arrondissements of Saint-Germain-des-Prés, Le Quartier Latin, and Montparnasse.[9]

In particular, Saint-Germain-des-Prés served as a mecca for jazz musicians and as a multicultural center of creativity, enticing not only African Americans but also American tourists, exiled artists, French literati, philosophers, and stars from all over the world. Clubs located here housed philosophy just as much as jazz. In these years, fresh after Nazi-occupied France, youngsters crowded the clubs of Saint-Germain-des-Prés, listening to jazz and associating it with freedom. So when the war was over, jazz was thoroughly embraced. It became the new norm to drink and party into the wee hours. Bodies grooved and notes swung while jazz brightened the dimmed smoke-filled caves.

While commingling in the vibrant, diverse network of artists and intellectuals in the Parisian jazz scene, African Americans also created bonds among themselves in the overlapping community most commonly known as *Paris Noir* (Black Paris). Tyler Stovall has described the sense of community forged in the first boom of jazz, the 1920s: "Two common experiences united African Americans in Paris during the 1920s. First and foremost, the city offered them a life free of the debilitating limitations imposed by American racism. . . . Second, for the most part black Americans in Paris chose not to remake themselves as black Frenchmen or Frenchwomen, but instead established an expatriate African American community" (*Paris* 26). As Stovall notes, African American artists in Paris created their own space (though it interwove with other cultural spaces). That community was linked heavily to the image of Paris, in particular, as a place with fewer limitations and more possibilities for success. Stovall's Paris Noir then is geographically set in this city as well as built on less tangible (but still fixated) ideals.

Some writers like William Shack have likened this interwar community to the culturally rich space of 1920s Harlem. Shack's book title *Harlem in Montmartre* connotes an almost supplanted community. Again, this community is tied to place, a relationship between places actually. Shack's vision of community emphasizes the continued relations between African Americans residing in France with their families and their homes back in the States. In the passage quoted above, Tyler Stovall also characterizes Paris Noir of the 1920s as a distinctive, Americancentric group—one not interested in assimilating per se but rather making use of Paris for its own gains. These characterizations of the interwar African American community in Paris as still relating to the United States, as purposefully distinctive from its French environment, and as geographically tied to particular cities continued with the migration of African Americans who came after World War II.

Paris Noir after World War II was a hot spot of black intellectualism and musical creation, just like its predecessor. African Americans of every artistic persuasion traveled to Paris to study, perform, and write. James Baldwin came in 1948 and seemed to inhabit the Saint-Germain-des-Prés hot spot Café de Flore, even more than his nearby apartment (Baldwin, *Notes* 127). Famed *Life* magazine photographer Gordon Parks made his home in Paris in 1950. In 1951 the cartoonist Ollie Harrington turned the Café Tournon into a famous spot, as he spent many a night swapping stories with writers Richard Wright and Chester Himes (Stovall, *Paris* 148, 188). Pianist Bud Powell came in 1959 and made Paris his home for years (Stovall, *Paris* 102). Romare Bearden was one of many African American painters who trained in Paris and exhibited work there through the 1940s and 1950s (Stovall, *Paris* 88). Thus, Paris was very much a center of black artistry at this time.

Since jazz clubs were mostly owned by the French, restaurants became the "new centers of black sociability" (Stovall, *Paris* 161). They were among the few institutions that African Americans managed, and they became central to community gatherings. In a letter in May 1949 Cavanaugh characterizes Richard Wright as clamoring for the opening of the club so he could get some fried chicken. For many of these African Americans Chez Inez was at the core of what I term a "culture of catching up." The culture of catching up entails a community mood that promotes catching up over food, music, discussion, and keeping in contact through correspondence or visits. The culture of catching up is a phenomenon I first observed when my mother and I were welcomed into the Parisian home of drummer John Betsch. He was glad to have visitors, to extend news on the jazz scene to me, to share recordings, and to discuss those we both knew stateside.

I found that even today food and music were still an essential part of this culture of catching up. Betsch cooked us an extraordinary meal, using fresh seafood and vegetables from the nearby market. While he chopped, he talked about previous musical engagements and his favorite artists. He'd stop occasionally to pass around a photograph, liner notes, and most often to let the music speak for itself by popping in a CD.

Chez Inez also fed its customers' stomachs while fueling their memories of home and loved ones. Serving up everything from red beans and rice for 100 francs (30 cents) and fried chicken and rice for 200 francs (61 cents), Chez Inez reminded African Americans of home and foods easy to come by in the U.S. South (Carson 107; Stanton 81). Cavanaugh, rather than being singular in this trend to bring back the remembered foods from home, was representative. While women like Cavanaugh took on this role, there were others like former G.I. Leroy Haynes, whose restaurant Chez Haynes was famous for its soul food until its closing after sixty years in 2009.

Food as a core survival strategy and tool for socializing is also depicted in the film representation of this era, *Round Midnight,* directed by Bertrand Tavernier in 1986. Based on the memoir of Francis Paudras and his relationship with Bud Powell, the film's protagonist, Dale Turner, often comes back to his hotel room, where his wife, Buttercup, or friend, Ace, have cooked up a mouth-watering meal indicative of the southern United States.

Whether at Chez Inez, Haynes Restaurant, or in private homes, African Americans found food to be a coping mechanism that reminded them of home. In her restaurant and in her home Cavanaugh helped feed a universal desire for home. She served soul food: chicken, collard greens, and spare ribs to name a few examples. The menu filled more than just appetites, though, as it provided a material connection to home. Marveline Hughes discusses how soul food can be traced back to African foods, like the seeds for black-eyed peas, that were brought to the United States during the Middle Passage; while soul food is "one preserver of Black culture," black women may also take pride in their recipes and in the empowerment they feel in feeding and nurturing their families (272–73). Through Chez Inez, Cavanaugh literally nurtured her fellow African Americans. More than that, she provided a material and memory-based connection to their lives in the United States. These ties to home were important for surviving a life abroad.

Talking to Laurent Clarke about his father, Kenny Clarke, I saw more examples of the culture of catching up at work in postwar Paris. He mentioned that his father and Dizzy Gillespie had never missed an opportunity to connect and keep each other informed. Laurent Clarke told me that there was "a whole bunch of musicians playing together in the 30s and 40s; whenever one of these guys had the opportunity to come to France, it was just another opportunity to get together. . . . They were bringing news. They didn't miss any occasion or opportunity to see each other" (L. Clarke). Also, he discussed his mother and how she joined musicians at her table. She seduced them with her chicken and chili. He remembered these get-togethers as humorous, with lots of teasing, swapping of stories, and good home cooking.

Cavanaugh also reinforced the culture of catching up through her correspondence (fig. 5). She described to Rosenkrantz how Bechet "really gassed po' Paree . . . [and] stopped 'em cold for 10 minutes" during the 1949 festival; in another letter she recounted that she'd "had a coffee with Kenny Clarke last nite. Everyone likes him here" (Letter to Timme Rosenkrantz, May; Letter to Timme Rosenkrantz, June). These letters demonstrate again that Cavanaugh was at the heart of activity among African American artists and was therefore very knowledgeable about this scene. They also show that the culture of catching up was not limited to Paris; this cultural practice connected with others abroad and widened the inner circle of the community.

This was the case for saxophonist Hal Singer, who revealed to me the role that the smaller, more localized jazz scene in Paris contributed to networking for him. Even though Singer had heard of, and even shared musical partners with, Kenny Clarke, it wasn't until Singer settled in Paris that he met Clarke and later played with him. So, in this case, the small size and the even smaller population of African Americans in Paris encouraged bonding that did not occur elsewhere. The culture of catching up was about reminiscing. It was about establishing community, not only community with those in Paris but with those far away.

In many ways Cavanaugh created a home away from home for African American artists. Whether with her club, letters, or cooking, she helped shape a community that was supportive of African American success and sociability. Performance studies and African American studies scholar E. Patrick Johnson discusses the possible dangers in African American communities of creating an "authenticating discourse based on skin color, cultural traditions (e.g., food preparation or 'soul' food), and experience narratives" (196). But Cavanaugh avoided much "authenticating discourse," for even though she built community among African Americans, Cavanaugh and other artists were not exclusionary in their activities. In the postwar African American community of Paris the elements of food, racial connection, and sharing of experiences were integral to the culture of catching up.

FIGURE 5.   Inez Cavanaugh corresponds with good friend pianist Mary Lou Williams. Mary Lou Williams Collection, Institute of Jazz Studies, Rutgers University.

But rather than distinguishing "real" African American culture or isolating themselves, many African Americans maintained bonds among themselves while simultaneously commingling in a vibrant, diverse network of artists in the Left Bank. This is perhaps one distinction from the more isolated and Americancentric model of community referenced in the aforementioned passages from Shack and Stovall.

Not only did Cavanaugh interact with a range of black artists; she also partied with figures like Jean-Paul Sartre, whom jazz critic Boris Vian brought to enjoy jazz at Chez Inez. She schmoozed with French film stars, too: "French singers and film stars like Juliette Gréco and Sacha Distel had been regular patrons, trying to copy her special way with a vocal, and it was the place where American musicians on Paris gigs loved to drop by on their way home" (Rosenkrantz, *Harlem* 219). Apparently, Chez Inez was so popular it even drew the French aristocracy. In the liner notes for Cavanaugh's 1968 album with Teddy Wilson, Rosenkrantz boasted: "It was where the Duc de Talleyrand drove up with an open-carful of noisy friends and had a chamber pot emptied on his head by an angry neighbor upstairs, shouting 'Las Bas Les Américains' . . . and the Duc de Talleyrand showing 'Mais, je suis français." So even dukes were known to come to Chez Inez and were just as rowdy at times as the reputed Americans.

Cavanaugh provided a bridge between the white French jazz community and the ever-burgeoning African American artistic population in Paris. Her local and international connections among multiple artists and communities is apparent in figure 6; on the cover of her notebook Cavanaugh's friend and pianist Mary Lou Williams scribbled Cavanaugh's Copenhagen address, key Parisian contacts such as Boris Vian and Charles Delaunay, and her network of friends and musicians in England and the United States. The notebook cover melds these multinational and cultural influences together in a way that resembles the function of Chez Inez. In its diversity of races and nationalities Chez Inez exemplified the concept of a jazz diaspora. The venue spurred ethnically hybrid relationships by offering a space for networking among white French musicians, critics, and African American jazz musicians. While I have yet to find records that clearly distinguish whether Inez owned or only managed Chez Inez, the very management of the club was hybrid, reflecting the ethnic backgrounds of Inez and her Indo-Chinese comanager. Alongside blues and jazz, Cavanaugh was required to feature a certain number of Indo-Chinese songs each night; the audience makeup of Chez Inez reflected a similar ethnic diversity as it welcomed interracial couples and people of all nations and races ("Paris" 71–72). The *Ebony* profile on jazz clubs in Paris revealed that this ethnically mixed club scene was the norm: "There are no all-Negro night clubs, as such, in Paris. Owners, bands, floor shows and customers are all mixed. Wherever Negroes work, there are always more mixed couples than all-white or all Negro couples on the dance floor" ("Paris Night Life" 71).

Cavanaugh exemplified interracial relations. Her long-held relationship with Timme Rosenkrantz bucked segregation. An African American woman with a white Danish man still caused a stir in the United States; in fact, interracial marriage was illegal in many states. The landmark *Loving*

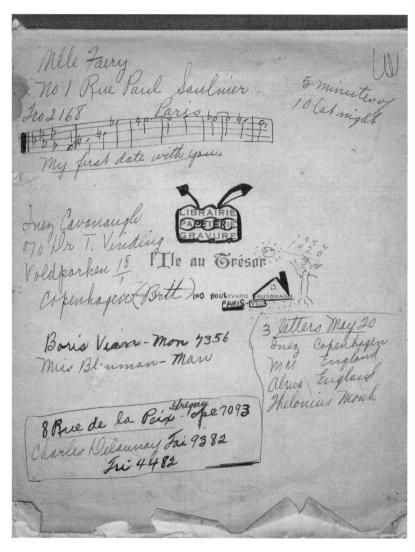

FIGURE 6.   The notebook cover of Mary Lou Williams. Mary Lou Williams
Collection, Institute of Jazz Studies, Rutgers University.

vs. Virginia case, wherein the Supreme Court invalidated state laws against
interracial marriage, was not decided until 1967. I have uncovered no
accounts or correspondence about discomfort with their relationship in
New York City. But the dismay of Rosenkrantz's grandmother may have
been the primary cause for their never getting married (D. Clarke, *Donald*

Clarke's). The couple spent more than thirty years together before Rosenkrantz died in 1969.

Their relationship and Chez Inez were important symbols and realizations of diversity in these jazz and Paris Noir communities. In addition to Chez Inez, Haynes Restaurant, another cultural hangout of Paris Noir, also exemplified miscegenation and became the heart not only of African American cultural memory and catching up but also of interracial connections:

> Another black GI who remained in Paris was LeRoy Haynes. He was a student of the arts when he came with the army, and he remained to study on the GI Bill. He soon met a French girl, Gaby, whom he married. She became his partner in an American restaurant in Pigalle that specialized in soul food. The place rapidly became the haunt of many race brothers who had more stories to tell than money in their pockets. LeRoy Haynes himself became a friend of Richard Wright, whose French-American Fellowship Association he joined, becoming its president in the early 1950s. (Fabre, *From Harlem* 165)

These venues offered ways of interacting and thriving that would have been blocked in the United States. Most important, many African American musicians (particularly men) came to Europe and sought out interracial relationships. I remember seeing a large black-and-white photo of Bechet in the French national library archives. He was beaming at the camera and tucked in close to his white German wife, Elisabeth Ziegler, as they rode a carriage through a parade in honor of their marriage in 1951 Antibes, France. In 1962 Kenny Clarke married a white Dutch woman, Daisy Wallbach, and had a child with her. Clarke's first marriage, to singer Carmen McRae, also produced a son, who would stay in the United States. In our conversations both Johnny Griffin and Hal Singer mentioned their long-term relationships with white European women.

Tyler Stovall has recognized miscegenation as a common theme across decades of African American presence in Paris: "The theme of miscegenation, with its echoes of both romantic liberation and racial revenge, runs like a red thread through the history of postwar African American life in Paris. It expressed not only defiance of America's color line but also a refusal to conform to the sexual practices of most black Americans" ("Harlem-sur-Seine"). Interracial relationships were a draw to African American musicians. These relationships added reasons to stay and helped combat loneliness while living abroad. Spaces like Chez Inez, and couples like Rosenkrantz and Cavanaugh, provided safe spaces to collapse racial divides, expectations, and conventions.

But William Gardner Smith recognized that the French were only super-ficially open to integration. Living in France for sixteen years and working as a reporter, he interacted in Paris Noir but also observed and eventually critiqued racism in France in his books *The Stone Face* and *Return to Black America*. Smith distinguishes relationships and marriage, noting that the French frowned on the latter; he also suggests that while African American men may have enjoyed interracial relationships, they were aware of the oft-exoticized and hypersexualized perceptions of the French women they attracted (W. Smith, *Return* 65).

Chez Inez was not the only place Cavanaugh encouraged friends to catch up and experience interracial and international mixing; she opened up her home, too. Cavanaugh and Rosenkrantz had been known for their parties and recording sessions in their Harlem apartment on W. 44th Street (Clarke). In their Parisian apartment they continued the tradition of inspir-ing, nurturing, and recording new talent. Conveniently located near Club du Vieux Colombier, where Cavanaugh performed often in her first years in Paris, Hotel Crystal was located on Rue Saint-Benoit, in the heart of Le Quartier Latin (Fabre, *From Harlem* 165). The apartment was apparently a popular resting spot for an assortment of African Americans: James Baldwin and Chester Himes; actor Canada Lee; singers Eartha Kitt, Ethel Waters, and Hazel Scott, as well as pianist Mary Lou Williams (L. Dahl 230). Situated as it was in the Latin Quarter, near the homes of many African Americans, it also helped foster creative innovation, as well as bonding—and not just among musicians but also artists of all media and African American exiles.

Cavanaugh hosted parties into the wee hours, and her apartment served as an unofficial practice space for several musicians. Errol Garner found daily inspiration at Cavanaugh's piano, once writing "Lamplight" in honor of "a subdued table lamp of hers" (L. Dahl 189). Her apartment acted as a musi-cian's studio and an unofficial salon, inspiring musical development and help-ing musicians to be in control of recording their own work. This availability was key, given the desire for creative freedom but also the negative produc-tion experiences that many musicians had had in the United States.

Drummer Art Taylor struggled with the white appropriation of jazz in the United States:

> They've got all the black musicians on the run. Black musicians all over Europe, running away from America. But that's part of the white power structure that's killing us and our music. Just like they've killed it with the so-called cool school, West Coast jive. They sold us down the line. Took the music out of Harlem and put it in Carnegie Hall and downtown

in those joints where you've got to be quiet. The black people split and
went back to Harlem, back to the rhythm and blues, so they could have a
good time. Then the white power structure just kicked the rest of us out
and propagated what they call avant-garde. (A. Taylor 67)

One of Cavanaugh's most prominent traits and survival strategies was the
promotion of black music and musicians. She was particularly proactive
with marketing herself. This prompted a joint project; she and Leroy
Haynes starred in Richard Wright's play *Daddy Goodness* (Fabre, *From
Harlem* 165). In a May 1949 letter to Rosenkrantz she shared another
opportunity: "The V.C. is about to put the other caves in the alley. Did I tell
you Dick Wright was asked by Pagliere (Open City) to do a special script on
V.C.? Pagliere and R.W. was in to see me. P said my scene in the documentary film is terrific, wants to do the sound over in a place with better acous-
tics. I'm to phone studio and they'll run it off for me." All of these examples
demonstrate a melding of disciplines and an opening of opportunities to
African American jazz musicians. They also portray Cavanaugh as a key
negotiator and publicist for her club and performances.

Of course, she might also have been considered opportunistic. In pianist
Mary Lou Williams's accounts Cavanaugh was sneaky, moody, and out for
herself, and the couple created a "perpetual open house" to secretly record
songs from artists and later sell them for their sole benefit (L. Dahl 168–
301, 170). Williams suggested that the couple stole recordings, sold them on
the black market, and did not pay her for her recording of *The Zodiac Suite*
(170–71). This may have been the cause of a falling out, as they had been
good friends.

Were the gatherings at Cavanaugh's apartment and Chez Inez nothing
more than cash cows for the visionaries behind them? After multiple failed
ventures in New York, from a radio program to a music magazine,
Cavanaugh and Rosenkrantz (nicknamed Robber Baron for his dishonest
practices) may have positioned "community" as just another tool to build
their finances (L. Dahl 169). What this perspective misses is a musician's
inherent need for self-promotion and opportunism to survive. With a mod-
est talent and mediocre success in singing, Cavanaugh undertook a range of
tasks to keep herself afloat. She accompanied others not only as a singer but
also in her interviews and writing. She followed, sought out, finagled, and
created opportunities, all the while staying in the background of big names
like Duke Ellington. These jobs did not give her a name or recognition. But
they left Ellington remembering her as "a very dear and important person,"
said his public relations representative Patricia Willard (quoted in D. Clarke,
Donald Clarke's).

So Cavanaugh tried many ventures in order to survive, and she also tried a range of businesses with Rosenkrantz, from restaurant management to recordings. Their business ventures failed on most occasions. But while they lasted, they forwarded talent—supporting Don Byas on tour, facilitating the recording of Errol Garner, opening Chez Inez in New York City and Paris, and debuting Timmes Club in Copenhagen to host and employ a range of American talents.[10] So Cavanaugh kept finding ways to promote herself and other talent in the process.

She also defied normative gender roles of mid-twentieth-century America. She worked in roles rarely inhabited by women at the time. She bucked American social rules of racial homogeneity by having a lifelong relationship with a white man. She dismissed the expectations of women at the time by not marrying Rosenkrantz and often living and traveling without him.

Accompanying and networking with men was one of Cavanaugh's successful survival strategies. In pictures she is often seen posing in a group or alongside a man (e.g., Aaron Bridgers, Sidney Bechet, Teddy Wilson, or Rosenkrantz). This perhaps points to stronger working relationships with men. In her letters to Rosenkrantz in May and June of 1949, she mentioned a range of opportunities from, and supportive of, men:

> Well I have just left the grand man of jazz [Sidney Bechet] at his hotel in Rue l'Université round the corner to dash home and write this additional note for him to carry on the plane today at 6 pm.

> Well everyone is . . . awaiting the opening of Chez Inez. Art Buchwald [*Paris Herald Tribune*] was in tonite. Is backing me to the hill [*sic*].

> Avakian promised to do a story on me for *Mademoiselle* when I open the joint and get photos of names . . . and a new dress or two. I finally found a modiste. Incidentally I anticipate trouble from Moune so I'm going to get working papers for Rue Champollion "toute suite" to protect myself, n'est-ce pas!!!

> Had a coffee with Kenny Clarke last nite. Everyone likes him here. Jacque Dieval offered me 3 days in Brussels at 8.000 F a day—but I turned it down as I can't afford to leave Chez Inez just now.

All of the above excerpts feature men, except for the reference to Guadeloupian singer Moune Rivel. (Cavanaugh had taken over her club, Perroquet.) The distrust for Rivel greatly contrasts with the excitement and support of the men listed. It further supports my perspective that being a black woman with power in this Parisian jazz diaspora was rare, created competition with other female performers and managers, and required survival skills.

But Cavanaugh's skills differed from those of her predecessors. Josephine Baker, Ada "Bricktop" Smith, Adelaide Hall, and Florence Embry Jones were among the small but influential group of African American women who became club managers in the interwar period. Josephine Baker is the most remembered (and most revered and reviled at the time). As I have noted, her *danse sauvage* translated her black performing body into a jungle animal for the French imagination. It was the start of her path to stardom in France and of recognition worldwide. (Cavanaugh's predecessors tended to draw on dance and were hypersexualized and exoticized by fans, the press, and artistic renderings.)

Rachel Ann Gillet's dissertation, "Crossing the Pond: Jazz, Race and Gender in Interwar Paris," pays attention to other African American female performers in Paris in the Jazz Age. She argues that black female entertainers, even those who did not dance, were often still described in terms of their physicality. She, along with other scholars of black female performers in this era, discusses the obstacles to respectability among other blacks in France that included the perception of African American female jazz performers as lacking in morals and not meeting the expectations of behavior and dress by the African American press and elite.

Compared to Josephine Baker, Cavanaugh lacked star power and a distinctive voice to make a name for herself. When she arrived in Paris in 1946, Cavanaugh was in her mid-thirties and a jazz-industry veteran. Baker, by comparison, was just nineteen. Also, Chez Inez and Vieux Colombier were jazz caves for eating, chatting, and listening to music, unlike the dance halls and clubs in which Baker performed. So Cavanaugh's survival skills were unique but successful as they helped her thrive in the male-dominated Parisian jazz scene until 1952.

BEHIND THE SCENES OF PARISIAN DREAMS: A RISE IN RACISM AND COGNIZANCE OF RACIALIZED DIFFERENCE

Letters from Cavanaugh don't reveal it. Biography snippets rarely mention it. But behind the Parisian dreams of racial equality lurked a different reality. Where were the French of African descent in these jazz clubs? And why were the French so fascinated with African Americans when they had their own black colonists and immigrants? Looking back on the collaborations that African Americans produced in this fruitful jazz diaspora, there were only white French and African American collaborations. Africans were not part of the mix, and while the beguine playing of Caribbean musicians thrived in Paris, they were not a major part of the jazz scene.

An economic divide marginalized French of African descent from participation. Catherine Bernard writes, "Africans in France were mostly workers on the docks in maritime cities. They were not politically organized and their isolation was one of the major reasons for their exploitation. Except for the writer Claude McKay, there were few interactions between these different communities" (Bernard 24). McKay actually portrays Africans as dockworkers in his book, *Banjo;* though the book illustrates musical play within this group of seafarers, no moves to play professionally are made. Also, James Baldwin described Algerians in roles as taxi drivers or janitors (Baldwin, *Nobody* 141). William Gardner Smith noted the high prices of clubs; because of the prices of drinks and admittance (though Chez Inez was fairly reasonable at 25 cents for beer), Parisian jazz performances were limited to wealthier French fans, tourists, and foreigners (Smith, "It's Six" n.p.). Thus, it seems that the economic status of most French of African descent and women was significantly different from African American exiles and visitors. Perhaps the low economic status of many North Africans kept them separated from this scene.

While some African American artists came with barely more than a dime to their names (stories of Langston Hughes and James Baldwin living at the bare minimum come to mind), their cultural capital raised their statuses above their means. Their Americanness raised it. African American artists overall were given stature and financial support that they did not have in the United States. In Paris they weren't read as starving artists, even if they literally were. Moreover, Baldwin, always the American tourist, could cross "social and occupational lines" in Paris easier than he could in the States (*Nobody* 139). These same opportunities were not open to French of African descent.

Some African American artists began to notice and remark on this racialized differentiation: Bechet visited Dakar and saw the poor race relations there and was wise enough to see that racism persisted not just in the colonies but in France as well. *Esquire* reporter Blake Ehrlich captured his voluntary avoidance of racism in 1950s France: "Bechet keeps in mind the places in Paris he feels Negroes aren't welcome, and he stays away from them. Most of the time he feels too busy and too old to start proving things" (93–95).

Pianist Art Simmons came to Paris in 1949, playing at the Paris International Jazz Festival with Kenny Clarke. Simmons often played at Chez Inez and accompanied Billie Holiday and Carmen McRae at the Mars Club (Fabre, *From Harlem* 203; Holloway). As house pianist at the Mars Club, he settled in Paris and did many recordings with the Parisian-based label Barclay Records. He made his career in Paris for more than twenty years and began to notice a distinction in how the French perceived African Americans:

> "Some of what we thought when we first came to Paris was probably naive," said Simmons. "Pretty soon, I noticed some of the French people talking in a terrible way about 'the Arabs' and 'the Jews,' and I started wondering what they said about me when I wasn't around. And there was something kind of superior in the way they embraced American blacks, a 'noble savage' attitude or something. But it was better than the situation in the States in a lot of ways. And I think it was better for other guys who were black like me but gay on top of it." (quoted in Hajdu 143)

Simmons was one of many who had been attracted to the illusion of a color-blind Paris but later noticed race consciousness rather than blindness.

African American journalist William Gardner Smith also came to France with the idealized notion that Paris was color-blind (Stovall, "Preface" 305). Michel Fabre describes Smith as not totally gullible about French egalitarianism but believing hard work on his writing would make for acceptance by the French; however, as Smith observed the reality of Algerians his opinion soon changed (Fabre, *From Harlem* 243–55).

He was one of the first African Americans to confront the disparate treatment of Algerians and to write an account of the Algerian War of Independence as it was actually happening (Stovall, "Preface" 305). From 1954 until 1962 Algeria staged a revolution against France. In his 1963 novel *The Stone Face* Smith describes one of the goriest battles on October 17, 1961, when two hundred Algerians met their deaths in Paris (Stovall, "Preface" 305). Though the war was primarily waged on Algerian soil, the book also highlighted the subjugation and resistance of Algerians living in France. The novel goes on to explore the African American protagonist's search for identity and the realization of racism in France that contributes to his disillusionment.

James Baldwin believed the Algerian War of Independence pitted African Americans against Algerians in the French imagination. He realized that the two groups were joined by similar struggles and therefore conjoined in the French imagination (Baldwin, *Conversations* 268). Baldwin was one of few African Americans to understand that his experiences were quite different from those of North Africans in Paris. He recognized the different treatment of Algerians, suggesting that Europe wouldn't seem half as free to him if he weren't an American (*Nobody* 141).

As an African American in Paris, Baldwin had never visited the homelands or directly experienced the culture of the North Africans he met. He saw and recognized as familiar the violent oppression and prejudice enacted on them, but he could do nothing to change it. He recognized that his American passport distinguished him as coming from a free country. While the practice of freedom in the United States did not live up to the ideals, in Europe it meant that he was categorized and thereby treated differently from colonized and postcolonized French of African descent (Baldwin, *No Name* 377–78).

Baldwin's revelations illustrate and parallel Brent Hayes Edwards's discussions of the communicative link between African American and Francophone African writers in interwar France. In *The Practice of Diaspora* Edwards highlights the shared interest in creating a Pan-African consciousness across the literary and political works of African American writers. He shows common experiences of prejudice and challenges to political autonomy in the works of African Americans like Claude McKay and Francophone African writers the Nardal Sisters from Martinique. Edwards also demonstrates the challenges to articulating shared experiences, goals, and strategies. He explains that "black modern expression takes form not as a single thread, but through the often uneasy encounters of peoples of African descent with each other" (Edwards, *The Practice* 5). Looking at this alongside James Baldwin's perceptions highlights Baldwin's unease in not fully understanding the heritage, perspective, and attitude of French of African descent. In this perspective Baldwin's "encounter(s) on the Seine" become "uneasy encounters" that are more like debates, conflicts, and points of incomprehension. Despite these moments of unease, however, Baldwin is also clear that common, collective, and imposed meanings are read on black bodies irrespective of national experience and context.

For example, Baldwin once experienced firsthand some of the disregard and unfair treatment meted out to North Africans in Paris. In his first year in Paris he was wrongfully accused of stealing hotel linen. After spending several days in jail, it was only his American status (and the help of his lawyer friend) that got the case tossed out. Through the process he learned that French policemen were not so different from American officers; their disrespect and cruel laughter began to seem universal. He saw a life of "privation, injustice, [and] medieval cruelty" that was not too far from his own (*Notes* 101–16). Baldwin came to understand that there was a difference in social status between African Americans and French colonists of African descent. The increased freedoms that African Americans enjoyed existed alongside limitations for French of African descent. The requirements were easy to understand: one had to be American—specifically *African* American.

African American writer and performer Maya Angelou experienced a similar disillusionment with racism in France. She brought Senegalese friends to the Parisian production of *Porgy and Bess,* in which she was a cast member. When she told her French host at the performance that they were African and not African American, the host showed a look of horror that she was interacting with Africans, and she disappeared (Angelou 184). Angelou had planned to settle in Paris with her son. But when she noticed France's own race problem, she left because she "saw no benefit in exchanging one kind of prejudice for another" (Stovall, "Preface" 305; Angelou 185).

The experiences of Angelou, Simmons, Baldwin, and Smith all point to the privilege of being an African American performer. By *privilege* I mean a differentiated and hierarchized attention by the French. French historians Sue Peabody and Tyler Stovall have discussed the malleable nature of racial relations—the shift between racialized difference—as a way to subjugate the colonized, to downgrade and position as inferior, and to deny access to rights and opportunities (*Color* 3). In these ways, and more, the French fed off of the racialized exclusion of its subjects while attempting to consume the exotic "other" that African American musicians represented.

The French saw African American jazz musicians, like Art Simmons, as guests that contributed to economic production in a time of recovery. Postcolonial studies scholar Didier Gondola suggests that African Americans were beloved because they introduced jazz to the French and that this musical form helped express the "cosmopolitan" nature of interwar Paris (208). For example, Kenny Clarke's prolific jazz production, mentorship, and interracial and international collaborations certainly promoted increased knowledge and participation of jazz by the French—thereby making France more cosmopolitan in its jazz scene and jazz more universal in its reach. But French of African descent were perceived as pushing against the French republic with their resistance to ethnic homogenization. Perhaps this was owing to a fear of being kicked out of France. This is what Tyler Stovall argues: "Black expatriates were acutely aware of their status as guests of the French. Throughout the twentieth century, the French government had welcomed foreign political exiles on the implicit assumption that they abstain from involvement in French politics" (*Paris* 254).

In the Cold War period, when a collection of French literati and politicians were protesting the spread of American culture in France, African Americans were not the targets of anti-American sentiments. This privileged distinction, however, fell by the wayside when the lines of ethnic distinction blurred, for African Americans were not always clearly read as American; at times they were mistaken for Africans. Then the difference between these groups collapsed, causing confusion in national and ethnic identification. Mae Henderson, for example, argues that Josephine Baker, who was chosen as the queen for the 1931 colonial exposition, often had her identity conflated with that of an African (117). Moreover, Melvin Dixon talks about how he appreciated most of the national nonrecognition. In an interview with Jerome de Romanet, Dixon said, "I was asked frequently whether I was from North Africa, from the Caribbean, from anywhere in the world, other than the United States; and I felt that that was very interesting, because it gave me a way to explore various attitudes towards America" (quoted in de Romanet 98).

The conflation occurs today as well. When an African American settles in France and his or her language approaches fluency, there are times that even France's longtime love affair with African Americans and African American cultural expressions is replaced by misrecognition and the all-too-familiar return of racism. All of these examples illustrate that differences amid people of the African diaspora are not always read accurately. They also point to a connection, whether recognized or unrecognized, between African Americans and other peoples of African descent. Didier Gondola's article "But I Ain't African, I'm American!" engages this issue. He contends that African Americans were actually linked to Africans in the French imagination. He opines that the French related to African Americans differently to counteract their treatment of their colonized people of color: "In France, colonial history has constructed Africans as 'niggers' and Europeans as victimizers. Once this 'nigger' status has been created, Europeans need to guarantee their status as usurpers. To that end, they use other minorities as auxiliaries to create a fiction that race does not matter and that culture is, in essence, what sets subjects apart from citizens, victims from victimizers. The auxiliary is constructed as the deracialized alter ego and naturally pitted against the 'nigger'" (202). In Gondola's opinion the African American thus acts as the foil to the black French and helps promote a race-free Europe. Accordingly, this Europe is not judged on the basis of skin color but on the distinction accorded a particular culture. But in allowing such privilege to African Americans, France actually positioned the black French in a hierarchical relationship to African Americans—indeed, as "niggers." As auxiliaries to the French white status as victimizer, then, African Americans were unconsciously complicit in the subjugation of the black French population, thereby placing African Americans in a "liminal" state. Gondola describes the liminal figure of the African American in the following way: "In early twentieth-century France, black American émigrés served as liminal figures. They were thrust in[to] what Shelby Steele calls 'a nirvana of complete freedom,' a world that was yet to define the racial and cultural arsenal that would in later years enhance whiteness at the expense of African immigrants" (202). Gondola's arguments suggest that there must always be a "nigger"—if not an African American then some "other" must always be created to fill that role. The recognition by African Americans of the unjust treatment of other people of color makes African Americans complicit in building their own status on the backs of others. Perhaps this is the reason Maya Angelou left Paris.

THE END OF AN ILLUSION: FROM JOBS GALORE TO MOVING ON

Since the entry of jazz in France in 1917, African American jazz musicians had enjoyed respect even greater than other artists owing to the French history of negrophilia (love of African diasporic culture). In contrast to primitivist art that popularized the Depression era, the French were unable to fully understand and imitate jazz rhythms despite their desire for it. So, even though Paris encouraged social mixing, when African Americans were present, they most often led the jazz bands. Talking to jazz musicians Hal Singer, Bobby Few, and Archie Shepp, all of whom played in 1960s Paris, I confirmed that the bands of these times were mixed. Often, however, they featured one, or a maximum of two, African Americans surrounded by French musicians. These African Americans were the big draws. René Urtreger told me that "the audience[s] were more pro-American jazz; they preferred American jazzmen to European jazzmen, more black American. . . . Of course some were really fantastic and first, I mean top genius, but some were less good I would say. Ils sont profité un petite peu de ça" (They benefited a little from that) (Urtreger; my translation). It was one of the reasons behind the respect and craze for jazz, this perception that African Americans could play better. During this post–World War II period essentialist mind-sets prevailed, and African American musicians were still considered by most as more capable than their French counterparts. Hugues Panassié illustrates this point in his revised edition of *Real Jazz*. He apologizes for not formerly recognizing that African Americans excelled in jazz, writing that "from the point of view of jazz, most white musicians were inferior to black musicians" (vii–viii). But in this era white French musicians improved their skills and performed more thanks to musicians like Kenny Clarke, who taught them skills in keeping time on the drums, for example. So while the bands remained mixed, in the 1960s the ratio of African American or white American performers to white French changed.

French musicians began to protest more vocally the competition for gigs that African American musicians prompted. French work quotas that started as far back as the 1920s were reinstated in the 1960s, and they kept American musicians from competing for all jobs. The quota required that only one performer could be American (Broschke-Davis 57; Moody 129). Discussing Don Byas's decreased job opportunities in France, jazz critic Mike Zwerin wrote, "Like Kenny Clarke, Byas had been winning American jazz polls. He did very well in Europe at first. After a while, however, he found that he wasn't 'exotic' anymore. He came to be considered a 'local.' His price went down. Locals tend to take locals for granted" (Zwerin, "Jazz" 541). This discussion of Byas as a "local musician" applies to his bandmate Inez Cavanaugh, too.

After slightly more than five years in Paris, Cavanaugh learned that only a few could exist in the spotlight of jazz on the Left Bank. Unfortunately, she was being crowded out to the shadowy edges. Just as Chez Inez had knocked Moune Rivel's club, Perroquet, out of the water in 1949, so, too, Cavanaugh now had to move on. So in 1952 it was time for her to leave. Italy was next on her itinerary. Over the next ten years she moved from Copenhagen to Rome, all the time writing to friends and asking for financial support. In 1968 she was finally back in New York. But by then she had lost her spark and calling as a manager, singer, and convivial host: "Inez had lost faith in her own ability to be hostess and cook her famous 'southern fried chicken' while serving as house vocalist—those things that had made her 'Chez Inez' club so famous in Paris in the 1950s" (Rosenkrantz, *Harlem* 219). Even though she was only selling cigarettes now at the famed Hotel Bolivar in Manhattan rather than performing there, she was in contact with Rosenkrantz by mail, helping him with arrangements to open "Timmes Club" in Copenhagen (Rosenkrantz, *Harlem* 218–19). She would soon move back to Copenhagen herself, recording a few songs on *An Evening at Timme's Club* with the Teddy Wilson Trio in Denmark.

In 1969 Rosenkrantz died in his hotel room in New York City; Cavanaugh sang "I'll Never Be the Same" at his Copenhagen memorial (D. Clarke, *Donald Clarke's*). She was later sighted in Rome, a bare skeleton, asking friends for money; then she disappeared (D. Clarke, *Donald Clarke's*). After much sleuthing, jazz biographer Donald Clarke and Rosenkrantz's niece, Bente Arendup, discovered what became of her. In 1980 she died of cerebral arteriosclerosis in Long Beach, California (D. Clarke, *Donald Clarke's*). The years of migrating and promoting herself from France to Italy to Denmark to the United States had come to an end.

Cavanaugh's story, or the pieces I have put together of it, offers some insight into the experiences of performing and surviving as an African American woman in post–World War II Paris.[11] Like Cavanaugh, a number of African American musicians stayed for a while. Then they left. The residency and mobility of musicians like Cavanaugh in Paris redefines traditional ways of envisioning home and community. Susan Friedman has written: "Blurring the boundaries between home and elsewhere, migration increasingly involves multiple moves from place to place and continual travel back and forth instead of journeys from one location to another" (261). So "home" is no longer necessarily *one* place but multiple places. Paired with Dwight Conquergood's discussion of "'place' as a heavily trafficked intersection, a port of call and exchange, instead of a circumscribed territory" ("Performance" 145), I have begun to think of the home of these African American artists as a relationship among places that shape and move a person. As Friedman suggests, many African American jazz musicians did not originally go to Paris thinking they would stay for long. They went for an opportunity. Paris was one place—a stop, among several, that could work. Some did make it work in Paris, attempting to settle in.

The memory of jazz's heyday in Paris persists today through the musicians who remain, like Nancy Holloway. In 2010 I interviewed the African American singer. Holloway arrived in Paris in 1953 after eight days aboard the ship *La Liberté*. She never returned to live in the United States. Like Cavanaugh, she used Paris as a springboard to sing worldwide, including places such as Beirut, the Ivory Coast, Senegal, Bangkok, and Singapore. But she ended up settling in Paris, singing in the Mars Club for the G.I.s and accompanying Kenny Clarke and Lou Bennett at the Blue Note. Her memories further realized the culture of catching up I had imagined, since she fondly reminisced about food and music as sites of connection: "Over here, we sort of all came together because of Haynes, because of the Haynes Restaurant, because of the Blue Note" (Holloway). It's where she'd see James Baldwin and was the most popular place in town. When we met in her apartment, she regaled me with the stories of others she'd known: Maya Angelou, Josephine Baker, Lena Horne, even Elvis. I was so impressed by the original paintings from an old beau and the photos of Holloway in her heyday that I became nostalgic myself.

I recognize, however, that this life was never perfect. There were struggles. This jazz diaspora meant negotiation. It meant having increased job opportunities but then watching them fall away. It meant thinking the French viewed you with respect but then recognizing that respect was built on a history of stereotypes. That respect was in relation and in contrast to a willful disavowal of their African colonists and immigrants. It meant competition. It meant longing for home.

This jazz diaspora was also two-sided, exemplifying community—both Paris Noir and the Left Bank jazz scene. It featured a diverse mix of artists, races, nationalities, and classes, and Paris was the time-honored "meeting place" where so many had stayed and collaborated. Cavanaugh's jazz diaspora was specific to an ethnic community, a musical scene, and a particular geography that is encompassed in Tyler Stovall's discussion in *Paris Noir*. Yet at the same time it was global. The participants were not just African American, and they brought their own cultural backgrounds and interests as they traveled, creating moments not only of entertainment but of potential cultural exchange. Inez Cavanaugh stayed, left, then disappeared. Nancy Holloway also stayed for some time, but in my most recent visit I learned she had returned to New York City. With figures like these, who stayed and didn't become well-known stars, there is less to work with. They don't get put in jazz biographies and histories, because of hagiography and minimal archival material certainly but also because they kept moving. Histories in the new millennium have proliferated about jazz outside the United States, from France to China to South Africa and beyond. There are countless studies of the African diaspora and a growing trend of study on those communities, in France and Germany, for example. But what of those diasporic communities that were spread out or spaced out or kept moving? Case studies like Inez Cavanaugh's reveal the importance of investigating situated, localized communities alongside moving, global ones when studying individual and collective stories of migration, as well as the travels of jazz.

Looking at the photos of Holloway, I remember the surprise I felt at never having heard her story. I learned so much about what that world must have been like. It fueled my desire to uncover more stories and understand how and why African Americans stayed and left—so that the stories of Cavanaugh, Holloway, and others who settled and kept moving don't disappear.

4. Boris Vian and James Baldwin in Paris

Are We a Blues People, Too?

> All I know about music is that not many people ever really hear it.
> And even then, on the rare occasions when something opens within,
> and the music enters, what we mainly hear, or hear corroborated, are
> personal, private, vanishing evocations.
>
> JAMES BALDWIN, "Sonny's Blues"

I once read an essay by Robert O'Meally that changed the game for me, touched me to my very soul. As professor of English and founder of the Center for Jazz Studies at Columbia University, O'Meally knows his music. He has spent years analyzing the work of visual artist Romare Bearden and Ralph Ellison's "jazz-shaped" approach to literature (Ellison, *Living* ix).[1] What so moved me was how music had influenced his own writing in "Blues for Huckleberry":

> Sitting in my English Department office at Columbia University with
> blues-master Robert Johnson on the CD player, I continued rereading
> *Huckleberry Finn,* and the bluesiness of Huck's tale sounded through
> the book's pages. Listening to Johnson and then to Bessie Smith and
> Louis Armstrong and Duke Ellington (yes, to the instrumental blues as
> well as to the lyrics of blues singers), I heard a story ringing true to the
> one in *Huckleberry Finn:* a journey toward freedom against odds
> undertaken for the sake of yearning for an often impossible love, with
> the readiness to improvise as the sole means of supporting the hope of
> that love. (O'Meally, "Introduction" 11–12)

O'Meally goes on to say that *Huckleberry Finn* is bluesy in its discussion of life's trials but also in its humorous delivery of good fortune and luck. In the relationship between Huck and Jim there is both solo and an improvised democratic coming together that swings. What's striking about the consideration of *Huckleberry Finn* as a blues novel, O'Meally reveals, is that it just predates blues, so there is no conscious effort on Twain's part to draw on a nascent musical form. Additionally, O'Meally's discussion of the stereotypical slave-like portrayal of Jim problematizes him as a liberatory blues figure ("Introduction" 12).

Still, O'Meally "heard a story ringing true" as he listened to the blues and reread this classic. He could hear the characteristics of the blues, of a blues sensibility, in the character of Huckleberry Finn and in his journey. O'Meally was more open to this awareness when concurrently listening to blues while reading. The more I read this piece, the more I am in awe of the power of the blues to "get into" the listener and open her or him up, so that the individual identifies with and connects with the material in a way not otherwise possible. How had listening—while reading—changed O'Meally's understanding of the text in comparison to the multiple times he'd simply read and taught *The Adventures of Huckleberry Finn?* As the epigraph from James Baldwin suggests, the blues has a way of evoking memories, both personal and collective, both painful and joyful. And on rare occasions the blues has the power to bring epiphany and triumphant knowledge to the artists (Baldwin, "Sonny's Blues" 861). The writer then draws on music to approach in some way that emotional zenith and clarity.

The power of the blues to enlighten, haunt, and, most important, connect drives this chapter. Like O'Meally, I am drawn to a text not normally known for its blues inflections and to the white, and in this case French, writer Boris Vian, who did not share racial or national identity with the African American subject matter in his novels. Like O'Meally, African American writer James Baldwin, the other key figure in this chapter, listens to the blues as he writes and is profoundly changed by the process of doing so. And, like O'Meally, I inevitably cannot help but probe the bluesiness of Vian's and Baldwin's texts.

Blues literature includes texts—from poetry to critical essays to novels—that employ blues music, whether in lyrical imitation, as metaphor, or as key thematic devices. It is noteworthy that Vian and Baldwin drew primarily on blues, rather than jazz, in the texts I analyze. Often blues and jazz are conflated, but jazz could not have emerged without blues. Blues became the building blocks for every type of black music (jazz, R&B, and rock 'n' roll).

So blues preceded jazz, developing in the nineteenth century, whereas the first sounds of jazz originated in the early twentieth century. Blues drew musical elements from minstrel performance, ragtime, and slave songs, so it should not surprise us that the musical form was first observed in slave performances on plantations in the American South (Baraka, *Blues People* 17–86). The music was born in the Mississippi Delta and spread in the 1930s and 1940s from the southern United States to the North to international locales, soaking up many styles, from Country to Delta to Chicago blues. Among some of the characteristics of blues are attention to lowered notes like the flatted thirds and sevenths in the blues scale, call-and-response exchanges, vocal polyphony, attention to a range of vibratos in instrument and voice, and the use of idiosyncratic instruments like washboards, jugs, and musical saws (Blesh 103–7). Early blues especially encouraged deliberate transgression of the horizontal borders of the staff and the vertical borders of the chorus (23, 188). Most important to this discussion, blues music advances a story—often times more explicitly than jazz. The vocal inflections of the blues singer and variations in tone of the blues instrumentalist produce great emotional value in blues songs. Rich storytelling in blues provides a raw, real, and at times gritty musical translation of life's travails and ironies. The blues inherently shares emotional truth—in this case, black interiority—that connects with fans, whether they are of the same racial and national heritage or not.

Significantly, blues literature has also become a space for sharing the stories of African Americans and advocating for civil rights. The use of blues in poetry and fiction, as with Langston Hughes's 1926 poetry collection *The Weary Blues* and Ralph Ellison's *Invisible Man* (1952), may be most familiar. In these cases authors have employed the creative use of instrument and voice to push a playfulness of words and to evoke sensory meaning. But they have also drawn on the blues ethos as a symbol of oppression and survival. The use of blues in nonfiction texts, such as Amiri Baraka's *Blues People: Negro Music in White America,* makes the political functions of the blues more apparent. *Blues People* introduced readers to the trends and migrations of black music across the United States and demonstrated the ways that music articulated African American identity—from the forced migration of slaves from West Africa to the growing acculturation and consumerism of jazz and R&B in American mainstream culture. Though *Blues People* set the stage for a discussion of the many musical and cultural contributions of African Americans in the United States, its frame was limiting. Ralph Ellison critiqued the limitation of the book's sociological methodology and mourned the lack of aesthetic analysis Baraka could have used: "The tremendous burden of sociology which Jones [i.e., Baraka] would place upon this body of music is enough to give even the blues the blues" (Ellison, "The Blues"). What about the music's migrations outside of the United States? What about people of other ethnicities who had learned, disseminated, and changed blues as it traveled from locale to locale? And what about the influence of different types of artists, like Baraka himself, who helped shape the perceptions of the blues and blues people?

In this chapter I extend and critique Baraka's conception of blues people by including a non-American and the non-musical genre of literature to this community. Conjoining the literature and experiences of Vian and Baldwin, I explore how the authors' in-depth listening to blues unearthed black rage and prompted confrontations with black identity in their writings. In the end their literary activism, musical literature, and geographical distance also complicate the concept of a blues people and shift the possibilities of a jazz diaspora to the written word.

SEPARATE BUT EQUALLY IN LOVE
WITH JAZZ AND BLUES

Born in Ville d'Avray on March 10, 1920, Boris Vian came to jazz at an early age. After hearing Duke Ellington's band play in Paris in 1938, he became obsessed with jazz music and the party lifestyle; in fact, he proclaimed that the 1938 concert, Dizzy Gillespie's big band tour in 1948, and Ella Fitzgerald's tour in 1952 were the three greatest moments in his life (Vian, *Chroniques* 300).[2] These moments were just the high points of his jazz-obsessed life. Vian befriended Ellington, naming him as his daughter's godfather, and Ellington inspired Vian to take up the trumpet, despite the threat it posed to his weak heart. Vian never wanted to be a professional musician but enjoyed playing trumpet for the Claude Abadie Band; the band recorded several songs, including "Jazz Me Blues" and "Tin Roof Blues," for the Swing record label (Arnaud 79–97). He, his brothers, and other band members graced clubs like Tabou, within the Parisian caves. From the 1930s until his death by cardiac arrest in 1959, Boris Vian performed, brokered relationships, and managed events in Saint-Germain-des-Prés, transforming the area into a central jazz hot spot in Paris after World War II.

The catalogue of Vian's contributions to the Parisian jazz scene is long. He aided Charles Delaunay with festival preparations and future Hot Club of France events (Tournès 300). He produced albums, including *Kenny Clarke's Sextet Plays Andre Hodeir* in 1957, which won the Charles Cros Academy Award (Haggerty, "Under Paris" 207). He introduced Miles Davis to film director Louis Malle, and the connection he forged between Davis and Malle led to the now-famous *Ascenseur pour l'échafaud* soundtrack (1958) (Tournès 313). Jazz fans were exposed to his biting wit, creative language, absurd and nonsensical imaginings, and erudite knowledge of jazz in his reviews for *Jazz News* and *Jazz Hot*. Starting in 1946, he had a weekly article in *Combat*, as well as his radio chronicles, which would later be printed in 1948 in *Jazz Hot*.[3]

In his radio broadcasts, jazz criticisms and promotion of recordings, festivals and tours in France, Vian was a gatekeeper of jazz. His guidebook,

Manuel de Saint-Germain-des-Prés, has stood the test of time as a lasting testimony of the key figures, clubs, and environment of jazz in 1950s Paris. He wrote jazz-inspired fiction as well. His novel *L'écume des jours* was a finalist for the Prix Goncourt.[4] Later in his life he would also excel as a French *chanteur* (singer). So he became renowned as a club owner, jazz trumpeter, singer, critic, radio announcer, novelist, and event promoter and had considerable access to jazz listeners and participants. The impact he had on jazz is remarkable, especially when we consider that he was a white, French, part-time musician who never even visited the United States.

At first glance James Baldwin was Boris Vian's opposite. He was African American and, though not a musician, was immersed in black music in the States. He was surrounded by blues and jazz musicians in his native Harlem and in Greenwich Village, where he lived as a young freelance writer. Born in 1927, Baldwin was a prolific writer, widely known for his critical essays on racism in the civil rights era (e.g., *The Fire Next Time* and *Nobody Knows My Name*). Throughout his career he wrestled with articulating African American identities, most often drawing on music. From *Go Tell It on the Mountain* and *Amen Corner* (featuring gospel hymns and churchgoing performances) to the jazz characters in "Sonny's Blues" and *Another Country*, Baldwin continually infused black musical idioms into his literature.

His work was equally influenced by migration and exile. Notably, all of the aforementioned titles were written while he visited Switzerland and resided in France and Turkey. His first relocation occurred in 1948, when he migrated to Paris. He lived and worked in the heart of the Saint-Germain-des-Prés and mingled with some of the same writers, intellectuals, and jazz musicians as Vian. In figure 7 LeRoy Neiman illustrates James Baldwin surrounded by characteristic Parisian sites and signage as he reflects and observes in the outdoor seating of Les Deux Magots (Two Chinese figurines), a popular café among intellectuals in Saint-Germain-des-Prés. Neiman's use of broken lines and partial shading portrays many of the figures and sites around Baldwin as incomplete or in progress. Yet Baldwin's figure remains in contrast, centered and distinguished with a rare use of color. Perhaps Neiman's artistic choice is meant to underscore Baldwin's ever-visible, influential race—whether in his American homeland or this foreign French setting. The illustration also reflects Baldwin's role as articulator and observer; he often took in his surroundings and compared what he saw abroad to his American experiences. Rather than a static photo of one moment in time, the illustration performs similarly to Baldwin's writing. Baldwin's oeuvre consistently invites, perhaps even pushes, readers to enter into dialogue with his topic and ponder it more fully. With each

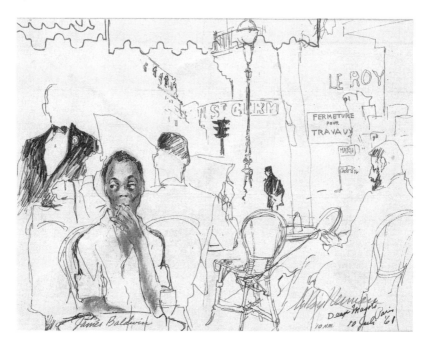

FIGURE 7.   In this drawing by LeRoy Neiman of 1961 Paris James Baldwin observes and reflects at the café and restaurant Les Deux Magots, which is located in the heart of Saint-Germain-des-Prés. © LeRoy Neiman.

viewing of the drawing, I also fill in the broken spaces and lines, adding my own perceptions to the postwar Paris that Baldwin evokes in his writing.

Baldwin shifted between France and the United States throughout his life, returning often to Harlem. But he was a frequent visitor and resident of France. French audiences became familiar with Baldwin's work. Many of his works were translated into French, and some (like *Evidence of Things Not Seen*) were supported by the French press, whereas the American press only had poor reviews (Fabre, *From Harlem* 210). Moreover, Michel Fabre discusses how Baldwin became a public intellectual, always asked to weigh in on debates about race in the United States but also on Africa; in 1985 the French showed their long-held esteem by honoring him with membership in the *Ordre national de la Légion d'honneur*—only African American visual artist Henry O. Tanner and dancer Josephine Baker had received this higher honor from the Legion of Honor before (Fabre, *From Harlem* 213). Baldwin firmly established himself in French social matters and was conversant about and active in American political issues. Eventually he made his home in Saint-Paul-de-Vence, a city in southeastern France near the

Riviera. He died there in 1987, but his body was transported back to New York for his funeral. Moving away from the United States enriched Baldwin's creativity and ability to discuss the injustices at home. Exile plunged Baldwin into a hyperawareness of his racial and national heritage, which was often prompted by listening to, and writing about, black music.[5]

Looking at these two men together suggests significant differences at first glance. Vian and Baldwin were from two different countries. Their racial backgrounds were very different. But they also had a lot in common. Their writings included the haunting sounds of recordings, the live, swinging music of Saint-Germain-des-Prés, and their imaginings and memories of the innovative New York jazz scene. For Baldwin the blues revealed greater consciousness about how black identity was perceived by white Americans, while blues and jazz jumpstarted Vian's vast imagination. He portrayed his imaginings of what it was to be black, American, and oppressed in the post–World War II period through a blues-playing character.

Their prose translated the sound and memory of the music, even though they were far away from U.S. blues hubs like New York, New Orleans, and Chicago. They were even removed from the settings of racial disparity portrayed in their literature. Baldwin and Vian metaphorically heard the blues through their memories and through migrating African American musicians. Both men were filled with rage by the lack of respect and decency experienced by African Americans, so they worked as political activists, using the commingling of literature and music to communicate their frustrations.

Those frustrations correlated directly to collective experiences of being black in the United States after World War II. The end of the war spurred a widespread proliferation of lynchings that illustrated a zenith in white supremacist violence and, consequently, in race riots as well: the lynchings of four African Americans off a bridge in Georgia in 1946 that was never prosecuted; the murder of more than one hundred African Americans and the ensuing race riot in Tennessee in 1946 that the NAACP, led by then lawyer Thurgood Marshall, successfully defended (although he almost didn't escape the threat of lynching himself); the 1947 lynching of Willie Earle, historically noted as the last lynching in South Carolina and the catalyst for the creation of antilynching laws in that state. These moments were not exceptions but the daily horror African Americans faced. Though Baldwin had not been to the South and Vian had never gone to the United States, this national narrative of violence influenced their writing. James Baldwin and Boris Vian used the blues and the written word to react against the dangers of lynching and to share their rage at racial prejudice in the safer, unrealized worlds they created on the page.

THE RAGE-FILLED BLUES OF JAMES BALDWIN
AND BORIS VIAN

> I could not get over two facts, both equally difficult for the
> imagination to grasp, and one was that I could have been mur-
> dered. But the other was that I had been ready to commit mur-
> der. I saw nothing very clearly but I did see this: that my life,
> my real life, was in danger, and not from anything other people
> might do but from the hatred that I carried in my own heart.
>
> JAMES BALDWIN, *Notes of a Native Son*

Rage threatened to consume Baldwin unless he ran away. He had just come
from a movie with a friend, when they walked into a diner. On once again
hearing, "We don't serve Negroes here," something snapped in Baldwin.
He was so consumed with rage that he threw a mug of water on the waitress. A white man rushed forward to pummel him. But he escaped out the
door and was helped by his friend, who led the pursuing police in the wrong
direction (Baldwin, *Notes* 72).

This incident in 1948 New Jersey marked a turning point in Baldwin's
career, leading him away from the United States. He later explained in
Nobody Knows My Name: "I left America because I doubted my ability to
survive the fury of the color problem here. (Sometimes I still do)" (137). So
he moved to Paris. While vacationing in Europe, he visited the Francophone
city of Lausanne, Switzerland. Ensconced in the Swiss mountains, he was
drawn to a record that he had willfully abandoned in the United States
(*Nobody* 138). Listening to Bessie Smith's 1927 song "Backwater Blues"
drew him back to his racial heritage and social conditions facing African
Americans in his homeland. His original disavowal of the record was likely
due to negative stereotypes that blues may connote (i.e., of being simple,
sexual, and not speaking to the high culture of African Americans) (138).
Baldwin described Smith's significant impact on him: "She helped to reconcile me to being a 'nigger'" (*Nobody* 138). As Josh Kun has explained,
"[Smith] was the summation of all the stereotypes, all the prejudices, all the
projected racial and sexual fantasies, all the watermelons and pickaninnies
and dialect speech, and all the externally imposed self-hate. It was Bessie
who both Okeh and Black Swan . . . turned down because her voice was too
rough, too Negro, too black" (94).

Smith's record represented a history of violence and suffering that
Baldwin attempted to escape. Assumptions about African American experience were disseminated through all popular media, but especially music,
which joined racialized assumptions with the emotional weight of the art

form. "Backwater Blues" made Baldwin uneasy. But this time he did not emotionally flee from its enlightening effect. His sense of identity was thrown into chaos, as the combination of migration, music, and black consciousness prompted an experience of dislocated listening.

"Dislocated listening" is a term I have created to describe a more attuned listening to, and understanding of, African American experience. This understanding occurs when there is a dislocation, a separation or movement away from home. This movement creates distance that prompts disorientation, discomfort, vulnerability, and openness to new experiences. In the process of this distancing, one begins to accept harsh realities of one's experience, specifically, in Baldwin's case, a history of suffering. Instead of pulling away, the person is prompted to engage with more attuned listening. One is able to connect with the experience on an almost visceral level.

Willfully dislocated from his homeland, Baldwin journeyed to Francophone Switzerland, a place starkly different from his urban African American world. Distance from the United States released him from some of his rage at the racial injustices of the 1940s, but the blues drew him back to his African American roots. The blues form, and Smith's stylizations, created discomfort and exacted a visceral toll. Ralph Ellison describes the blues as "an impulse to keep the painful details and episodes of a brutal experience alive in one's aching consciousness, to finger its jagged grain, and to transcend it, not by the consolation of philosophy but by squeezing from it a near-tragic, near-comic lyricism" (Ellison, *Living* 129). Blues lyrics are tragicomic because they make us remember the pain of our history while helping us to get through it.

For example, Smith sang about lust in a comic way, as with her rendition of "Nobody in Town Can Bake a Sweet Jelly Roll like Mine." The song's double entendres involving food and sex provide irony and humor. Her famous rendition of "St. Louis Blues" creates the opposite effect as she sings mournfully about the loss of her man. Her blues tunes are tragicomic in their consistent attention to both humor and sorrow.

Added to this tragicomic sensibility is the discomforting impact of the blues. The genre's privileging of rough and raw timbre over polished smoothness spurs a discomforting effect. In particular, Smith's voice was grainy, gritty, and soul stirring. It somehow reached inside the listener; that's what happened to Baldwin, I suspect. As he returned to a song he'd long avoided, what Ellison calls the "jagged grain" of black music moved him. The blues opened him up and revealed a new level of understanding about his African American heritage.

Writer and cultural critic Albert Murray's extension of blues and jazz as "esthetic equipment for living," as the survival tools for "confronting, acknowledging, and contending with the infernal absurdities and ever-impending frustrations of 'black existence,'" is helpful here (Murray 58). Smith's grainy voice pushes James Baldwin to acknowledgment and discomfort. The roughness of Smith's voice interprets both textual meaning and a visceral, embodied experience. Her voice cuts across histories to connote past, present, and future struggles. In hearing her "jagged grain," Baldwin had to reconcile his past, a reconciliation that he had successfully avoided until visiting Switzerland.

But geographic dislocation prompted an objective and subjective understanding of his blackness. "Backwater Blues" paralleled the movement between Baldwin's experiences. "There ain't no place for a po' ol' girl to go . . ." shifts to "I packed all my clothes, throwed them in and they rowed me along" (B. Smith and Johnson). As the lyrics suggest, Baldwin escaped his home because he could not see himself in it clearly.

Or, he attempted to escape. Baldwin later recognized that his migrations made ever more present the fact that his home was never far away. Baldwin once commented, "You never leave home, you take your home with you" (*The Price*). He couldn't get away from the knowledge that his home was right there in the song. By listening to this song he located himself in his past, and he was actually drawn back to it. Smith and Baldwin both inhabit these spaces where they are not supposed to be, yet they have this rare mobility and liberation. In both cases liberation meant separating from home, fleeing—or did it?

Migration to France was perceived as a liberating act of survival for so many—from Henry Ossawa Tanner, the first artist to make his home in Paris, to today's multitudes. As we have seen, Paris served as a place that beckoned African Americans with the allure passed down from stories of freedom, seductive articles of artists' success, and experiences of growth and recognition in visual, literary, and musical performance from the artists who migrated there. From this genealogy of African American migrating artists, Richard Wright bears the most resemblance to James Baldwin in his reasons for migrating. Wright had also described the madness and violence African Americans internalized as a result of racism; his work did much to add to sociological and social realist studies of racism in the United States. In his seminal novel *Native Son* he fashioned a young black male protagonist growing up in urban Chicago and detailed the destruction of daily and pervasive racism on his psyche and his behavior. By escaping when he did, Baldwin had hoped to avoid such dangers. In his own life, too, Richard

Wright migrated to France with similar hopes in mind. Writing from Paris between 1950 and 1951, Wright detailed his decision to migrate in "I Choose Exile":

> I am a native born American Negro. The first 38 years of my life were spent exclusively on the soil of my native land. But, at the moment of this writing, I live in voluntary exile in France and I like it. . . . During the years of my life in America I felt that in time my country would settle down to humane living with a code of civilized values. But my sojourn in France made me realize that I had deceived myself. I know now that America has no such future, that it is inescapably different from Europe and that no conceivable stretch of historical time will make it like Europe. . . . Yet, deep down, during all those years, I felt that there was something organically wrong with a nation that could so cynically violate its laws in meting out cruelties upon a helpless minority. America's barbaric treatment of the Negro is not one-half so bad or inhuman as the destructive war which she wages against the concept of the free person, against the Rights of Man, and against herself! (R. Wright, "I Choose" 1)

Wright's impetus for migration and his ensuing reflections indicate several things: he would become a mentor for Baldwin as the latter made his way to Paris. On the first day of his arrival Baldwin was taken to meet Wright and the editors of *Zero* magazine at Les Deux Magots (Baldwin, *Nobody* 255). But Baldwin's resulting critique of *Native Son* in his *Zero* magazine essay "Everybody's Protest Novel" strained, then actually ended, their relationship (*Nobody* 226). In sum, Wright was the veteran intellectual on African American experience and an example of how to thrive in Paris. He was known to frequent Les Deux Magots and to hold literary court there. Baldwin's journey would be different: his favorite spot was on the second floor of the café next door, Café de Flore. He wrote there partly to avoid his cold, tiny apartment at the Hôtel de Verneuil (Campbell 26). The café was also a central spot for writers like Jean-Paul Sartre, with whom Baldwin also dialogued since both used literature to philosophize on issues of colonization and subjugation of people of African descent. But rather than settling into café culture, Baldwin also took walks around the city (and interacted with those outside of this musical and intellectual social set). He drank and conversed into the wee hours, as he was wont to do wherever he was (Fabre, *From Harlem* 2; Leeming 47). In the process Baldwin developed a perspective about U.S. race relations that differed from Wright's.

Richard Wright left *for* France. It allowed for greater freedoms, and he had given up on the possibility that the United States would ever evolve in attitude or in action. He perceived more equality for human rights in France; his life and dialogue with philosophers there like Albert Camus and Jean-Paul Sartre widened his interests and changed his focus to universal human rights. This widened sensibility still took the shape of a fictional and nonfictional exploration of African American experience. His work was now very much in dialogue with European writers and philosophers after his move to France.

James Baldwin's time in France also offered him space for expanded interests. He balked at being a stereotypical race writer and became annoyed with being recognized as an exemplar of addressing the "race question." This took the form of multiple journals and presses asking for reviews and commentary on what he believed was a flat, predictable inquiry into how to right race relations in America. Such a perspective was also his main contention with Wright. Baldwin thought that Wright painted flat, negative images of African American experience that lacked agency. In "Everybody's Protest Novel," Baldwin critiqued *Native Son* for contributing to the perception that African Americans lack humanity:

> Below the surface of this novel there lies, as it seems to me, a continuation, a complement of that monstrous legend it was written to destroy. . . . For Bigger's tragedy is not that he is cold or black or hungry, not even that he is American, black; but that he has accepted a theology that denies him life, that he admits the possibility of his being sub-human and feels constrained, therefore to battle for his humanity according to those brutal criteria bequeathed him at his birth. But our humanity is our burden, our life; we need not battle for it; we need only to do what is infinitely more difficult—that is, accept it. The failure of the protest novel lies in its rejection of life, the human being, the denial of his beauty, dread, power, in its insistence that is his categorization alone which is real and which cannot be transcended. (*Notes* 18)

This passage reveals the greatest difference between Baldwin and Wright and actually suggests the role of blues and jazz for Baldwin—that is life. Recall Albert Murray's characterization of the blues as "equipment for living" (58). Baldwin's rage and subsequent move from the United States, as well as his mental return to his experience there through listening to Bessie Smith, represented his larger philosophy on living, on surviving. For Baldwin, unlike Wright, moved *from* the United States. But even in France he still remained in the States in his mind. Listening to the blues pulled up his and others' experiences as an African American in post–World War II America. He didn't close the door on it, as Wright did, but used the music and the migration to expand the possibilities of living.

In contrast, Boris Vian wrote about African American experience with violent death—murder, in fact. He also made his start based on the literary precedents of Richard Wright. With his 1946 novel *J'irai cracher sur vos tombes (I Spit on Your Graves)*, Vian marked himself as an African American as he took on the nom de plume of Vernon Sullivan. Portraying himself as Sullivan's editor (until the secret was discovered), Vian played both an advocate and victim of civil rights injustices. As a white Frenchman who had never visited the United States, it was hard to imagine that he could represent an experience so different from his own. But his obsession with jazz and blues created an empathy with African American experience that pushed him into activism. Under the protection of a pseudonym he attempted to illustrate the rage and victimization of African Americans, specifically black rage.

J'irai cracher was a vitriolic, hate-filled, sexually rampant, black protest novel written in approximately two weeks (Vian, *I Spit* xiii; Arnaud 138). In the character of Lee Anderson, Vian created an African American male protagonist bent on vengeance over his brother's lynching for loving a white woman. In response Lee enacts violence against a white community.

Surprisingly, most were not shocked to learn that Vian wrote the book. His tendencies for wordplay, absurdity, and experimentation foiled any real disguise. But the content caused a scandal. The racism and sexual deviation in *J'irai cracher* was so extreme that the response was cataclysmic. "Terrible," said the journal *Franc-Tireur* (Arnaud 142). "Blacker than noir, this Molotov cocktail of race, sex and hatred burns off the page," writes a critic today, more than fifty years later (Healy).

Vian's language was incredibly graphic, sensational, and arguably pornographic in the rape and murder scenes. Critics immediately condemned the novel as sexually explicit and excessive in its violent descriptions. *J'irai cracher* woke up the moral police (the Cartel d'action sociale et morale, a group that brought action against groups and figures that challenged French society's social and moral standards). The book threatened the French sense of decency. Vian was charged with crimes of indecency for creating "an outrage against good morals" and was fined 100,000 francs, the equivalent of about $200 today (Campbell 81–84). While this controversy was a huge annoyance, it also brought attention to *J'irai cracher,* as well as other works.

Most impactful was how the novel provoked the French public. It provided a realistic look at the state of racism in the United States and articulated, in French, a very visceral picture of the ills of racism. With *J'irai cracher* Vian overtly attacked segregation and racialized violence in the United States. He used his pen to show the real threats of being black in America and the potential of an exploding rage. In one scene near the end of the novel he characterizes Lee's reactions to a racial slur:

> I tried hard to control myself when she called me a dirty nigger and said
> that Dexter had told her that, and that she had come with me to warn
> Jean, and that she hated me more than anybody in her whole life. . . . I
> bent over her. I think I must have snorted and panted like a wild beast and
> she began to scream. I bit her right between the thighs. I had my mouth
> full of black stiff hairs. . . . My face was smeared with blood and I sat back
> on my haunches a bit. I'd never heard a woman scream like that; all of a
> sudden I felt that I was shooting off in my shorts. . . . She thrashed about
> so violently I thought my left forearm would be jerked off. I now felt
> such a rage that I could have skinned her alive. (Vian, *I Spit* 155)

At this moment Lee plunges into rape, murder, and death. He unapologetically thrills and scares his first victim with sexual advances and brutishness. The writers of *Black Rage*, psychiatrists William Grier and Price Cobbs, consider this type of rage as an escalating grief, rooted in death and dehumanization. The grief is reshaped into self-hate and aggression against the perceived perpetuators of the torturous experiences (Grier and Cobbs 176). Lee is a hyperbolic embodiment of this rage. He lashes out against white American society at large for the lynching of his brother, identifying this group of friends (particularly the women) on which to exact revenge. Without conscience—with glee actually—he kills, rapes, teases, and delights in his victims' suffering. What is so immoral is his lack of pity. He continues to relive the murder of his brother with each attack. The last moments in the novel emphasize animalistic violence without reason or compassion. They show Lee as living on instinct and as primarily a hypersexualized being. Throughout it all, Lee's vengeance is further fueled by Jean's repugnant reaction to his being black and his deflation at Lou's spitting of "nigger" at him.

Amid his planning and vengeful reveling there is one bright moment—his memory of Tom dancing as a young man to the song "When the Saints Go Marching In." The memory takes him to a happier time with his family—potentially a time of preracial recognition in his youth, when he was accepted. The New Orleans jazz standard has an energy and vibrancy that keeps Lee going as he starts to feel the pain from a gunshot wound and fights to stay conscious as he drives. Although not a funeral dirge, "When the Saints" is a popular song for funerals in New Orleans. It is a fitting song choice because, in the tradition of spirituals and gospel music, it offers hope and signifies a journey to a better place: heaven. As Lee recalls this memory, he unwittingly makes his drive to death.

This last scene demonstrates Vian's knowledge of the tragicomic quality of black music (Ellison, *Collected* 129). In this passage music serves as a survival tool, as it does for so many African Americans from slavery to the present day. In the blues and jazz of Saint-Germain-des-Prés Vian heard how beautifully the music spotlighted pain and survival despite it all. He heard how these musicians swung life in the face of battle. In the concept of Murray again blues and jazz become "esthetic equipment for living," particularly good for confrontation (Murray 58). Vian's novel also reflects Ellison's tragicomic sensibility as it bleeds with death yet shows signs of life, humor, and joy in the scenes of dancing, guitar playing, and music-infused memories.

As with Baldwin's reflections about his rage-inducing encounter with a white waitress, Vian's protagonist lashes out but in an ever-consuming rage. He goes where Baldwin never threatens yet fears to go. Lee commits mass murder. Still, both Baldwin and Lee obscure their rage—Baldwin by avoiding Smith's music and the history of racialization it recalled, Lee by hiding his African American heritage and his brother's lynching.

But Lee's rage was not original. Vian had, earlier in the year, translated a short story for Richard Wright, and the character Lee seemed like a quick imitation of Wright's protagonist in *Native Son*, Bigger Thomas (Campbell 240–41). Vian also created a seemingly unfeeling black protagonist who lashed out with rape and murder against a white woman and was led to destruction by the wearing effect of years of degradation. While Vian (like Wright) proposed to shed light on the harrowing social condition of African Americans, he did damage by representing the same stereotypes and problems against which he was rhetorically fighting. Vian emphasized the perception of blacks as subhuman, of having one's very humanity unrecognized. In *J'irai cracher* Vian reproduced that rage in the way Wright had done with *Native Son*. From Baldwin's perspective Vian's representation of blackness lacked humanity, and the rage he emphasized reproduced the problem (*The Devil* 509).

Despite *J'irai cracher*'s simplistic imitation of African American literature, Vian did spotlight some harsh, gruesome experiences of being black in the United States. Baldwin critiqued it but also pointed out the book's strengths in his review: "Vian's social details, as concerns American life, are all askew. . . . In spite of the book's naiveté, Vian cared enough about his subject to force one into a confrontation with a certain kind of anguish. The book's power comes from the fact that he forces you to see this anguish from the undisguised viewpoint of his foreign, alienated own" (Baldwin, *The Devil* 507). While Vian recreated violent stereotypes of African Americans in *J'irai cracher*, he also explained the rage felt by blacks to a French audience far removed from this experience. But it was under a veil

FIGURE 8.   Boris Vian plays the trumpet at Club Saint-
Germain-des-Prés in 1949. Keystone-France / Getty Images.

of white and foreign privilege that he took this authority, an authority he was accustomed to in his work as a jazz critic.

Vian had crafted a career as a keen, witty critic of authentic blues and jazz, and *J'irai cracher* spoke to his essentialist perceptions of race. His jazz criticisms portrayed his belief that blacks played the best jazz. In fact, he believed that his own trumpet playing never had a chance of reaching the highest level, partly because of talent but also because of race. Vian was recognized as a passable trumpeter by most (fig. 8). Along with opening Tabou, he also played at Club Saint-Germain. Kenny Clarke has recalled how Vian loved the Dixieland style but still tried to add modern accents to appease him (Haggerty, "Under Paris" 203). But Vian considered himself only a friend and promoter of real jazz musicians rather than a successful player. Vian scholar Celeste Day Moore describes Vian's racialized downgrading of his skills when she writes: "He lamented his participation in a jazz band that he saw as a far cry from the quality of all-black bands. Reflecting a particularly racialized ranking of jazz, Vian wrote that his band could play only as well as 'nègres de trente-septième ordre'" (negroes of the thirty-seventh rank) (Moore 23).

His essentialist opinion and his outlandish humor emanated from this 1948 *Combat* article. In "Should White Jazz Musicians Be Executed?" Vian wrote, "The problem is the following: black music is increasingly encumbered by sometimes harmonious but always superfluous and usually avoidable white elements. Should we continue to congratulate and encourage the whites in question, should we criticize them or simply tell them to go take their suspenders and hang themselves?" (Vian and Zwerin 46). Vian's comments here are incendiary, satirical, and intentionally offensive. They typify his oft-times-biting wit and strong opinions. They also reflect his core perspective that white musicians could never really compete with African American musicians and that racially pure jazz, that is bands with only African Americans, were the strongest.

Vian's journalistic critique comes through in the voice of his character Lee:

LEE: All the great popular composers are colored. Like Duke Ellington, for example.

JEAN: What about Gershwin, Kern, and all of those?

LEE: They're all immigrants from Europe. . . . They're the ones best able to envelop it. But I don't think you'd find a single original passage anywhere in Gershwin's work—one that hasn't been copied or plagiarized. Just try and find one in the *Rhapsody in Blue,* for example.

JEAN: You're funny. . . . I just hate the colored race.

(VIAN, *I Spit* 95)

Here the portrayal of African Americans is quite different from the portrait of raw rage in the earlier passage. Lee defends African Americans' artistry and intelligence as he puts them up against some of the most renowned composers. In passages like this Vian's rage comes through. He, too, raged against racialized difference and violence but also against the lack of respect and recognition accorded jazz. As the essay "Should White Jazz Musicians Be Executed?" shows, Vian not only fashions a vengeful and violent protagonist, but he crafts violent comments that can kill in their harshness and extreme exclusion. With *J'irai cracher* and his essays and broadcasts Vian attempted to uplift the perception of blacks as contributing to popular culture through dance, song, and musical composition. Sometimes he drew on the tools of violence and polemical retort as his literary weapons of justice.

While Vian showed no reticence in criticism or literature expressing his opinions about the contributions of African Americans to popular culture, it is interesting that he felt the need for a pseudonym in order to write about other aspects of African American experience. Actually, *J'irai cracher* was not his first instance of literary passing with a pseudonym; he wrote three additional novels, including *Les morts ont tous la même peau* (The dead all have the same skin) the following year. The topic of *Les morts* was even more extreme; it featured another mixed protagonist passing for white. The half-brother of the protagonist (who has darker skin) threatens to uncover his secret, and violence again ensues.

Despite all of the problematic aspects of *J'irai cracher* (the perpetuation of stereotypes, imitation of Wright's work, passing for an African American writer, and offending the morals of the French), Baldwin sensed rare wisdom in the novel. He described it as "not sexual fantasy, but rage and pain: that rage and pain which Vian (almost alone) was able to hear in the black American musicians, in the bars, dives, and cellars, of the Paris of those years" (*The Devil* 506). While Vian imagined black rage and pain from a distance in France, he drew on blues to write himself into an African American experience. With Lee, Vian created a blues-playing guitarist who used his musical proficiency at singing and playing to help him quickly make friends in town. The music also heightened Vian's understanding of what it meant to be black in America.

Blues became a path to empathy for Vian, prompting him to take on African Americans' battles against racism. The music he shared with African Americans created a bond and prompted a unique, empathetic type of hearing. Jon Cruz's phrase "pathos-oriented hearing" pinpoints Vian's musically prompted activism: "It is the kind of hearing that coincides with and undergirds the interest of the abolitionists (black as well as white) who are the first to take a keen and strategic interest in—and who in a sense 'discover'—black music as a font of meaning. The shift from noise to meaning is accomplished by the emergence of the pathos unleashed by nineteenth-century humanitarian reformism, out of which the antislavery movement developed" (Cruz 61). While Cruz specifically discusses slave songs and how accounts show differing strategies for using the music, the model applies well to Vian, too. He used his literature to critique Jim Crow racism and to join the civil rights movement from France. But his criticism from France and his lack of firsthand knowledge of the United States made his critique somewhat inaccurate.

His expertise in jazz helped him experience the issues through "pathos" and empathy, even if not directly. Vian attached meaning to the blues and jazz he saw performed live and heard in recordings. With *J'irai cracher* he used blues and jazz strategically to frame and help explain African American experience for his white French audience. As Baldwin noted, Vian identified with their plight because he heard the tragicomic sensibility in the music and inevitably in the experiences of African Americans. The blues and jazz served as "fonts" of history and memory of African American experience. The music unearthed, in both authors, rage against racism and self-rage over absorbing years of racial degradation. Yet at the end of it all, these authors also illustrated the comic quality of African American histories and experiences. That dichotomy of the blues, which emotes sorrow while inevitably uplifting the heart and spirit, lived on through the music. The tragicomic sensibility of the blues helped Baldwin and Lee survive.

Ralph Ellison and Albert Murray elucidated the tragicomic sensibility of the blues, but they did so in order to foreground the possibilities and contributions of the blues rather than the oppression it sought to transcend. Situated far from Paris, in New York City, Ralph Ellison and Albert Murray composed blues and jazz literature for political suasion, too, but they did so in order to uplift the perceptions of African Americans. Long after war's end, in 1970, Ellison and Murray persisted in promoting the contributions of the blues, jazz, and the African American culture they grew out of. In an essay entitled "What America Would Be Like without Blacks," Ellison affirmed the influence of African American culture in the United States, claiming that American culture "would be lacking in the sudden turns, shocks and swift changes of pace (all jazz shaped) that serve to remind us that the world is ever unexplored" (Ellison, *Shadow* 234). Albert Murray foregrounded the positive, contributory effects of the blues in *The Omni-Americans: Black Experience and American Culture*:

> But it should be clear that what U.S. Negro musicians express
> represents far more than the fact that American black folks been 'buked
> and been scorned and nobody know de trouble dey seen. Distinctive as
> it is, U.S. Negro music, like U.S. Negro life, is, after all, or rather first of
> all, also inseparable from life in the United States at large. . . . As for the
> blues, they affirm not only U.S. Negro life in all of its arbitrary
> complexities and not only life in America in all of its infinite confusions,
> they affirm life and humanity itself in the very process of confronting
> failures and existentialistic absurdities. The spirit of the blues moves in
> the opposite direction from ashes and sackcloth, self-pity, self-hatred,
> and suicide. (147)

Murray's perspective of the blues counters Baldwin's and Vian's representations of blues as rage-filled and carrying memories of oppressions.[6] Here he goes one step further than the tragicomic sensibility of the blues, though, and points to the danger of seeing it as individual and self-oriented expression. As he describes, the blues is not self-oriented and mired in "self-pity, self-hatred, and suicide." Murray's blues expresses the collective aspirations of humanity instead. Murray claims that the blues is more than representative or characteristic of U.S. culture, and the blues cannot be separated from U.S. culture. Instead it is life affirming, characteristic of humanity, and born specifically out of human interaction in the United States.

What interests me is the very different approach yet always already similar goal these writers had in employing blues literature for political purpose. Vian and Baldwin both struck out against the United States and made the ills against African Americans more apparent and poignant by drawing on the sensory nature and perceptions of the music. But they did it from abroad. Ellison and Murray also drew on the blues for the same aims of integration and equality, but they pointed to the music's undeniable ties to the fabric of American culture. Their blues literature was inclusive and lacking in rage and attack. Instead, their blues forged community.

EXTENDING BARAKA'S *BLUES PEOPLE*

When Amiri Baraka first wrote *Blues People* in 1963, he created a seminal testament to the migration, dissemination, and impact of "black music" on American culture. Despite the multiple migrations and the growth of jazz, Baraka performed an authenticating narrative, arguing that jazz was the rightful possession of African Americans and that its Afrocentric background should be honored (203). The text was one more representation, and there were many from poetry to plays to essays, of his Black Nationalist efforts.

Baraka's perspective was passionately supported and critiqued. Ralph Ellison supported Baraka's aims to show the relationship between the evolution of the African to the African American and the way the music evolved as example and influence with the musician. However, he critiqued Baraka's viewpoint that the more mainstream and middle-class blues and jazz became, the more it lost its blackness. Ellison underlines the point that Baraka's blues people are not complex enough to take in a multiplicity of classes and the mix of the races through miscegenation:

> One would get the impression that there was a rigid correlation
> between color, education, income and the Negro's preference in music.
> But what are we to say of a white-skinned Negro with brown freckles,
> who owns sixteen oil wells sunk in a piece of Texas land once farmed by
> his ex-slave parents who were a blue-eyed, white-skinned, redheaded
> (kinky) Negro woman from Virginia and a blue-gummed, black-

skinned, curly haired Negro male from Mississippi, and who not only sang bass in a Holy Roller church, played the market and voted Republican but collected blues recordings and was a walking depository of blues tradition? Jones's theory no more allows for the existence of such a Negro than it allows for himself; but that "concord of sensibilities" which has been defined as the meaning of culture, allows for much more variety than Jones would admit. (Ellison "The Blues")

In contrast to Baraka, Ellison still comes back to the African American as the center of blues and jazz, but he sees the Americanization, commodification, and miscegenation that occurs not as a downside or a diminution in the value of blues and jazz but as inevitable and true. Ellison's blues and jazz are interwoven in and inseparable from the diversity of the United States, whereas Baraka would want to separate them.

A departure from even an African American–centered foundation to blues and jazz would counter both these authors' viewpoints. In his 1995 book *Jazz: The American Theme Song* James Lincoln Collier questioned whether jazz should even be labeled "black music." Despite the prevalence of this perspective among many American jazz fans, critics, and musicians, Collier found it to be a pernicious myth that was absorbed by the American social consciousness; he challenged this conception of jazz that would not include its white fans and would deign to label a cultural artifact as having a particular ethnicity (185–89). Collier perceived the African American identity of jazz as a political construction risen out of the mid-twentieth century and proposed by militants like Baraka; it was in direct contrast to a confidence and authority of white musicians in Dixieland-style playing and a racialized distinction of "hot" jazz as more emotional and different but not better or distinctive as authentic jazz (187–88). Collier's identification of the midcentury as a moment of change in the discursive performance of jazz is particularly relevant to my concerns here. His argument, although different from my own, points to the political uses not only of musical performance but of its perception, and it underlines again that this postwar moment spurred a change in the political function and perception of jazz and blues. Putting Vian and Baldwin in dialogue with Baraka and Ellison (and the modern-day voice of Collier) feeds into the question of just what the racial and national identity of jazz and blues is and thereby who can play it, who can write about it, and who can exemplify it. In short, who are really a blues people?

Perhaps in response to Collier, but certainly with the benefit of time and retrospect, Amiri Baraka's view of jazz as "black music" changed. Or, more accurately, his definition of *black* evolved. In his introduction to the 1999 reprint of *Blues People* he departed from his previously essentialist view-point:

> There is one thing that I have learned, since the original writing of *Blues People,* that I feel must be a critical new emphasis not understood completely by me in the earlier text. That is, that the Africanisms are not limited to Black people, but indeed, American Culture, itself, is shaped by and includes a great many Africanisms. So that American culture, in the real world, is a composite of African, European, and Native or Akwesasne cultures, history, and people. . . . Actually, *Blues People* is a beginning text. There is yet much work to be done to properly bring the music into the open light of international understanding and collective social development and use—despite the massive commercial exploitation and proof that there is, indeed, as *Jazz Times* projects in its 1998 convention, "The International Business of Jazz." (Baraka, *Blues People* x–xi)

I have taken on part of Baraka's call to "bring the music into the open light of international understanding." I believe that blues people are character-ized by and formed out of migration and music making. Exploring some of the "many Africanisms" Baraka cites on foreign shores is particularly nec-essary given that both blues and jazz also traveled to Europe in the earliest days of their production. The work of Vian and Baldwin pushes against the Americancentric housing of blues music and literature. Vian's work also tests expectations of who can write about "black music."

As a non-American passing for African American, and helping to sustain the jazz scene in France, Vian positions himself in a world of blues people. As an African American writing from France, and yet inextricably drawn to the music of his racialized history, Baldwin extends himself beyond the American home of blues literature. Both Vian and Baldwin take blues peo-ple to the next level, challenging and critiquing their confines.

Vian's *L'écume des jours* and Baldwin's "Sonny's Blues" are prime examples of jazz diasporas. Jazz diasporas are geographically and histori-cally located cultural spaces that offer a flexibility, negotiation, and shifting of racial and national identity for migrating African American jazz musi-cians and communities of jazzophiles with whom they collaborate. Jazz diasporas extend the concept of blues people by collapsing national and racial borders and redefining musical communities. Vian and Baldwin both extend the possibilities of jazz's national and racial identity through liter-ary jazz diasporas.

In 1947 Boris Vian created a fantastical, anticonformist jazz world in the novel *L'écume des jours* (Froth of the daydream). On a starlit evening in

Paris's Latin Quarter in 2013 I went to see the film adaptation of the book, *L'écume des jours / Mood Indigo*, directed by Michel Gondry. As I stepped out of the neighborhood cinema, the yahhhhh-yah-yah-yah of a muted trumpet and a rambling, walking bass resounded in my head. *L'écume des jours* describes the journey to love for two characters, Colin and Chloe, and their subsequent marriage and changing dynamics as Chloe falls ill. In the novel and film the protagonist exists in a world that literally runs on the beats of jazz, and everyone thrives on the music. For example, the film features a piano cocktail based on the mood created from a live performance on a piano.

The film pays tribute to Duke Ellington in many ways, from the subtitle *Mood Indigo* (one of Ellington's biggest hits) to the portrait of Ellington that Colin placed above his safe. Ellington's popular 1940 rendition of the song "Chloe (Song of the Swamp)" is embodied in name and character through Chloe. The book follows Colin's search for love, his journey to gain Chloe's attention, and his descent into the working world of a soul-crushing capitalistic, mechanistic job.

Gondry chose Bobby Few to sing and play Ellington's composition "Sophisticated Lady," a romantic song of love and woe. Few is an African American pianist and a mainstay of the contemporary Paris jazz circle, as well as a global success. It is as if Few stands in for Ellington in the film, adding a modern interpretation of his music. Gondry channels Vian in the way that he is still making a space to spotlight African American talent. For Few stands in as representative of the history of African American musicians that inspired Vian and prompted him to empathize with the plight of African American musicians (Willett 76, 80).

The film augments the novel by imagining, onscreen, Vian's musical and intellectual environment but also by demonstrating his support of African American musicians. Creating a new, imaginative world fueled by jazz, *L'écume des jours* also illustrates the thriving jazz and intellectual scene that Vian negotiated in post–World War II Paris. Vian's character Chick is obsessed with the books and lectures of Jean-Sol Partre (a parody of Sartre). Vian's parodic representation of the French philosopher speaks to his close friendship with Sartre in real life. Vian played a key role in diversifying the Left Bank, by ushering in the literary greats and intellectuals Sartre and Camus to the jazz world. Both spent time at Chez Inez, Tabou, and Club Saint-Germain.

As one of the main figureheads of the existentialist movement, Sartre represented a multitude of young, enthusiastic *zazous* intent on living for the moment and banishing the sorrow and pain of the war.[7] The same jazz

caves that shook with music and wreaked of smoke also shook with philosophical debates on existentialism. Vian characterizes this happy-go-lucky
crowd with his zany, bizarre style. The book and film present a tragicomic,
inventive, and music-laden world.

The world that Vian creates on the page is a jazz diaspora, as he uses
fantasy to imagine a safe space for jazz-crazed fans and marginalized intellectuals. This space of escape is where the independently wealthy Colin can
thrive for a while, just sipping on jazz for sustenance. Colin escapes, for
some time, the demands of the real world until Chloe's illness forces him to
work in the factories; thus, he becomes a cog in the machine of capitalism.
Vian portrays jazz as the respite from a systematic, soul-crushing, capital-
ist-driven way of living. The novel creates a space where one of the greatest
jazz composers, Duke Ellington, is honored as the very beat that keeps life
running. In sum, Vian creates a jazz diaspora inclusive of white French
philosophers and hip, imaginative writers, and the pedestal is raised for
African American jazz musicians like Duke Ellington.

Of most significance is the way that *L'écume des jours* (and its success as
"high" literature) uplifts the perception of jazz and further incorporates
music into French literature and French society. With *J'irai cracher* and
L'écume des jours Vian creates a jazzy world where his literary improvisation gives jazz wings and allows it to signify in new and engaging ways. He
also challenges authenticity claims by blurring the lines of who can write
about this music and know about its possibilities. Yes, as a critic he has demonstrated expertise in the music, but in *L'écume des jours* he goes further
than he had with *J'irai cracher*. Instead of pretending to be black to gain
authority, he steps into a role of authority immediately and becomes a soloist on the bandstand. Rather than being the metaphorical rhythm section
that simply supports African American icons, he expands the parameters of
jazz and creates a new soundscape on the page. Figures such as Vian uplift
the status of jazz by including it in critically acclaimed high literature. This
incorporates jazz and blues even further into French society, thereby
obscuring the classification of this music as American or African American.
With *L'écume des jours* Vian expands the concept of "blues people" by placing himself and his white, French literary protagonists in this blues and jazz
community.

But Vian wasn't African American. Even so, when he passed for black
under the pseudonym of Vernon Sullivan, his literature momentarily
entered the genre of African American literature. He had never even been
to the United States. Actually, he hadn't migrated anywhere. Including him
in a community of blues people presents a quandary. So recalling Robert

O'Meally's blues reading of *Huckleberry Finn* proves helpful. As with *Huckleberry Finn, J'irai cracher sur vos tombes* was not written by an African American, nor was it entirely about blues music. But the influence of blues and jazz seeps through Vian's literature, radio shows, and world-view. He problematizes a limiting view of blues and jazz as Afrocentric cultural expression and prompts a reframing of the concept of blues people. He demonstrates how blues people are influenced by the transnational, interracial, and interdisciplinary trafficking of black music—especially in France, given the large role that France played in promoting, critiquing, and hosting jazz and jazz musicians from the early twentieth century onward. Vian also shows how jazz diasporas can include those who have not come from the United States but who share an empathetic rather than a geo-graphical bond. For Vian's migration is empathetic through his passing for black and in the fantastical world of privilege he creates for jazz in *L'écume des jours.*

But Vian doesn't fit neatly into the model of a jazz diaspora. Rather than serving as a survival tool for him as a writer, jazz became a tool of libera-tion—a way to free his African American brothers and play even more with literary constraints. In *J'irai cracher* he has the option of momentarily pass-ing for black, which his white privilege allows. Vian's skin color and cultural background inevitably protect him from expectations, judgments, and vio-lence based on racial prejudice against blacks; he can always step out of blackness, having the *choice* of consuming or attempting to assume black-ness. The jazz diaspora of *L'écume des jours* is fantasy and is quite a depar-ture from performing live jazz and living as a blues people. Vian and his protagonists are always distanced in some way from an authentic experi-ence of blackness, via their different racial and national identities and fan-tastical leaps. So Vian remained distanced from African American experi-ences, but he was not the only one.

James Baldwin had willfully distanced himself. Disavowing the blues and emigrating from the United States, he had separated himself from the rage and pain of racism in the mid-twentieth century. While there were some things he pushed away in his long-held disavowal of blues songs like "Backwater Blues," he was simultaneously immersed in a world of blues people. He was a product of the innovative, thriving Harlem and Greenwich Village jazz, art, and literary scene, and his writing continually returned to those influences. Yet Baldwin migrated to France to escape the treatment of African Americans in the United States. In Paris he frequented the clubs and events in the Paris Noir community, prizing his friendship with African American painter Beauford Delaney, who had been a mentor and good friend since Baldwin's early days in Greenwich Village. He also wandered beyond the rich musical and literary scene of Saint-Germain-des-Prés.

Baldwin would spend the rest of his life moving between northern and southern France, Turkey, and the United States. Distance from the United States offered clarity and safety for him to compose. His friend and secretary Bernard Hassel revealed that Baldwin "came because he wanted to be a writer and couldn't be a writer in America" (*Price of the Ticket*). Baldwin published in journals such as the *Partisan Review* and *Harper's Magazine*. Selected essays were compiled in *Notes of a Native Son* in 1955. They revealed his encounters with the black French and their harsh treatment in Paris, reactions to his darker skin in an all-white Swiss town, and the realization that African Americans could never fully shed their American heritage and be "real Parisians." These essays accompanied investigations of life in America, such as "The Harlem Ghetto," "Journey to Atlanta," and "Everybody's Protest Novel." The organization of *Notes of a Native Son* suggests that Baldwin's attention to Europe and the United States was commingled, married even. These essays tell us that Baldwin was unable to shed his interest in U.S. affairs, despite living abroad.

The blues allowed Baldwin to find a home and settle down, despite his geographical in-betweenness and incertitude about articulating African diasporic experiences. The music rooted him to his African American heritage and helped him more clearly articulate it. He captured this history and drew on music as a survival tool in his writing and his life. Like Vian, he created jazz diasporas on the page. His stories created interstices of existence for a people continually battered by their real-life social environments. These stories paralleled in some ways his personal confrontation with his African American heritage and history through dislocated listening. Baldwin's recognition of home from Europe and his inability to remove himself from the "menace" of his American heritage reappear as key themes in his short story "Sonny's Blues."

Composed in 1957 Paris, "Sonny's Blues" recounts the life of its eponymous protagonist, a fictional African American jazz pianist, and his struggles to escape prejudice, poverty, and drug addiction in Harlem in the mid-twentieth century. "Sonny's Blues" presents a tenuous relationship between two brothers: one unnamed brother tries to assimilate into the mainstream and embrace middle-class American culture; the other, Sonny, strives to escape his condition and clearly express his feelings and life in blues and jazz performance. More than a snapshot of the different traps and struggles of urban African American life, "Sonny's Blues" is about miscommunication and the struggle of African Americans to communicate and understand African American experience, especially amid a marginalized position in the United States.

In "Sonny's Blues" Baldwin portrays two brothers who struggle to really "hear" each other. One brother is a teacher assimilating to escape the traps of poverty, and the other is a jazz pianist resisting the mainstream through drugs and music. The story commences with the unnamed brother finding out about Sonny's time in prison for drugs. While "Sonny's Blues" does not directly correlate to Baldwin's travels overseas, it does emphasize, in several ways, the importance of migration, starting with both brothers' exile from the Harlem ghetto.

"Sonny's Blues" exemplifies a jazz diaspora as it presents the confines of national and racial identity yet also illustrates the liberatory collective power of music and migration to push past these limitations. The older brother flees first, hoping to attain a better chance for success in a middle-class neighborhood. He distances himself psychologically from Sonny and his struggles: leaving him behind with his wife and family while in the army, failing to communicate with Sonny, and being closed off to Sonny's profession as a jazz musician. Most important, he leaves behind the struggles of his family and of Sonny to survive; "Sonny's Blues" reveals the brother's process and eventual musical reckoning with that dislocation.

In the following passage the older brother describes the confines that Harlem represented for them:

> So we drove along, between the green of the park and the stony, lifeless elegance of hotels and apartment buildings, toward the vivid, killing streets of our childhood. . . . But houses exactly like the houses of our past yet dominated the landscape, boys exactly like the boys we once had been found themselves encircled by disaster. Some escaped the trap, most didn't. Those who got out always left something of themselves behind, as some animals amputate a leg and leave it in a trap. It might be said, perhaps, that I had escaped, after all, I was a school teacher; or that Sonny had, he hadn't lived in Harlem for years. Yet, as the cab moved uptown through streets which seemed, with a rush, to darken with dark people, and as I covertly studied Sonny's face, it came to me that what we both were seeking through our separate cab windows was that part of ourselves which had been left behind. It is always at the hour of trouble and confrontation that the missing member aches.
>
> We hit 110th Street and started rolling up Lenox Avenue. And I'd known this avenue all my life, but it seemed to me again, as it had seemed on the day I'd first heard about Sonny's trouble, filled with a hidden menace which was its very breath of life. (Baldwin, "Sonny's Blues" 838–39)

In "Sonny's Blues" Harlem reflects a space of darkness, in which African Americans are situated in nearly inescapable poverty and hopelessness. This Harlem is laden with the dangers of drugs and crime—a city that is too often left to deteriorate and where little is invested financially. Baldwin emphasizes the stagnancy, danger, and agency of this Harlem. As a car rolls through this neighborhood and the reader simultaneously is introduced to Harlem for the first time, Baldwin uses striking language, discussing the city as having "killing streets" and the people as "encircled by disaster" and sitting in a trap. This trap is "filled with a hidden menace which was its very breath of life."

So Baldwin uses increasingly and overwhelmingly negative terms to describe Harlem. But the reader is also aware that the two brothers have escaped Harlem's grip and the vices that prevailed there. Baldwin pairs his emphasis on traps with distance—a moving distance. The most obvious example is the car passing through 110th and Lenox but never engaging. Notably, the brothers look out through separate windows, reminding us of their disconnectedness from their childhood home. This keeps them from interacting and protects them from this present; still the memories of their past life menace them.

Baldwin compares the brothers' escape and dislocation from Harlem with amputation and leaving behind a limb. The implication is that the trap and dislocation cause tremendous pain—not unlike the emotional intensity in Bessie Smith's voice that spurs a visceral reaction in him. But this particularly violent metaphor represents more than just discomfort; it suggests a brutal and painful psychological tearing away of one's upbringing and heritage. Baldwin's language choice "as some animals amputate a leg and leave it in a trap" riffs on Fanon's phrasing in his 1952 book, *Black Skin, White Masks*. Baldwin would have come into contact with Fanon's work. Fanon was living in Paris at the time of publication, plus he participated in some political events supported by Francophone African writers and intellectuals like the first Congrès des écrivains et artistes noirs (Conference of Negro-African Writers and Artists) in 1956 Paris. In the chapter titled "The Facts of Blackness," Fanon writes, "I discovered my blackness, my ethnic characteristics; and I was battered down by tom-toms, cannibalism, intellectual deficiency, fetishism, racial defects, slaveships. . . . I took myself far off from my own presence, far indeed, and made myself an object. What else could it be for me but an amputation, an excision, a hemorrhage that spattered my whole body with black blood? But I did not want this revision, this thematization. All I wanted was to be a man among other men" (*Theories* 259).

Here Fanon describes his internalization of racialization and the toll that a history of racialized perceptions, expectations, and oppressions has taken on him psychologically. He describes his torturous prompt to separate himself from these performances of race. His words envisage a ripping away from and a desire to be perceived anew as human rather than marked by racial differentiation. Baldwin's choice to reference amputation in "Sonny's Blues" recalls this same psychological struggle. While Baldwin does not spend much space discussing racial or socioeconomic difference in the passage, the word choice and other moments of "Sonny's Blues" recall the impact of racial prejudice. This life of racial and economic oppression is just what Baldwin's characters try to escape—though they are never psychologically able to leave home, just as Baldwin wasn't.

The unnamed brother left years ago, becoming a teacher and settling in a housing project near his school and away from the ghetto (Baldwin, "Sonny's Blues" 839). Sonny's first attempt to escape was through travel to Greece when he joined the military and traveled away from Harlem and toward liberation (851). Their current distance, yet return home, prompts a realization in the older brother that some part of his history is caught in the "menace"—the obstacle that Harlem represents. Sonny also struggled with the ghettoized, segregated environment. Temptations of vice entrapped him, and it seemed impossible to fully escape these external conditions. Yet there was also liberation to be found in his blues. Baldwin was liberated in listening to the blues, and Sonny gained liberation by performing it. In the last scene of the short story Baldwin shows the potential for liberation, through a reckoning and eventual acceptance of one's past and one's place in history.

Sonny has been in prison for a year, separated from his environment and family because of drugs. He is then invited to return to the Harlem ghetto. He sits in a Harlem club and is asked to play the blues. His yearlong distance from the piano has created nervousness, an inner "torment." It is a visceral struggle, a feeling of discomfort and vulnerability that makes him stumble and stutter his way along. Baldwin details the pain etched in his face, as the brother recounts: "And the face I saw on Sonny I'd never seen before. Everything had been burned out of it" (Baldwin, "Sonny's Blues" 24).

But gradually, as the concert progresses, the band starts to play together. And Sonny is no longer alone and isolated; he dissolves into the group. Together, they tell their story of African American culture; they try "to make us listen." Their story, like a tragicomic blues, reveals "suffering" and "delight," "light" and "darkness." Sonny struggles and suffers alongside the band until his chance to solo. In this moment both Sonny and his brother undergo a transformation as Sonny's playing takes him to a musical and psychological zenith while the brother's experience of listening expands his formerly limited perspective:

> He hit something in all of them, he hit something in me, myself, and the music tightened and deepened, apprehension began to beat the air. They were not about anything very new. He and his boys up there were keeping it new, at the risk of ruin, destruction, madness, and death, in order to find new ways to make us listen. For, while the tale of how we suffer, and how were are delighted, and how we may triumph is never new, it always must be heard. Then they all gathered around Sonny and Sonny played. . . . Freedom lurked around us and I understood, at last, that he could help us to be free if we would listen, that he would never be free until we did. Yet there was no battle in his face now, I heard what he had gone through, and would continue to go through until he came to rest in earth. He had made it his: that long line, of which we knew only Mama and Daddy. (Baldwin, "Sonny's Blues" 24)

This moment is akin to Baldwin's own reconciliation, for Sonny can hear how to free the brother and the band from the torment of the historical struggle of being black in America. Sonny struggled with his racialized past—his ghettoized, segregated home and the tempting vices of drugs and crime that had entrapped him and led to prison. It seemed impossible to fully escape those external conditions. Those were Sonny's blues.

Those moments of tragicomic recognition were rooted in oppression, from which one could never fully remove oneself. Yet there was also liberation to be found, for Baldwin reminds us that the tragic merges with the comic, heartache reaches out for joy, and the down and out meets the trick to survive. Baldwin shows clearly in this scene the potential for dislocated listening, the liberation through a reckoning and eventual acceptance of one's past and place in history.

But Sonny must hear across history, back to his parents and remember the struggle they conveyed to him. But what does it mean to hear across history? Or to hear across nations? "Sonny's Blues" becomes a "performed effigy," in the words of Josh Kun. Discussing James Baldwin's reaction to "Backwater Blues," Kun writes, "Records like Smith's are 'performed effigies,' audio surrogates that sound forth distant absences and conjure up distant pasts" (Kun 94). Like "Backwater Blues," "Sonny's Blues" is a performed effigy. It "sound[s] forth distant" and not so distant historical collective traumas, from the moment when the brothers recall the traps of living in the ghetto as children to Sonny's realization of his particular place in history beside his mother and father as they negotiate and overcome conditions of racialization (Baldwin, "Sonny's Blues" 842–43). With "Sonny's Blues" Baldwin creates on the page a community of ancestors talking through the music, performing through Sonny. In this way "Sonny's Blues" is a classic jazz diaspora text that forges the forces of movement and music together to make clearer that which Baldwin says "no American is prepared to hear" (Baldwin, *Notes* 19). Just as Sonny struggles on that piano, we also see Baldwin grappling with his racialized history. He continues to write about Harlem amid the cafés of Paris, unable to leave behind this collective history. But the music, combined with migration, inevitably allows Baldwin to collapse the confines of racialization and expand the communities of people that can identify with African American experiences.

In sum, Baldwin and Vian introduce the possibilities of an extended community of blues people by articulating African American experience in a way that connects rather than isolates. By connecting these two authors' works and lives, I have proposed a relationship. The relationship connects these two but also African Americans and white French and even the United States and France. Baldwin was still tied to race relations in the United States from France, whereas Vian created links between his French heritage and the heritage he heard in the music and imagined through his writing. Considering Baldwin's work in a French setting and discussing Vian's pre-conceptions of African Americans reaffirms a relationship between these two national communities that are ever-embedded in African American music and musical literature. Michelle Wright encapsulates this relationship in her characterization of Baldwin as transatlantic:

> "Encounter on the Seine" underscores the transatlantic structure of the African American Subject, pointing to the ways in which geographic displacement brings to the fore the meanings and meaninglessness of modernity and its civilizing project. Through these encounters Baldwin posits the importance of transatlantic discourse in cutting through the simplistic mythologies of oppressed and oppressor pinned to the linear chronology of progress. . . . In contrast to the impulsive understanding of the white Frenchman and the embarrassed white American, the transatlantic African American Subject embodies and reflects the complicated ties between the Old World, the New World, and the African Diaspora. (228–29)

I would add that Baldwin, as well as blues and jazz, clearly demonstrates the transatlantic nature of African Americans. For years he resisted reflecting on many of the negative connotations of African American experience. He needed migration and music to characterize his racialized history and memory. Performing and listening to blues and jazz helped Vian imaginatively migrate to the United States and attempt to capture the rage and beauty of African Americans living there. For Vian the music was transatlantic, too, forcing a connection and identification even without the direct experience of being black in the United States. Michele Wright's characterization of African Americans as transatlantic subjects opens up the dialogue on the experiences of African Americans, of a blues people, arguing that it is too limiting to discuss jazz and blues culture in only one race, one place, or one medium. This music has mobility. Blues people keep moving, keep connecting, keep relating . . .

5. Kenny Clarke's Journey between "Black" and "Universal" Music

As a national and global commodity, black music has penetrated the boundaries between and among cultures around the world. As such, it becomes bound up in an intricately spun web of cultural, social, and political battles over origin, ownership, circulation, and performance.

E. PATRICK JOHNSON

Seventy-five years later, jazz is still a paradox in the terms J.A. Rogers set out in 1925: It is a music rooted in American and, more specifically, African American experience; yet it is indeed too "fundamentally human" to be racial and too international to be understood solely as a product of the United States.

ERIC PORTER

Sometimes a song seduces you, intrigues you, and takes you on a journey . . .

My journey into the world of universal jazz tripped out its first steps on my hearing of "Box 703: Washington, D.C." Featured on the December 1961 album *Jazz Is Universal,* by the Clarke-Boland Big Band (C-BBB), this song is like a bumpy, lively journey right on down the road to D.C. A band of trumpets blurt. The drums undergird, swinging and spinning almost off-kilter. The walking bass commingles, bouncing the song along, and the single muted trumpet trips along with the da-ding dinging of the drums keeping time. Add to that a frenetically swinging, yet in-sync, band. The solo sax creates a musical path, spitting out its story as trumpets spurt out accents. On each hearing I am left with a scorched path. For this song is hot, the trumpets assert, screaming and screeching in unison at the end.

As the first song on *Jazz Is Universal,* "Box 703: Washington, D.C." commences a geographical journey from the U.S. capital to Overbrook, Kansas, as the album ends with the C-BBB's rendition of James Moody's composition, "Last Train from Overbrook." This album also sonically moves forward with its swinging propulsion. Most significantly, *Jazz Is Universal* represents a significant movement between perceptions of jazz as "black music" and as "universal" music.

The band's drummer and cofounder, Kenny Clarke, exemplifies this paradigm shift. A combination of childhood daydreams, memory of his wartime tours, and escalating racism in the United States spurred his migration to France in 1956. Even though he left the epicenter of jazz production in New York City, he soon created a vibrant and influential jazz diaspora in Paris. Kenny Clarke became the cornerstone of the Saint-Germain-des-Prés jazz scene, a house drummer for the Blue Note and Club Saint-Germain, the most represented drummer at Vogue records, and the go-to guy for such groundbreaking projects as the *Ascenseur pour l'échafaud* soundtrack (fig. 9). He both mentored French bands and persuaded African American performers to visit Paris. Ultimately, he created the foundation for countless collaborations between American and French jazz musicians.

In the 1960s he moved his expertise beyond the boundaries of Paris, disseminating jazz to such places as Cologne and London, where he promoted the C-BBB, a band consisting of members from a plethora of countries, including England, Sweden, Holland, and the United States. With their seminal album the C-BBB promoted the message that jazz was not just black or American music. This was just one symbol of the multiple ways the African American drummer mobilized jazz in Europe from what had been termed "Negro music" to "universal" music. Through his introduction of bebop in France in 1948, his own migration to France in 1956, and his mentoring and collaborations with European musicians until his death in 1985, Kenny Clarke created a jazz diaspora that was more inclusive of diverse races and nationalities. His jazz diaspora was universal. It is the widest and most encompassing jazz diaspora in this book, and it retains the enduring impact and influence of ethnic particularism (i.e., jazz as uniquely African American music). Yet in this postwar era Clarke's expanded jazz diaspora also collapsed national and racial signifiers of jazz and began to challenge African American participation in jazz in Europe. The term *universal* holds within it tension between these two perspectives.

This chapter reflects on tension between and shifts in perspectives. Each subsection describes examples of experiences and rhetoric that prize African American identity, yet these sections also discuss the Europeanization and globalization that Kenny Clarke's life and music come to connote. The chapter elaborates on both the man and his music; the two narratives often run parallel or shift back and forth—for the man and the music are constitutive of each other. Given the breadth of Kenny Clarke's impact on postwar jazz in Paris, the chapter also shifts between earlier and later periods. Sometimes different historical moments reveal contradictory or shifting opinions.

FIGURE 9.   Kenny Clarke takes a break from a Barclay Studio session to pose for the camera in 1959 Paris. © Herman Leonard Photography LLC / CTS Images).

On January 2, 1914, Kenneth Spearman Clarke was born in Pittsburgh, Pennsylvania, where he was raised in a musically gifted middle-class family. His father played the trombone, his mother the piano. As a little boy Clarke learned piano from his mother and retained those skills throughout his career (Hennessey, *Klook* 7). He learned the drums between the ages of eight and nine and quickly made a name and reputation for himself in Pittsburgh. But he'd always wanted to get out of Pittsburgh. Jazz offered a way out and the discovery of his niche: "He disliked the ambiance of a steel mill town. He did not fit in; he felt uncomfortable in his environment and could not communicate with the people around him. Alienated and isolated, he had dreams of being somewhere else, of leaving Pittsburgh," writes biographer Mike Hennessey (*Klook* 39). So in the 1930s he moved to New York, where he made his claim to fame in the bebop jazz genre.

As one of the now-famous crew of Minton's Playhouse (between 1942 and 1944 in New York) he innovated the bebop jazz drum style—earning the nickname Klook because of the unique sound of the accent he added on the drums (DeVeaux, *Birth* 218). Jazz critic Leonard Feather recounts Clarke's first bebop explorations: "Later, in Minton's as Kenny developed the idea of using the bass drum pedal for special accents rather than regular rhythm, and the top cymbal to maintain the steady four beats, Teddy Hill would imitate the sounds he produced. 'What is that kloop-mop stuff you're doing?' he'd say. That's how it sounded to him—Kloop-mop!—and that's what they called the music itself before it became known as bebop, says Hill" (Feather, *Inside* 8).

Kenny Clarke was at the top of his game in the 1950s. He cofounded the Modern Jazz Quartet with pianist John Lewis in 1952, and he recorded with Charlie Parker, Milt Jackson, Mary Lou Williams, and Sonny Rollins. He was thriving in New York, so his migration to Paris in 1956 was a bit surprising.

But it shouldn't have been. For Kenny Clarke had always dreamed of France. At the age of twelve he was growing up in Pittsburgh but daydreaming about Paris: "I wanted to go to France. I had to read about it. I kept thinking about it: France, Paris, must be nice. I was twelve" (Broschke-Davis 39). World War II provided a passport to France for Clarke. It gave him another taste of a life that he had long admired. The war had presented opportunities for Clarke and other African American soldiers to see life abroad.[1] During his military stint Clarke had traveled throughout the United States and to several European cities, performing with a jazz band while stationed in Camp Seibert in Alabama; singing with a vocal quartet during his tour of Tetworth in Liverpool; and creating a twelve-person choir in the 13th Special Service Unit in Rouen (as well as in cities in Germany and Belgium) (Hennessey, *Klook* 53). During his wartime tour in France he experienced a land with more freedom and more welcoming people than his homeland. In Clarke's opinion Europeans treated artists differently, giving them respect that was lacking in the United States. He found "a certain quality of life" and "peace and quiet" (quoted in Zwerin, "Kenny" par. 3).

When Clarke had a four-day tour in Paris with his military band in 1944, he was hoping to revisit some of the people he'd met during his tours in

1937 and 1938 with pianist and bandleader Edgar Hayes. In 1944 he would meet, for the first time, Charles Delaunay, founder of *Jazz Hot* and an influential jazz critic and event promoter (Hennessey, *Klook* 54). This meeting spawned an invitation to the Paris International Jazz Festival and a long recording commitment with Delaunay's Vogue recording label.

Clarke was also impressed with the European lifestyle: "I promised myself that I would return as a civilian some day and spend some time there. In fact, the whole European way of life appealed to me. The tempo of life is slow and easy, and the people are not so superficial" (quoted in Hennessey, *Klook* 54). This visit countered the racism and limitations he was enduring in the United States and its military.

The war showed Clarke and other African American soldiers a different way of life in Europe, a life that seemed less defined by racial difference. In his interaction with the French during the war, Clarke saw the kind of community in which he hoped to thrive. He once said to an interviewer, "The people, that was what I was counting on, I found the people I had dreamt about.... I wanted to stay in Europe as early as 1937 when I first went there. I probably would have stayed then. I had offers to stay, but the war was coming. I decided to come back" (Broschke-Davis 46).

When Clarke was first drafted into the army, his treatment in the American South drove him to go AWOL during his military service in Alabama, but after 107 days Clarke unenthusiastically returned to complete his term (Hennessey, *Klook* 52–53). After his discharge in 1946 he returned to the jazz scene in New York. Although work was prevalent, the challenges of living and working in a racist environment still plagued him. For the most part white Americans did not respect or appreciate that he had served his country in the war; instead, Clarke and other African American soldiers were violently targeted after World War II.

In his pen-and-ink illustration "The Return of the Soldier" African American artist Charles White poignantly documented this postwar suppression of freedoms and increased violence in 1946: a mound of distinctly angled figures, drawn in sepia hue and chiaroscuro shading, are the first shapes that greet the eye. A closer look reveals three allegories that illustrate the inescapable, entangled danger in black and white relations after World War II. A Klan member stands with smoking printed scroll in hand, perhaps symbolizing the fragility of constitutional equal rights in the hands of the Klan's de facto justice. He peeks over the shoulder of a policeman, touching his shoulder and leaning to the side almost as if he is another arm of the law. But justice is symbolized as the greatest threat for African Americans in this illustration. The policeman takes up much of the picture as his hulking form points a gun downward and in the center of the art-work. Surrounding the guns are three African American soldiers still in their uniforms yet now kneeling or lying rather than saluting tall and proud. One soldier reaches up as if scratching or clawing, while his eyes point downward in defeat. Another soldier looks up with questioning opened mouth. His fingers curl and enfold himself—potentially protecting against backlash. The last soldier lies beneath them all, looking up, in dan-ger of being stomped on or crushed.

"The Return of the Soldier" reveals the collaboration between the Klan and the police in oppressing African Americans and multiple forms this oppression took, from de jure constitutional law to the violent potential of de facto justice. White's illustration documented real quotidian struggles rather than highlighting unique events. With lynchings and mob riots from Freeport, New York, to Columbia, Tennessee, the freedoms African American soldiers had tasted abroad were revoked across the United States.[2]

This was the return to the United States that Clarke faced. It stood in contrast to more positive experiences he had touring and performing in France after the war. Multiple offers came: tours in 1948, the Paris International Jazz Festival in 1949, and the recordings and concerts that kept him there for months later.

Yet Clarke still did not relocate. He found one survival strategy, however, that would sustain him for the rest of his life: religion. Clarke converted to Islam and changed his name to Liaquat Ali Salaam. He believed that the Christian faith was not inclusive of blacks; converting was a way of lashing out at the hypocritical Christian world's treatment of blacks (Broschke-Davis 63; Hennessey, *Klook* 56–59). His conversion could be taken as a sign of his support for Black Nationalism, given this was an era of increased popularity and visibility of groups like the Nation of Islam. But even though Kenny Clarke was devout in his daily prayer rituals, he was not fanatical and did not promote a political agenda; although he identified in part with the political movements of Malcolm X and black Muslims, the Muslim religion supported his view of life and sustained him (Hennessey, *Klook* 56–59).

Also, showing an identification card with "Muslim" as opposed to "Colored" potentially prompted better treatment by police who "were per-suaded that they were visiting Arab dignitaries" (Zwerin, "Kenny"). Muslim identity in this postwar era of the United States yielded greater cultural capital than was normally afforded to African Americans. Clarke remained a devout Muslim until his death, often talking about his beliefs with band members and even bestowing his son with the Arabic name of Laurent Salaam Clarke (Chautemps; L. Clarke).

But religious commitment was not enough for Clarke to discount the inequities he faced as an African American jazz musician in America. He felt manipulated and disempowered by racism in the jazz industry, once saying, "As fast as you create something, white so-called musicians take it away from you and exploit it, because they have the money. They have radio, television, records. They pass off everything you create as their own. They know if they expose it on television, everyone will think the white man created it . . . all the cheap imitations on television and they get by with it. You create something and you see who has it the next day" (Broschke-Davis 59). He was bitter that the jazz industry was controlled by whites and particularly that whites appropriated music produced by African Americans. Though jazz gigs were all too prevalent for him in mid-1950s New York, Clarke lacked the power to control production. He believed African Americans had fueled the jazz industry, but jazz had come to be represented by white Americans. Author of *Paris Noir: African Americans in the City of Light,* Tyler Stovall describes the power struggles Clarke saw at work in the New York jazz scene:

> The jazz scene in New York was rigidly run by an elite of primarily white music promoters, who decided who would or would not play the city's leading clubs, and kept black jazz performers firmly under their control. . . . The problem ultimately was white control of black music, and by the 1950s exile from America seemed a way to escape this control. "The music has gotten into the wrong hands," wrote Clarke. "Musicians everywhere are sitting home by the telephone waiting for a white man to call them for a gig, and the only future I see in our music is for black people to have their own thing going; otherwise it's no use." (*Paris Noir* 177–78)

In some ways Clarke was running away from white Europeans, too. That was the reason he quit the Modern Jazz Quartet (MJQ). The MJQ was moving away from core jazz elements and toward a marriage with classical music (Broschke-Davis 53). Clarke blamed his growing dissatisfaction with the quartet on John Lewis's desire not to play jazz but to model music after the classical greats. Calling out Lewis, Clarke claimed, "He can play jazz fantastically if he wants to, but he doesn't like to. What he likes is Bach and Chopin. It's insane to say that I was bored in the MJQ. I wanted to play jazz, but there was no way with those damned arrangements. So I left" (quoted in Monson, *Freedom Sounds* 97).[3]

In *Jazz Exiles: American Musicians Abroad* Bill Moody adds several other reasons for Clarke's migration from the States, including the popularity and spread of drugs among jazz musicians; the payment in drugs rather than money from record companies; the danger of being blackballed for calling out the advantage that promoters were taking of his friend Dizzy Gillespie; the changing jazz industry; and memories of the favorable reception of him in Europe (60). All of these life events were signs that Clarke was finally done.

With a gig at the Savoy and Miles Davis banging on his door with yet another opportunity, Kenny Clarke left New York in 1956; he accepted an offer to play for Michel Legrand on a short-term contract in Paris (Zwerin, "Jazz" 534). The temporary gig with Legrand turned into permanent Parisian residency, and Clark never again visited the United States for more than a few months at a time (Zwerin, "Jazz" 534; Broschke-Davis 61–62). He would remain in France until his death on January 26, 1985, at his home in the eastern Parisian suburb of Montreuil-sous-Bois.

As Tyler Stovall has aptly described him, Kenny Clarke was "a self-conscious refugee from racism, disheartened and disgusted by the powerful white establishment's mistreatment of his music and his people" (*Paris Noir* 178). He differed from Sidney Bechet, who said he would return to the States if given the opportunity (Ehrlich 95). Bechet existed in a jazz diaspora that allowed him to perform different subjectivities that helped him survive and thrive in France. Kenny Clarke had already created an image of France in his mind from childhood and his later visits, and he seems to have sought out that image when he settled in France. It was an image of settling down, of finally fitting in, which was quite different from Sidney Bechet's restless yet targeted negotiation of subjectivities. In contrast, Clarke proudly represented his race and made use of it in Europe to ironically go *beyond* the limitations of race—at least the limitations for African Americans in the United States. In *The Black Atlantic: Modernity and Double Consciousness* Paul Gilroy elaborates on desire for exile shared by African Americans: "Whether their experience of exile is enforced or chosen, temporary or permanent, these intellectuals and activists, writers, speakers, poets, and artists repeatedly articulate a desire to escape the restrictive bonds of ethnicity, national identification, and sometimes even 'race' itself" (Gilroy, *The Black Atlantic* 19). Clarke migrated to Paris "to escape the restrictive bonds of ethnicity." By migrating, he took an active stance against the treatment of African Americans in the United States with the hope of a different life in France.

By the time Ursula Broschke-Davis interviewed him in 1982 and 1983, Kenny Clarke had lived in Paris for twenty-five years. His impression of life there after all those years was ambiguous. Clarke had both realized his dreams to migrate and reconciled himself to inescapability of racial disparity in France. "He felt respected as a human being, and he received fantastic receptions as an artist. . . . He actually found Paris to be as he had imagined it," writes Broschke-Davis, adding that "Clarke had found his personal happiness in Paris" (46, 61). Yet Clarke also revealed something else to her: "I am way out of the European society. I am not accepted. I just stay on the outskirts. In a sense no white society is going to accept a black man. The sooner black people figure that out, the better off they will be" (58). One man, two contradictory feelings about France. He was happy in Paris and had the life of calm and the people with whom he wanted to interact. Yet he was ever the outsider. These two sentiments seemingly oppose each other, but they actually coexist in the performance of universalism.

For Clarke secured universal rights, as represented in the ideals of the American Constitution's "We, the people" and the motto born out of the French Revolution, "Liberté, Égalité, Fraternité" (Liberty, Equality, Brotherhood). He was treated as a human being rather than degraded and deemed inferior. His music was valued and absorbed into French culture, and he had assimilated into French culture after years of living and raising his family in France. But Clarke's foreign heritage would always distinguish him racially and nationally from the hegemony of the white French. A history of exoticized, primitivist perceptions of African American jazz musicians also contrasted perceptions of black French in the metropole. So Clarke strongly symbolized African American experience rather than eluding racialized boundaries in France. His race connected him to his American homeland and would forever distance him, marking him as "the other," abroad.

BETWEEN "BLACK" AND "UNIVERSAL" MUSIC

Kenny Clarke's race forever distinguished him in France, but it also forged the path through which he and jazz assimilated into French culture and European culture at large. I espouse the term *universal* throughout this chapter to describe several aspects of jazz's and Clarke's assimilation in France and Europe. I have been asked a few times about my use of this term. Some have inquired whether the term fully encapsulates my meaning or if it is helpful given all the political meanings it also conveys. Neither *international* nor *global* is sufficient, however. While this chapter describes the globalization of jazz through Kenny Clarke's performances, it explores more than the path from American root to European route that jazz has made. *Cosmopolitan* is a more accurate term. In *Making Jazz French: Music and Modern Life in Interwar Paris* Jeffrey Jackson sees the acculturation of jazz in interwar France as a sign of France's cosmopolitan perspective. He writes about the French "willingness to look beyond the borders of France and bring a new music into their own culture. This cosmopolitanism was possible because French culture was not fixed or timeless but resilient and flexible, even after the turmoil of World War I" (201). Jackson's cosmopolitan France is adaptive and open in its absorption of culture and changing of identity. This adaptability is certainly a characteristic of a jazz diaspora.

The hope conveyed in postcolonial studies scholar Anthony Appiah's use of *cosmopolitanism* has also influenced my perspective: Appiah introduces his book *Cosmopolitanism: Ethics in a World of Strangers* with the expressed goal "to have made it harder to think of the world as divided between the West and the Rest; between locals and moderns; between the bloodless ethics of profit and the bloody ethic of identity; between 'us' and 'them'" (xxi). Appiah's goal prompts a reconsideration of divisions and reflection on the values, morals, and cultures we share rather than our differences. *Jazz Diasporas* is also fueled by my desire to illustrate multiple ways that living in France affected African American musicians and the musical and social culture they linked with the United States.

Cosmopolitanism has also been employed to describe a merging of ethnic identities. In one of several investigations of Josephine Baker, film scholar Terri Francis describes the "cosmopolitan, modern figure" that African American intellectuals like Alain Locke made and how they contributed to French national consciousness; she later discusses "cosmopolitan Paris" as a result of an influx of immigration. Additionally, Tyler Stovall uses *cosmopolitan* to detail the diversity of the Paris Noir community across the ages: "Indeed, the diversity of the community went so far as to include many who were neither black nor American, from spouses and lovers to patrons of jazz clubs and soul food restaurants. People participated in many different ways, but at some level the community was open to all interested in black American culture. Finally, the community was cosmopolitan not just in its internal makeup but also in its broader perspective" ("Harlem-sur-Seine" n.p.). All of these uses of the notion of cosmopolitanism speak to the capacity of a jazz diaspora, to house the negotiation of multiple identities and to encourage the merging of various racial, national, and artistic communities.

Last, musicologist Steven Feld's *Jazz Cosmopolitanism in Accra: Five Musical Years in Ghana* offers the most intriguing use of the term as it relates to our present concerns. Feld's cosmopolitanism encompasses the effect of transatlantic dialogues between American and African musicians—in their unknown paralleling, piggy-backing, and innovating. Through the case studies of several Ghanaian musicians, Feld reveals "the vicissitudes of a music whose dynamic origins were overtaken, in terms of both acoustic and social complexity, by diasporic dialogues, global crossings, and transnational feedback" (59). So, too, with my own ponderings. Kenny Clarke's jazz journey takes us through battles over national and racial authenticity to imitation to collaboration to innovation—and back and forth between them all. His journey to universal jazz is very much cosmopolitan in Feldian terms. In sum, *cosmopolitan* is relevant and representative of my research, and it may be most familiar to readers and scholars of cultural studies—particularly texts on migration. Because of this familiarity, its prominence in key jazz scholarship like Feld's, and the ways that *cosmopolitan* contributes to and dialogues with my thinking on the *universal*, I have discussed it at length here. However, *universal* offers more, and at times contradictory, layers of meaning. In doing so, the actual uses and performances of the term *universal* have discounted its moral ideals in a way that *cosmopolitan* does not reveal. It is just this complex nature of the term that is particularly useful.

Using *universal* rather than *cosmopolitan* is a performative choice. For *universal* as a word and ideology performs in multiple ways. By employing the word, I am recognizing these multiple functions while also attempting to make *universal* perform more explicitly and honestly than other rhetorical choices. In this perspective *universal* does not merely connote global but black-cum-global-cum-cosmopolitan-cum a host of contradictory and complementary significations. In this chapter the term *universal* comes to mean the widespread identification with jazz as freedom music, the widening of who can "authentically" play jazz, merging European classical elements in jazz, the collective African American desire for and pursuit of human rights, the joint efforts to articulate and fight against shared oppressions of people of African descent, the French republic's immigration policy of inclusion, and the globalization of jazz.

In Nazi-occupied Paris French jazz critic and promoter Charles Delaunay used the term *universal* in the report he sent to the American magazine *Down Beat*. He claimed that jazz did not belong to one race nor to one nation; instead, he wrote, "jazz is much more than an American music—it is the first universal music" ("Delaunay" 131). Claiming that the music belonged to hearts of all humanity, Delaunay saw jazz as representative of everyone. Surviving the war would make French jazz fans even more cognizant of jazz as a symbol of both oppression and freedom. Jazz was survival music, and it was the theme song for the young in the sixth arrondissement of Saint-Germain-des-Prés. French students, intellectuals, writers, artists, and foreign visitors toasted freedom in jazz-filled caves. They drew on jazz's ability to overcome sociopolitical constraints. For them jazz was a war cry and a cry of joy at the achievement of liberation.

The French editors of *Jazz 47* shared and helped shape this universal impact of jazz in the magazine's 1947 tribute: "Black music? American music? Jazz became the rallying cry of young people from all over the world. It is the new blood that spreads around the globe and its pulsations simultaneously beat in the earth's arteries; whether in Valparaiso, Shanghai, Johannesburg or Stockholm, amateurs, musicians, records or radio, this blood beats in unison to the new rhythm of the 20th century" ("Le jazz en Europe" 54–55; my translation). Although French jazz critics had long boasted authority in their knowledge of the music, they progressed to claiming jazz as everyone's music in this postwar era. This universalizing discourse included a more confident assessment of French jazz musicianship. Five years after war's end Delaunay wrote that although jazz was originally created and primarily disseminated by African Americans, French musicians had begun to absorb a black sensibility of the music and to make an impression on the French jazz scene (Delaunay, "Faut" 18). Under the helm of Kenny Clarke and other African American musicians residing in Paris, young French jazz musicians gained confidence in their playing and assumed a more influential role in performing or representing jazz worldwide—thus more readily joining the universal jazz community that French jazz critics had assertively claimed. French critics' discourse of universalism represented a shift in their previous criticism of French jazz as imitation and promotion of jazz by African Americans as "authentic" jazz.

Another use of *universal* comes from a popular trend by avant-garde jazz musicians in the 1960s. In *What Is This Thing Called Jazz? African American Musicians as Artists, Critics, and Activists* Eric Porter identifies the universalist perspectives of African American jazz musicians John Coltrane, Eric Dolphy, and Ornette Coleman, who wanted to experiment with merging European harmonic conventions with jazz elements. Porter discusses Coltrane's tendency to steer clear of politicizing his music with Black Nationalist aims; he also quotes a 1962 *Down Beat* interview wherein Dolphy describes music as a connector that mirrors the thoughts and hearts of others outside the United States as well as within (Porter 197). Given this perspective, Porter notes: "The universalist approach to art expressed by Coltrane and Dolphy, however, still presented a challenge to those who wished to limit the meaning and function of this music to an African American context, just as Coleman's demand that musicians have the freedom to incorporate classical and folk elements was potentially at odds with a black aesthetic" (197).

This use of *universal* relates to Kenny Clarke because it was just this type of musical exploration (the Europeanization of jazz) that he eschewed in his departure from the Modern Jazz Quartet. It seemingly opposes his resistance to the MJQ's turn to classical elements, which he had left behind in the mid-1950s. Ursula Broschke-Davis elaborates: "It is ironic that Kenny had to leave a black jazz group and the cradle of black music to go to Europe to play the music he loved—the music that 'swings.' But the fact was that American jazz musicians black and white were trying to Europeanize jazz. On the other hand, European jazz lovers were searching for the true soul of jazz" (53). At least they were until the end of my period of study in 1963. But it appears that not only European fans, musicians, and critics had expanded their perception of jazz; Clarke had, too. Clarke's work with the C-BBB and his mentorship of French jazz musicians contributed to a universalist perspective similar to the avant-garde jazz musicians mentioned above.

Despite this era of expansion in the perceptions of jazz, jazz from its very beginnings had always signified freedom. As I have mentioned, during World War II fans the world over had clung to jazz as a symbol of the struggle for freedom by African Americans and a signal that they, too, could survive. Another way that the word *universal* frames this chapter is in the shared desire for human rights espoused by all the African American artists featured herein. Similarly, Kenny Clarke's primary motivation for migration to Paris was the hope for respect, humanity, and access to universal rights.

African American cultural historian Robin D.G. Kelley discusses this shared frustration of seeking freedom in the United States and the dream to move to a better place: "At least in our minds, we joined a long line of black thinkers who believed that to achieve freedom we first had to get out of Dodge" (*Freedom* 16). Here Kelley references the desire by African American intellectuals to leave behind the restraints of the United States and find a homeland in Africa. Though the homeland I reference is Paris, the sentiment of feeling excluded and needing to "get out of Dodge" to better assess the United States is the same. This mentality seems somewhat universal among African American intellectuals, especially James Baldwin and Richard Wright.

In a letter to Mrs. Shelton in 1951, Wright articulates a positive view of the Cold War from the isolation of his Parisian setting: "My main point is that the few paltry grants of freedom which white Americans allow Negroes today come from outside pressure and not from their belief in American ideals" (Wright, personal letter 2–3). In this sense universalism conveys the shared ideal of Paris as a color-blind haven and a way to prompt change in the United States through cultural competition and success away from home.

The term *universal* also articulates common experiences of blackness and political movements that articulate and act on shared racialized oppressions. Paris has historically served as a conducive site for discussions about global black consciousness and for proposing unified activities and actions. Noted African American writer, intellectual, and sociologist W. E. B. Du Bois and member of the French Parliament from Senegal Blaise Diagne organized the first Pan-African Congress in 1919. It would spur additional meetings throughout the world thereafter. In 1935 the poets and one-day politicians Aimé Césaire from Martinique, Léon Damas of Senegal, and Léopold Sédar Senghor from French Guyana met while studying in Paris; there they commenced the first issue of the literary journal *L'étudiant noir* (The black student). The journal created an important space for discussion about global black consciousness. Additionally, with his 1939 book *Cahier d'un retour au pays natal* (Notebook of a return to the native land) Césaire introduced the concept of *négritude*. All three would contribute a perspective. While differing in their particular uses of the term, they all employed *négritude* to promote pride in blackness, desire for unified action by people of African descent, and characterization of blackness as beautiful, powerful, and connected to the earth and nature.

The impact of negritude transcended the 1930s and 1940s and influenced those hoping to effect black autonomy, power, and freedom in the Francophone world and globally. While Kenny Clarke did not affiliate himself with particular political parties or causes, his actions and words paralleled certain political strides toward universal blackness.

In the aforementioned examples *universal* has represented aspects of race and ethnicity. But it has also performed an erasure, or at least a masking, of ethnic distinction. Changes in immigration policies spurred by the end of the war contributed to a more ethnically diverse population in continental France. In her book about migrant rights in the French republic Mary Lewis explains the motivation for this increased immigration:

> Reviving democracy and the promise of universal liberty and equality became vital to the task of post-war reconstruction. Migration policy, too, was overhauled. Or so it seems from a superficial glance: Regulations now explicitly aimed at encouraging permanent immigration, not just temporary migration, and a new National Immigration Office was founded to coordinate policy among ministries. . . . While all modern democratic republics claim liberty and equality before the law as core political principles, republican rhetoric in France implies that these are more perfectly realized there than elsewhere, for the republic recognizes no differences among its citizens. In short, France's republic is "one and

indivisible" because all those things that breed division are deemed irrelevant to public life. (243)

World War II and the resulting wars of independence from Indochina and Algeria most prominently changed the ethnic makeup of the French republic. In this breakdown of the French Empire came ripples of conflict, prejudice, and divisiveness not just in former French colonies but in the metropole as well. The Paris Massacre on October 17, 1961, was one example of a lack of tolerance building to the brink and leading to blood in the streets. Kenny Clarke was an immigrant in the midst of this turmoil of an "indivisible" France. Perhaps his life there was one of privilege. For his jazz experience and American citizenship distinguished him from others. But he was also distinguished as a racialized other assimilating into a French republic, which had been reinvigorated by universal policies yet ethnically embattled by the hypocrisy of its universal values.

Last, my primary use of *universal* is perhaps the most obvious; that is, *Jazz Is Universal.* The album symbolized diversity in ethnic backgrounds and musical experiences in the C-BBB, but it could also serve as a capstone in Clarke's thirty years of mentoring and collaborating with European and American musicians that further contributed to the globalization of jazz. This spread of jazz recordings, concerts, and musical skill started long before his migration in 1956; it built on multiple connections between French fans and musicians and touring and residing musicians like Clarke.

"RUE CHAPTAL (ROYAL ROOST)": KENNY CLARKE'S FRENCH BEBOP CONNECTION

Clarke first demonstrated his admiration for Paris in a major way with the 1946 bebop hit "Rue Chaptal (Royal Roost)." Fresh from military service and still living in the United States, he connected two locales in jazz history. With "Rue Chaptal (Royal Roost)" he put Paris on the map as a prominent jazz hot spot by using a French title, spotlighting the Hot Club of France headquarters and spurring jazz production in France. "Rue Chaptal (Royal Roost)" was a single on the album *Epistrophy,* recorded by Clarke and his 52nd Street Boys in New York City. The album became a cutting-edge standard of the bebop style. It was also Charles Delaunay's opportunity to introduce the French to bebop, after jazz production and distribution had lapsed during World War II. Recorded in New York but issued only in Europe at the time, "Rue Chaptal (Royal Roost)" was just one example of how Clarke was beginning to position jazz and himself in France.

The song was known by most as "Royal Roost," and it was named for a club featuring bebop jazz in 1940s New York. The eponymous club was located at 1580 Broadway and featured everyone from Charlie "Bird" Parker to Max Roach. Bebop at the Royal Roost was so noteworthy that the venue was named Bop City in the 1950s (Cahn).

Along with "Salt Peanuts," a joint composition by Clarke and Gillespie that agitated divisions between French jazz fans with its 1947 export, "Rue Chaptal (Royal Roost)" spurred many other encounters between bebop and the French. Clarke would soon get an opportunity to tour in France when he finally met Delaunay during a European tour, as part of Gillespie's seventeen-person big band. It proved to be a watershed moment in the history of jazz in France, when Gillespie's big band toured Nice and Paris in 1948. This tour introduced the bebop style and its post-1942 innovations, on which France had largely missed out because of the war and the geographical divide. Plus, Delaunay's promotion of the Parisian concert competed with the first jazz festival after the war in Nice. (Louis Armstrong was a headliner, and it represented more traditional jazz.) Yet the 1948 concerts left French fans in awe and furthered the schism between those who liked traditional jazz and those who preferred the modern bebop style (Delaunay, *Delaunay's* 171–72). It was also a moving moment for the African American musicians performing.[4] Pianist John Lewis described it as "one of the best performances and experiences of [his] life" (Gillespie and Fraser 333–34). Kenny Clarke had played with the band from October 1947 through February 1948. "Kenny called it the 'highlight' of his career; he felt that it was one of the major reasons why he was so well received in Europe and it contributed to his decision to settle permanently in Paris eight years later," writes Ursula Broschke-Davis (50).

Some of the sharp and memorable reactions to bebop were due to its differences from other jazz genres. Bebop was different from earlier styles like swing, since it could never be labeled simply "dance" music. Bebop could be too quick to spur dancing. It was complicated and challenged the best musicians to maintain the pace and complex rhythms. "Radical changes in the rhythmic foundation, in particular the more aggressive and polyrhythmic role of the drummer, make bebop distinct," writes Scott DeVeaux (*Birth* 218).

Bop drumming was unique in a few different ways: "the first was the consistent use of the ride cymbal to create a wash of sound within the ensemble; second was the gradual removal of the bass drum from its timekeeping role; and third, the evolution of coordinated independence" (Owens 180). As part of the regular crew of Minton's playhouse until 1944, Clarke had performed alongside Charlie Christian, Charlie Parker, and Dizzy Gillespie, among others, to create the bebop genre. He innovated a bebop drumming style that maintained a "shimmering pulse on the ride cymbal, occasionally punctuated by vigorous accents on the bass and snare drums" (DeVeaux, *Birth* 218). Clarke was known for his minimalist, two-beat rhythms and brushes that allowed the soloists more free-play (494). In honor of Clarke at his death, music and cultural critic Stanley Crouch encapsulated Clarke's style: "Clarke's approach was light, crisp, and more varied in its responses to the horns than the heavier tuning and the restrictive role of other drummers. Since he kept the pulse on the cymbal, his left hand was free to work out spontaneous rhythm enlargements that he often coordinated with his bass drum" (50).

With his distinctive bebop drumming style, experience in the cutting contests and concerts at 1942 Minton's Playhouse, and French-bound recordings in the mid-1940s, there was no doubt that Kenny Clarke was the perfect representative of bebop. Beyond his skill and experience, however, Clarke's racial background also played a role in French perceptions of bebop. The seventeen-strong band showcased primarily African American musicians, except for musicians like the Afro-Cuban percussionist Chano Pozo.[5] Clarke and his bandmates were put on a pedestal for this difference, creating a stir of excitement and tension in white French audiences, who did not find the same skill level in French jazz production. The composition of the band visually seemed to affirm essentialist and primitivist beliefs that had long held sway among French jazz critics.

Many French jazz critics already believed blacks had an inherent ability to perform jazz better than whites. This essentialist mentality undergirded primitivist perspectives that African American musicians were exotic, primitive, and led by simplistic, natural instincts in contrast to the complex mechanization of the industrial world.[6] Essentialist claims emphasized the importance of legitimizing jazz, of locating and promoting "authentic" jazz. Both Hugues Panassié and Boris Vian believed that blacks possess an "instinctive feeling," an inherent soulful quality, that allows them to create the best music (Panassié, *The Real Jazz* 21; Vian, "50 Years" 61–62). As we have seen, Vian, who also played jazz trumpet, was convinced that he and other white musicians could not rise to the same excellence as African American musicians (Zwerin, *Round* 46). Other critics in this period, however, tried to move past essentialist claims. Charles Delaunay promoted jazz as universally identifiable by all people and advocated French jazz musicians as progressing in their path to authentic jazz (Delaunay, "Faut" 18; "Delaunay in Trenches" 6).

The very ideological bent of the bebop genre also contributed to a racialized reading of the music by French fans. Bebop represented a subversion of jazz musical traditions and political dissent against the U.S. status quo of segregation and racism. Amiri Baraka writes: "The period that saw bebop develop, during and after World War II, was a very unstable time for most Americans. There was a need for radical readjustment to the demands of the postwar world. The riots through the country appear as directly related to the psychological tenor of that time as the emergence of the 'new' music" (*Blues People* 210). Not only was the U.S. a major world power struggling to expand its world leadership and power; it also struggled at including African Americans as equals in U.S. society.

Before its quick rise to overt commercialism and mainstream acceptance, bebop (like jazz itself) was avant-garde and pushed boundaries. Beboppers scoffed at playing to elite audience tastes and making danceable music; instead, they offered up a "sharp and, to many, an uncomfortable edge" in their performances (Ramsey, *Race* 106). This edge and sharpness was a result of experimenting musicians attempting to move past the obvious, tried-and-true characteristics of jazz with their playing. Bebop also countered the icon of the amenable musician with that of a cool, knowing musician who used music as a weapon. In "Double V, Double-Time: Bebop's Politics of Style" Eric Lott explains: "Bebop was about making disciplined imagination alive and answerable to the social change of its time. . . . Militancy and music were undergirded by the same social facts; the music attempted to resolve at the level of style what the militancy combated in the streets" (457).

So bebop resisted the American mainstream and preceding musical genres in multiple ways. The musical form kept the music avant-garde for a while; the sheer speed of most bebop disqualified everyone but the most adept and creative of musicians. The militant nature of the music countered the happy-go-lucky caricature of the black entertainer. The music also challenged people to do more than dance. For as Clarke once said, "There was a message to our music. . . . The idea was to wake up, look around you, there's something to do" (DeVeaux, *Birth* 251). Baraka also recalls the emotional impact yet political salience of bebop: "There was in all of the Bop that grabbed me that quality of high intelligence being transmitted. Brought home with the flailing emotion of the music. . . . Not only did the music get down and through me at an intense emotional level, even an intense physical level, but it carried ideas. Heavy ideas" (*Digging* 225). Bebop offered a confident, complicated, and unforgiving resistance against racism and racial injustice. It was a music that moved people intellectually and spurred movement politically.

Cultural critic Scott Saul argues that hard bop, a subgenre of bebop, acted as an important musical voice in the civil rights protests of the 1960s. The subgenre emphasized brass instruments, drew on elements of soul and R&B, and in several cases featured hard-hitting, assertive drumming. David Rosenthal points out that some hard boppers created songs with emotive interpretations and slow and moody tempos as well (Rosenthal 44–45). Saul describes hard bop's ideological signification as freedom music: "Like the movement it grounded new appeals for freedom in older idioms of black spirituality, challenging the nation's public account of itself and testifying to the black community's cultural power. And, like the movement again it worked through a kind of orchestrated disruption—a musical version of what civil rights workers called 'direct action,' which jazz musicians experienced as a rhythmic assertiveness and a newly taut relationship between the demands of composition and the possibilities of improvisation" (Saul 2–3). For its correlations to "direct action" and aggression bebop (and hard bop with it) had a reputation of being unpatriotic. Because of its connotations of subversion, nonconformity, and overt resistance, some critics and fans perceived bebop as fighting against American values rather than trying to repair the breaks in American democracy. Dizzy Gillespie disputed the perception "that beboppers tended to express unpatriotic attitudes regarding segregation, economic injustice, and the American way of life.... Damn right! We refused to accept racism, poverty, or economic exploitation, nor would we live out uncreative humdrum lives merely for the sake of survival. But there was nothing unpatriotic about it. If America wouldn't honor its Constitution and respect us as men, we couldn't give a shit about the American way. And they made it damn near un-American to appreciate our music" (Gillespie and Fraser 287).

Gillespie's comment alludes to several important points regarding Kenny Clarke and other African American boppers who migrated to Europe. Migrating abroad could hold more weight and be more temptation for the bebop musician, like Clarke, who felt the weight of negative nationalist societal judgments in addition to dealing with racism. The bebop musician may have desired the great attention paid to this music outside the United States, particularly given the battles between New Orleans–style jazz and bebop fans that still brewed and in contrast to perceptions of bebop's lack of patriotism in the United States. This draw to migration may have expanded particularly as the 1950s came and went and France (still behind musically because of the war) was diligently playing and learning bebop. Gillespie also links bebop to the life of the African American musician. He suggests that performing bebop was not just "survival" but active resistance against "economic exploitation" in the jazz industry and racism in the States.

Performing the music and certainly disseminating it (with the aforementioned connotations and functions bebop performed) was a political act of dissent against economic and sociocultural inequities experienced by African Americans in the United States.

The 1948 French tours with Gillespie and Clarke showed the success of African Americans in performing, traveling, and innovating with bebop. It illustrated the achievements and further potential of the musicians and the music, unbound by "restrictive bonds of ethnicity" in Gilroy's terms. As Clarke enjoyed experiences of great reception and revisited the place he'd dreamed of and positively recalled after tours, he would not escape experiences of prejudice or pressures of civil rights engagement. Racialized differentiation and oppression persisted in France. It was just of a different stripe.

JAZZ, A PATH TO UNIVERSAL BLACKNESS?

"Why don't you learn French, dirty nigger?" shouted a fan at Gillespie's big band during the 1948 jazz festival (Hennessey, *Klook* 81). French jazz history has mostly overlooked or overwritten this moment of racial discord. Accounts from African American and French musicians alike have romanticized the import of these concerts. The invasion of jazz in France did stir up tensions in the French crowd because of its musical differences—it also stirred up age-old racial prejudices and stereotypes.

The above epithet uncannily recalls the opening of Frantz Fanon's seminal essay "The Fact of Blackness" in his 1952 book *Black Skin, White Masks*. A black psychiatrist and intellectual, Fanon details the psychological effects of colonization on French of African descent in Martinique. Born in 1925 Martinique, Fanon received his training in 1940s France and worked in Algeria in the mid-1950s during its War of Independence. In war-torn Algeria he wrote *The Wretched of the Earth* in 1961 and explored the identification of blackness, specifically in the context of the white French and their colonists. In *Black Skin, White Masks* he described the ways that French of African descent were marked and objectified in his native Martinique: "'Dirty nigger!' Or simply, 'Look a Negro!' I came into the world imbued with the will to find a meaning in things . . . and then I found that I was an object in the midst of other objects. Sealed into that crushing objecthood, I turned beseechingly to others. . . . The movements, the attitudes, the glances of the other fixed me there, in the sense in which a chemical solution is fixed by a dye. I was indignant; I demanded an explanation. Nothing happened" (257). Here Fanon describes how blackness is read on his body, suggesting that the stares fix him into place. As the other reads blackness on his body, he loses his ability to move without recognition and his freedom to assign his own meanings to his own body. The looks are based on skin color and promote the subordination of blackness to whiteness. Fanon comes to the realization that the black man cannot alter this objectification. His difference will always be perceived, and his blackness will always be considered in relation to whiteness.

Fanon's experience deconstructs the signification of blackness and the internalization of this difference by both the viewer and the viewed. In his perspective blackness is created through whiteness, held inferior in relation to whiteness, and made ugly, animalistic, and unintelligent in comparison; this blackness is called out based on a folklore made up of a racialized history of stories, stereotypes, and fetishism that all merge to create this portrait of the black man as other.

Growing up in colonized Martinique Fanon perceived himself as French. His life in Martinique offered some geographic distinction from continental France but not difference in national pride or belonging. He embraced that national identity while also learning from poet and politician Aimé Césaire about negritude as a high school student. He balanced both French Caribbean and African identities in his perception of self. But Fanon's experiences changed. In *Black Skin, White Masks* he documents the rampant racism he later experienced under George Robert's Vichy regime from 1940 to 1943 in Martinique; the distinction was also made that Robert and the surge of French settlers he brought were much more prejudiced and degrading in their treatment of Martiniquais of African descent than French living on the continent (Macey 14–15).

Fanon willingly left Martinique when given the opportunity to fight for the Free French Forces during the war. He thought he would be supporting a cause against racism and fascism. After being sent to Algeria to receive officer's training, his perspective changed. In "Frantz Fanon, the Resistance, and the Emergence of Identity Politics" Dennis McEnnerney explains: "Although Fanon believed he was equal to other French citizens, he learned unhappily during the Second World War that he was French *and* an 'inferior' other. Working through the experience of the internal resistance after the war, he then learned how to understand the difficulty of resisting the fantastic republican universalism that obscured French racism" (McEnnerney 275).

I have gone into detail about Fanon because his writing identified and denounced racism specifically as experienced by the colonized. His writing made links between the different treatment of Caribbeans of African descent, Africans, and African Americans. His work also contributed to a call for universal blackness—that is, a united front in articulating the value of blackness and pondering the causes and effects of this racialized difference.

The differentiation of blackness, this making and seeing different and therefore living different, was internalized by Kenny Clarke, too. In his 1980s interviews with Ursula Broschke-Davis, Clarke revealed his disillusionment and reconciliation of a division between whites and blacks and between Westerners and those of African descent. "There is no room for blackness in the Western world," he commented (61). Broschke-Davis also shared his perceptions of African Americans as "aliens"; she added, "He saw the solution in the individual; all the individual can do is find a spot for himself as an outsider" (61). This contrasted greatly with Clarke's persistent dreams of Paris as the place to be and his identification of Paris as a place of escape from exploitation. Fanon and Clarke shared a similar view about the impossibility of exceeding racial constraints in France.

Despite the similar prejudices and perspectives these two populations of African descent endured, for the most part African Americans in post–World War II Paris did not protest the mistreatment of French of African descent. Didier Gondola presents examples of key African American figures, like W. E. B. Du Bois, who conveniently never mentioned racism against the Senegalese. While writing for *Crisis,* the official magazine of the NAACP that he had founded, Du Bois advocated diversity within French troops, but he turned a blind eye to the minimal training given to the Senegalese (Gondola 207). This seems particularly bizarre since these colonized people were fighting for the same freedoms that African Americans sought in Paris.

As a journalist for Johnson publications, William Gardner Smith had to translate reports of violence against Algerians. His job put him in direct contact with ills in French society. Author of *From Harlem to Paris: Black American Writers in France, 1840–1980,* Michel Fabre describes the identification and latent political support that Gardner Smith had with Algerian victims of police brutality and prejudice: "The dark-skinned expatriates were gradually led to take the side of the Algerian 'rebels' with whom the police tended to confuse them when checking papers in the streets, before respectfully glancing at their U.S. passports. Smith refrained from airing his views in interviews. He would have run the risk of losing his job and being expelled from the country for interfering in French politics. Yet his sympathies, like those of Gibson [writer], Wright [writer], Harrington [cartoonist], and many other brothers, were with the Algerians" (Fabre, *From Harlem* 248–49).

It is interesting that primarily writers protested the French treatment of its colonists in this postwar era. The journal *Présence Africaine* and the first

Congrès des écrivains et artistes noirs (Conference of Negro-African Writers and Artists) that it promoted in 1956 created literary and physical spaces for dialogue about global black consciousness. With the combined support of African and African American scholars—such as Aimé Césaire, Léopold Sédar Senghor, Alioune Diop, Richard Wright, and James Baldwin—these organizations and movements spoke of universal injustices and hoped to mobilize people of African descent from all around the world.[7] At the 1956 conference Césaire summed it up well: "'No one is suggesting that there is such a thing as a pure race. . . . We are not Negroes by our own desire, but, in effect, because of Europe. What unites all Negroes is the injustices they have suffered at European hands" (quoted in Baldwin, *Nobody* 168–69).

But African American musicians tended to avoid the fracas. Kenny Clarke told Ursula Broschke Davis, "It's nothing I can do about it. So I just follow my line. I know no white society is going to really accept a black man, so I just stay out of it" (Broschke-Davis 58). So Clarke did not speak out. He had reconciled himself to the fact that there would always be inequality. Except for Louis Armstrong, who signed a letter of support for the 1956 Congrès des écrivains et artistes noirs, I have found few examples of African American jazz musicians participating in political dialogues about shared experiences of racism and political dissent with French of African descent (Jules-Rosette, *Black Paris* 50).

In glaring contrast the 1950s and 1960s were decades that particularly showcased jazz protest songs about racial inequality in the United States: some about civil rights conflicts and some making connections to Africa as a spiritual and ideological home for African Americans. Songs like Louis Armstrong's "Black and Blue" and Billie Holiday's "Strange Fruit" had in the interwar period drawn on jazz to critique U.S. race relations, but the postwar period was littered with more politically motivated musical outbursts. In 1957 Charles Mingus wrote "Fables of Faubus" to protest the actions of Arkansas governor Orval Faubus, who in the same year had used the National Guard to bar African American students from entering the Central High School of Little Rock ("With an Even Hand"). The lyrics of the song were so explicitly critical that Columbia Records refused to publish them:

> Oh Lord, don't let 'em shoot us!
> Oh Lord, don't let 'em stab us!
> Oh Lord, don't let 'em tar and feather us!
> Oh Lord, no more swastikas!
> Oh Lord, no more Ku Klux Klan!

Columbia did release the instrumental version in 1959, but "Fables of Faubus" was not recorded with vocals until 1960 on the independent label Candid ("With an Even Hand"; Proyect).

With the 1960 album *We Insist: Freedom Now Suite* fellow drummer Max Roach and vocalist Abbey Lincoln landed a visual and aural punch at instigators of racialized violence. The album cover showed African American men sitting at the lunch counter and waiting to be served by a white American waiter. The cover illustrated the antithesis of Jim Crow justice, which outlawed African Americans from entering the front door and sitting in the same sections with white Americans. In one song, "Triptych: Prayer, Protest, Peace," Lincoln's vocal interpretation ranged from moans to screams, effectively eliciting emotion in the listener and signifying slavery—or bondage at the very least.

In 1963 saxophonist John Coltrane kept alive the memory of four African American girls in his song "Alabama." He musically mourned their death from the Ku Klux Klan's bombing of Birmingham's 16th Street Baptist Church. In 1964 Nina Simone angrily sang about church bombings, too, and a catalogue of other things from search dogs to the assassination of Medgar Evers in Jackson, Mississippi, that inspired the song "Mississippi Goddam."

The mid-1960s, with their musical protests and Martin Luther King Jr.'s March on Washington, were a watershed moment in the civil rights movement. The desire to return to the United States and articulate dissent through march, speeches, and song pulled heavy on many African American artists who decided to return. Ingrid Monson writes of an obligation, what she terms "a culture of commitment," that was felt by many African American musicians on the front lines of marches (*Freedom* 217). She describes their hesitancy in marching but their great attention to fund-raising events instead:

> Although jazz musicians were among the most active supporters of civil rights causes and were substantially more outspoken than R&B musicians in the early 1960s, they were nevertheless notably absent from the front lines of the Southern grassroots civil rights campaigns. . . . One exception to this trend was Billy Taylor's participation in "Salute to Freedom '63" in Birmingham, Alabama, in August 1963. The concert, which featured Ray Charles, Johnny Mathis, Billy Taylor, and Nina Simone, drew some fifteen thousand people to benefit the SCLC, SNCC, NAACP, CORE, NUL, and NALC. . . . In many ways, benefit concerts offered a relatively easy form of activism. Musicians could contribute to the cause by allowing the civil rights movement to capitalize on the cultural prestige of their music. (Monson, *Freedom* 218–20)

Being away from the States had to put even more pressure on those abroad. At least it did for James Baldwin. He put an ad in the *International Herald Tribune* to advertise a meeting in support of conducting a civil rights march in Paris, in support of the upcoming March on Washington on August 28, 1963. The ad produced a group meeting of two hundred African American artists led by the actor William Marshall. The group discussed the possibilities of a march and sit-in and produced a petition in support of the march and published it in Anglophone newspapers. The petition was also sent all across Europe and gained 550 names. The march did not take place because of the challenge of applying for official permission and other laws for peaceful protest. But on August 21, 1963, Baldwin did walk along with a smaller group of approximately eighty to one hundred others, including William Marshall, blues singer and pianist Memphis Slim, jazz pianist Hazel Scott, and jazz clarinetist and saxophonist Mezz Mezzrow, to deliver the petition to the American embassy. A few days later Baldwin returned to the States to support the March on Washington (Dudziak, *Cold War* 189–91).

But some African American artists, like Kenny Clarke, remained in France. They did not dissent—at least not in an overt fashion. Ralph Ellison explains that beboppers were not ultrapolitical to begin with, "whatever their musical intentions—and they were the least political of men" ("The Blues"). Kenny Clarke was neither vocally nor lyrically a political exponent of negritude, Black Nationalism, or civil rights marches. But his success with an all-black band and his ability to disseminate and fuel interest in bebop in Europe (when interest was moving in other directions in the United States) was a political act of protest. My point is akin to Tyler Stovall's key motivation and argument in *Paris Noir: African Americans in the City of Light*. Noting that much discourse discusses blackness as a problem, Stovall writes to elaborate on the "success story" of the black community in Paris from the late nineteenth century to the late twentieth (xv). *Paris Noir* acts as the antithesis of the American dream, showing that blacks left America to achieve upward mobility and in some cases found it (xv–xvi). Clarke's "success story" performs political change. The French jazz fan's desire to learn bebop further affirms its worthiness as an art form. The invitations for Clarke and others to come teach jazz rhythms positions these musicians at a higher status, as mentors. Clarke and the African American bebop musicians were sought out for their superior skill and knowledge rather than seen as inferior, as jazz music had been perceived in its earlier days. In the years to come Clarke would integrate this once "black music" into the French musical mainstream. Perhaps musical assimilation could lead to social integration, forwarding not only universal jazz but also universal rights.

OUR MAN IN PARIS: THE ASSIMILATION OF BEBOP AND KENNY CLARKE IN FRANCE

> He is something of a celebrity in Paris, particularly so in St. Germain, the students' quarter. And he's most accessible to his admirers. People of all kinds waved, shouted greetings, or stopped to speak with "Kennee" at a sidewalk café facing Club St. Germain, the night club where the Clarke group appears six nights a week to the delight of Parisian jazz fans and visiting tourists. First an African engaged the drummer in conversation about his work problems. A little later, a svelte, well-formed young woman slowed down for a "hallo" before continuing on her undulating way. A French musician stopped to question Clarke about a forthcoming recording session and then inquired where the drummer planned to spend his next four-week vacation. It all struck a familiar chord. The scene was out of a typical Warner Bros. picture, vintage 1930s, when the show-business celebrity or champion boxer or top-level hood or successful trial lawyer returns to "the old neighborhood," usually on New York City's lower east side. The only difference was the locale—and that the people treat Klook this way all the time.
>
> BURT KORALL

Our Man in Paris came out in 1963 and featured saxophonist Dexter Gordon, Kenny Clarke, pianist Bud Powell, and bassist Pierre Michelot. While Gordon graced the album cover, the title *Our Man in Paris* may have more accurately applied to Clarke, who had risen to the top of the Parisian jazz scene after his return in 1956. In 2003 the radio program *France Culture* produced a three-part radio series called *Jazz à Paris, années 50*. In the first episode, "La batteur Kenny Clarke," host Alain Gerber described the contributions of Clarke and Bechet as "centrale de la vie musicale" (central to musical life). Although the two musicians differed in personality and musical genre, they both immersed themselves in the French jazz industry. They taught, mentored, were sought after, rarely had trouble getting gigs, and were well known and beloved in the Parisian jazz community. But it was Clarke who became a conduit for the assimilation of bebop through his recordings, mentoring, collaborations, and desire to assimilate into French culture.

Clarke's dedication helped make France a home for jazz—so much so that he was no less a star than Bechet. Dizzy Gillespie once remarked: "I don't *think* Kenny is doing better in Europe than he would be over here. I *know* so. He could not get that kind of money here. I know so. He records in Europe—that's where he lives. And everybody respects him over there. . . . He is the king" (Broschke-Davis 55).

Clarke felt that Europeans treated artists differently, offering them the respect and money that they deserved, and many shared the belief. Saxophonist Johnny Griffin was a fellow C-BBB bandmate of Clarke's and expressed similar motivations for his migration to Paris and then later to Rotterdam, Germany: "The way people treated black musicians—or jazz musicians in general—was comparable to the respect they accord to classical artists. Coming back to New York, I ran into the same old hassles; . . . I'd enjoyed a period of relaxation and felt I could have a more dignified life in Europe, so I took off in the summer of 1963" (Moody 66).

The return of Clarke went a long way in improving the French knowledge of rhythm. Delaunay had identified the end of the war as the turning point in French musicians' understanding of the syncopated rhythms of jazz; he was constantly inviting Clarke and other African Americans to stay in France and teach them (Delaunay, "Preliminary"). For, as I noted in chapter 2, one has to have a strong understanding of time-keeping in order to depart from it. Clarke's style provided soloists and ensembles with the steady time they needed but also avoided crowding the soloist, giving him or her more freedom to experiment (Thigpen 17). His drumming influence extended to those with whom he played. *Jazz Magazine* critic Frank Ténot explains: "In France, he helped raise the level of our musicians. Moreover, we didn't know how to play the drums before he arrived. Those who listened to French jazz before were hit by the nice mediocrity of the rhythm sections" (Ténot, "Frankly" 34–35).[8] He also opened a drumming school at Conservatoire Saint-Germain-en-Lays from approximately 1967 to 1972, and he created an innovative method for drumming that is still in practice today (Haggerty, "Under Paris" 200; L. Clarke). Clarke provided the French with a skill that they needed and pursued.

But Clarke's tutelage went beyond the drumming school. He used the Blue Note as a home base, where he could be contacted and queried about such things as teaching stints at universities and mentoring of young French musicians (Haggerty, "Under Paris" 209). He served as an unofficial teacher, playing with the best young musicians in France, including French bassist Pierre Michelot, Algerian pianist and composer Martial Solal, and French pianist René Urtreger. He helped cast the spotlight on primarily French jazz bands, boosted the confidence of European jazz musicians, and helped transform the perception of French jazz musicianship following

World War II, and his collaboration with Delaunay made a substantial impact in the French recording industry.

Delaunay's Vogue label featured Clarke as the central figure in its bebop production. Clarke played with French and American musicians on fourteen of the recordings for the label from 1948 to 1951. His contribution accounted for 25 percent of the total recordings produced by Vogue in that era (Tournès 226). Clarke worked with a myriad of producers and musicians throughout his career, and he avoided teaming up with any one person. But his work with Delaunay was pivotal in the introduction and development of bebop in France.

Most impressive was the multitude of musicians Clarke played with and mentored. He played as house drummer for the Blue Note and Club Saint-Germain and was also the drummer for the Blue Note band nicknamed Les Trois Patrons (The three bosses). This trio included several combinations, but the most prominent was arguably Clarke on drums, African American Bud Powell on piano, and white French bassist Pierre Michelot (Hennessey, *Klook* 137).[9] The band kept the Blue Note swinging from 1959 to 1960 and was one of the most memorable of Clarke's collaborations.

The creative production in this golden age of Paris was disproportionate to the actual number of jazz musicians living there. In our 2005 interview Laurent Clarke suggested that the teachings of this tight-knit group (which tended to attract and play with top-notch stars) ultimately expanded the opportunities of jazz production in France. Paris became known for creating collaborations, and Clarke was in the thick of those collaborations.

His most famous collaboration was for the soundtrack of Louis Malle's film *Ascenseur pour l'échafaud* (Lift to the scaffold), which was first recorded in December 1957. Miles Davis was already visiting Paris and playing at clubs with Clarke, Barney Willen, Pierre Michelot, and René Urtreger and would bring them along on the film soundtrack. Boris Vian put Davis in touch with Malle and Jeanne Moreau, and they devised the first nonscripted and improvised film soundtrack (Tournès 313). Davis's process of watching the film—and spontaneously generating mood for the music—was inspired by a similar soundtrack project done by The Jazz Messengers the year before; both succeeded in changing the role of jazz musicians as subordinate characters in films, giving them behind-the-scenes authority to improvise and create a mood for soundtracks (Hennessey, *Klook* 129–30; Michelot).

The result was a spontaneous and powerful performance that far outlived production of the film noir–style movie. There was no standout attention by film media to the common film noir style and plot, even though

Malle won the prestigious Louis Delluc prize for the film. The actual sound-track would get rave reviews, however. Clarke was forever tied to this groundbreaking album.

One could argue that Clarke trained French musicians as a means of survival—that is, in order to have solid bandmates to better secure and sustain gigs. But I think he desired to bridge the gap between American and European play. He persuaded, welcomed, and kept time with many visiting American musicians. As house drummer for the Blue Note in the 1950s, he played with such greats as Chet Baker, Lester Young, Don Byas, Lee Konitz, and Stan Getz (Hennessey, *Klook* 137–38). One French musician in his house band, René Urtreger, recalled to me Clarke's popularity and big draw appeal: "He was the person who made the famous people come . . . like Sonny Stead, Dexter Gordon, Lester Young. . . . They knew, everybody knew who Kenny was" (Urtreger). Clarke's recognized stature, popularity, and experience as a veteran all contributed to his creation of a diverse jazz community in Paris, which further enhanced the education of young French jazz musicians.

In Paris Clarke also found what he needed to finally settle down. He married Daisy Wallback, his Dutch love, and they settled together in a house in 1962. They welcomed a son, Laurent Salaam-Clarke, into the world in 1964. Each of these actions says much about his desire to become a working and paying member of French society (Hennessey, *Klook* 145, 151). Most significant, he purchased a home. Many of the musicians I have interviewed and studied did not stay in France, save up sufficient funds, or want to pay for a house. But Clarke really wanted to settle down. His biographer, Michael Hennessey, recounts how Clarke saved his low wages until he was finally able to afford a house in the Paris suburb Montreuil-sous-Bois (145). With his home, marriage, and new son Clarke was fulfilling his dreams and expectations of Paris.

He also began to be perceived as French by others. Fellow African American jazz musicians and Paris residents trumpeter Benny Bailey and saxophonist Donald Byrd discussed their memories of him: "Of course, he became the man in Europe. He had known Paris since the thirties and he had absorbed the culture, the way of life," said Byrd (quoted in Hennessey, *Klook* 232). Bailey added: "I have this memory of him appreciating the comfort of his nice little house in Paris, smoking his pipe and enjoying a glass of wine" (quoted in Hennessey, *Klook* 228).

Clarke's acculturation in France was uncommon, because he learned the language well. He not only collaborated with the French publicly, but he also interacted with them on a daily basis in his private life. In addition he raised his child in the French school system and in the suburbs outside Paris, where people spoke little English. Though many African Americans who migrated to France married Europeans, most failed to master the French language and did not venture far from their Parisian neighborhoods. Clarke's life was different in that he did not superficially migrate to France. His heart, affairs, and interests were firmly embedded there.

But Clarke was also still *our man* in Paris. He was still very strongly tied to his African American heritage and personified American jazz. He may have bitterly migrated from the United States, but he still cared about the people and the music scene he'd left behind. Though he refused to be politically vocal about the civil rights movement, he revealed: "I must admit that I'm not interested in allying myself with causes. I'm a Negro; I know what's happening. I don't turn my back on realities because I'm 3,000 miles away. But . . . as far as I'm concerned, it's the music that's important. That's the legacy we leave behind" (Korall 17). He protested with his musical production. With songs like "American Rhythm: Klook Klux Klan" he could subtly protest from French shores without retribution.[10]

Actually, he helped expand the space for African American musicians in Paris. That space was originally carved out in the 1920s and created anew by the first African American musicians to migrate to Paris after World War II, like Don Byas and Inez Cavanaugh. Clarke drew in African American performers (e.g., Elvin Jones, Sonny Rollins, Ben Webster, and a young Nathan Davis) with job opportunities, introduced them to the greater freedoms and opportunities in France, and made sure they had a place to settle and some food (Hennessey, *Klook* 138–39, 147). He became a mentor and friend to Nathan Davis immediately when Davis arrived in 1962. Clarke even encouraged Davis to return to the United States in 1969 in order to accept the opportunity to teach at the University of Pittsburgh; the closest Clarke ever came to moving back to the United States was in his brief teaching stints at the university at Davis's invitation—though Davis could not get him to make it a permanent visit (Moody 126–27). So Kenny Clarke helped to pave the way for many Americans, with his collaborative contacts, excellent skills, reputation, and generosity.

As "Our Man in Paris," Clarke made the French look good. His success in Paris added fodder to the illusion that Paris was a color-blind haven for African Americans. By supporting African American jazz musicians, French critics and fans saw themselves as advocating racial equality when the United States was failing in that arena. By doing so they could ignore their own racial prejudices and shift negative attention back to the United States. Many African Americans, including Clarke, played along with the illusion of Paris as a haven from overt racism perhaps to protect their unique liberties in this provisionary home (Stovall, *Paris Noir* 254).

Clarke occupied a privileged position, enjoying a *de jure* Europeanness. He was the privileged "other" standing in direct contrast to the black French. He attained a peaceful life, which was the antithesis of the powder keg times of French colonial battles and U.S. civil rights clashes. He did not compose songs that directly attacked the Algerian War of Independence or use music to assertively protest U.S. civil rights inequality. Despite his political inaction, he was aware of the imperfect and exclusive *liberté* of French society. He just believed the best he could do was to move out, to escape.

JAZZ IS UNIVERSAL

> Many young Afro-American musicians streamed into Paris in the mid-sixties. They were an angry generation. They felt that American black musicians were being exploited in Europe just as they had been in the United States. They claimed that the Afro-Americans had been hired to teach the Europeans to play jazz so they could establish their own jazz scene and build up their own jazz industry. The Europeans' intention, the blacks said, was to build European jazz stars, just as the intention of the American industry was to build white jazz stars.
>
> BROSCHKE-DAVIS

"Klook became a fairly regular commuter on the 7:43 a.m. Trans Europe Express from Paris to Cologne" (Hennessey, *Klook* 146). Germany was home to the C-BBB, and Clarke was on the road at least three times a month, often outside of French borders. Clarke's notoriety, networking, and support of African American musicians became a lifeline for jazz in a changing musical climate and with a growing focus on rock 'n' roll. Enticing other African Americans to the 1949 Paris Jazz Festival and to the Blue Note ensured fresh talent.

But it was not enough. Parisian clubs closed or morphed into discos in the late 1960s, and French musicians replaced many Americans as part of a French union quota instituted to ensure more opportunities for French musicians (Hennessey, *Klook* 154–55).[11] Bill Moody elaborates: "Union leaders Michel Hausser and Gil Lafite claimed they represented some fifty French musicians. Their campaign was based on a 1933 law that said foreigners must not represent more than 10 percent of a night spot band. The law also, however, provided for exceptions that allowed that number to increase to 30 percent" (62). Although the quota was dismissed by many French clubs (as they believed it hobbled the quality of their performances) and European jazz fans protested, it still threatened to change the face of jazz.

In the 1960s African American artists still drew big crowds, but the bitterness from French musicians could be felt even more. Nathan Davis recounted one signal experience he had: "Yeah, I remember one time I came off the bandstand just before it started. This one saxophone player came up to me, blocked my path, and said, 'You're taking work because you're black.' All that kind of stuff. It was really embarrassing because the club was crowded and Saturday night. I told him he could go and work in America if he wanted and mentioned some French musicians who had done so. 'Jean-Luc Ponty, Martial Solal, Michel Legrand, these cats work, so just go'" (Moody 128). With the increase in French jazz players and the crackdown by their union came diminished opportunities for other African American musicians residing in Paris—though Kenny Clarke was apparently still thriving. In response many jazz musicians (including Clarke) used Paris as a springboard for other hot spots like Berlin, Geneva, London, and Rome. When Clarke recorded *The Golden Eight* in 1961 with a group of eight international musicians, the ensuing opportunities and support resulted in the C-BBB.

The C-BBB became the epitome of racial and national collaboration in jazz production. Depending on the performance, it could cull thirteen to seventeen musicians from seven to twelve countries, including the United States, England, Austria, France, Turkey, Holland, Sweden, and Germany; Mike Hennessey once deemed the band "a miniature United Nations" (Hennessey, *Klook* 161–68; Hennessey, "Clarke-Boland" 22–24). The C-BBB was a big band of many talents, featuring multiple trumpets, saxophones, and even two drummers. In comparison to Gillespie's 1948 big band, African Americans made up a mere quarter of the personnel. The band included a fair number of Americans, but a variety of ethnicities were represented.

Clarke drew an amazing range of jazz musicians from around the world to Paris as a result of his collaborative contacts, excellent skills, and reputation. Bandmate Johnny Griffin described Clarke's role this way: "they had so much respect for Kenny Clarke—and that was an intensely unifying element. He was what you might call the uncommon denominator!" (Jewel).

The band's uniqueness, popularity, and musical distinction can also be attributed to its Belgian cofounder, Francy Boland. Boland was trained as a classical composer, but later on in his career he composed jazz songs, most notably for Count Basie and Glenn Miller (Brown). Boland scripted complex harmonic compositions that only the best could play. Benny Bailey described Boland's composition style: "Everything he writes seems so simple, so normal; but just try to dissect his colours and you end up pretty badly: all the secrets lie between the lines. It is the simplicity, the concentration on essentials, that is his strength" (Brown). *Jazz Is Universal* solidified his credibility as a composer who knew how to swing (Hennessey, "Clarke-Boland" 22). Fans could hear the influence and legacy of jazz—of Count Basie and Duke Ellington—in Boland's compositions. The band performed so well because of the wealth of talent on the table. Zoot Sims, Derek Humble, and Ake Persson had thriving careers of their own, and it took them all a year to finally set a recording date; yet when they came together, individual egos were lost (Jewel). Musically this band was so stunning because of its swinging double drum set—often featured at the end of concerts—and the synchronized five-sax solo that set apart the 1967 song and album *Sax No End*. Their sound was so complex, tight, energized, and rhythmically crazy that decades later it's still hot.

The C-BBB gathered most often in Cologne, Germany, to record, and they toured throughout Europe—from London to Prague—from 1961 until 1972. In eleven years the band recorded an unbelievable thirty-nine albums. Who knows how much longer they would have continued if not for money issues. As Michael Hennessey suggests, funding such a big band was costly; tellingly, they never made it to the United States for this reason ("Clarke-Boland" 24). Ironically, they were once sponsored by the U.S. State Department to perform in Spain, Belgium, and Sweden (Broschke-Davis 56).

The multinational, multiethnic, and multitalented makeup of the C-BBB challenged perceptions that "real" jazz was Americancentric or Afrocentric. As the liner notes professed, "Jazz is universal today. Everyone knows it, affirms it or writes it. This album is irrefutable proof" (Clark-Boland Big Band, *Jazz Is Universal* 24). The album proved that good jazz was not only housed in the United States. *Voice of America* radio host Willis Conover wrote: "Today the jazz language has become a *lingua franca* bypassing a score of spoken tongues. One of the happier aspects of this mission is the absence of conscious proselytizing: jazz, by its very existence, drew the world to itself" (quoted in Hennessey, "Clarke-Boland" 23). Conover's opinion points to the changing tide of just who was perceived as playing authentic jazz.

Clarke played a key role in spurring this discursive and perceptual shift to universal jazz. By the early 1960s, French jazz musicians could compete more readily with African Americans as authentic jazz producers rather than imitators. When the next huge wave of African American musicians came to Paris in 1962 and 1963, the distinction of many of them (except arguably the most famous) as authenticators of good jazz was changing. Just thinking back to Gillespie's 1948 big band, which featured 100 percent black participation, seemed to exemplify this change. It had been nearly fifteen years since the racial slur against his all-black band, the shock of bebop that silenced the crowd, and Delaunay's persistent desire for Clarke and other African American musicians to stay in France and teach French musicians syncopation. *Jazz Is Universal* symbolized a turn in jazz discourse and production in Europe. Clarke brought together savvy jazz musicians from all over Europe and helped position jazz as universal via the C-BBB.

One important example of Clarke's contribution to universal jazz was his collaboration and relationship with C-BBB colleague Kenny Clare. Note the similarity between the names *Clare* and *Clarke* and the shared given name; rather than just causing confusion this similarity contributed to claims of appropriation. Clare was a white British drummer, born in 1929 London. He got his start backing bands on English radio. Clare began to replace Kenny Clarke in the C-BBB when Clarke was unavailable for recordings or performances.

Their relationship started off as the bond between mentor and protégé. Clarke supported Clare, and they got along well. They began performing an unrivaled double-drum set in the C-BBB after a few years. In a 1968 interview with Tony Brown, Clare described his almost bumbling, error-prone audition and the amazement he felt at being called in to replace Clarke when he could not make a gig. The awe and respect that Clare felt for Clarke was apparent: "So many people would like to be able to get that very springy kind of beat that Klook has. I would. When I'm with him, I can play like that exactly, without even thinking about it. Soon as I'm away from it, I can't do it any more. Strange. I can't figure it out" (Brown). Clarke also felt an intuneness with Clare; he viewed himself and Clare as "soul brothers" who thought on the same level with their drumming (Clarke quoted in M. Jones).

Clarke actually recalled listening to one C-BBB recording and asking when he had recorded it. The recording featured Clare, but even Clarke couldn't tell the difference (Thigpen 21). The similar sound and name made the two (at face value at least) almost interchangeable to the novice jazz fan. The confusion caused by the similar names and the credibility that Clare unwittingly acquired when his name was misread, misunderstood, or mistaken for Kenny Clarke's benefited the band. It allowed Clare to double for Clarke without taking the responsibility of intentional misleading. In fact,

Clarke revealed to Ursula Broschke-Davis that he moved away from performing as much with the band and Clare's name went on advertising materials instead (Broschke-Davis 57).

This conflation of a distinctive style by a black performer, subsequently replicated by a white performer, is at the heart of the globalization of jazz. Notably, it is also one function of a universalist narrative to consume what has been perceived and portrayed as an inherently ethnic art. As musicologist Ingrid Monson explains, "the appeals of white musicians to universalistic rhetoric can be perceived as power plays rather than expressions of universal brotherhood" (*Say Something* 203). In some perspectives the consumption of (and identification with) minority culture into mainstream culture was actually advantageous to the spread and reinvention of minority culture. Such is the argument of ethnomusicologist Charles Keil. In his 1966 book *Urban Blues* Keil shared his now oft-cited concept of "appropriation-revitalization":

> Negro music, since the days of the first recordings but especially during the last two decades, has become progressively more "reactionary"— that is more African in its essentials—primarily because the various blues and jazz styles are, at least in their initial phases, symbolic referents of in-group solidarity for the black masses and the more intellectual segments of the black bourgeoisie. It is for this reason that each successive appropriation and commercialization of a Negro style by white America through its record industry and mass media has stimulated the Negro community and its musical spokesman to generate a "new" music that it can call its own. In every instance the new music has been an amalgamation of increased musical knowledge (technically speaking) and a reemphasis of the most basic Afro-American resources. (43)

Keil's elaboration was in direct response to another perspective of appropriation that perceived this cultural consumption as a loss in power and credit attributed to African American performers. In relation to Clarke the assimilation of jazz in France threatened an erasure of African American contributions to the music. This erasure could take the form of unequal pay, decrease in opportunities, and diminution of recognition among other outcomes. With *Blues People* Amiri Baraka emerged as a prominent proponent of this perspective. Throughout the book he claimed that white American culture owed a debt to "black music," because blues, jazz, and R&B had been stolen/appropriated from their original creators. Baraka recognized that white American jazz musicians might not always have modeled themselves after African Americans, but he still argued that their sound could always be linked back to an African American originator:

> But the entrance of the white man into jazz at this level of sincerity and emotional legitimacy did at least bring him, by implication, much closer to the Negro; that is, even if a white trumpet player were to learn to play "jazz" by listening to Nick LaRocca and had his style set (as was Beiderbecke's case) *before* he ever heard black musicians, surely the musical debt to Negro music (and to the black culture from which it issued) had to be understood. As in the case of LaRocca's style, it is certainly an appropriation of black New Orleans brass style, most notably King Oliver's. (*Blues People* 151)

In Baraka's opinion African American artistry had historically and continually been whited out (and without much recognition of the fact) in what he elsewhere termed the "great music robbery" (Baraka and Baraka 331). Discussing the loss of ethnic distinction and commendation that occurred in the incorporation of early rock 'n' roll and R&B songs into the mainstream, Baraka expounded, "Labor is being stolen, resources vandalized, and the colored still ain't got nothin' but bad reputations" (Baraka and Baraka 332).

I should note here that some of Baraka's writing was heavily influenced by his political and artistic investment in ideologies of black nationalism. Calling out the lack of credit and the diminished earnings paid to African Americans, especially in relation to white bands covering their material, furthered an agenda of African American uplift in this moment that preceded the height of Black Nationalism. Baraka's political bent was a timely symbol of the 1960s, signifying then and now the rise in overt uses of music, literature, and art to convey pride, power, and beauty in African American culture.

Though Clarke took a non-political stance, his experience does relate in some ways to Baraka's opinions, as well as to Keil's. Fellow African American jazz musician and Parisian resident Donald Byrd also believed that Clarke's music was being stolen. Byrd was an African American jazz trumpeter who migrated to France in 1962. The Paris that greeted him was very different from the rhythm-starved era that first captured Clarke's attention. "The thing with the European musician was," exclaimed Byrd, "as soon as they stole the Afro-American musicians' stuff, especially Kenny's, they would go out playing like black cats and then they would try to keep the blacks from working" (quoted in Broschke-Davis 58).

The jobs for black artists also dried up in Paris. The quotas came back into effect. Clarke had many gigs outside Paris, where he'd become what Mike Zwerin calls a "local musician"; the downturn in jobs was due to the gradual decrease in appreciation for musicians who were always there and available (Zwerin, "Jazz" 541). So "local musicians" like Clarke began to travel more. They also could lose out in comparison to touring musicians, who might make more because of the boost of excitement and attendance temporary gigs could prompt. That was the case with Louis Armstrong, recalled Nathan Davis: "I remember a scene at the Antibes Jazz Festival. Louis came over and they wanted Klook to play with him for a lot less money. Klook said, 'I love Pops, but they give him all the money. I'm not going to do it'" (quoted in Moody 129).

With the wave of immigrants that came to Paris in the 1950s and 1960s there were more musicians looking for work. All of this created greater competition for jazz gigs in Paris. But since jazz clubs were mostly white-owned, and with the French working to improve their performance of jazz rhythms from touring and residing African American jazz musicians, there was bound to be a good deal of imitation. But were Clarke's work and opportunities being appropriated?

Ursula Broschke-Davis describes Kenny Clarke as "especially bitter that many white jazz musicians seemed to learn to play by 'stealing'" (47). In support she adds Clarke's own statement: "Whites still can't play jazz. So you know how they sounded then. They all sound like Guy Lombardo to me" (47). Yet in a contemporaneous interview with journalist Burt Korall in 1963, Clarke had countered just this type of authenticity claim on jazz: "Something unhealthy is happening to jazz in America. . . . I hear a lot about Crow Jim, reverse segregation. . . . How can any musician in his right mind put down Stan Getz and people like that? It's a bunch of you know what. One race can learn from another. No one race has everything. This attitude could do jazz a lot of damage" (quoted in Korall 17). Additionally, I once asked his son Laurent Clarke whether he thought his father's music was "stolen" from him. He said his father saw the imitation as "recognition of the influence he had on bebop music more than unfair competition" (Clarke interview).

Clarke's differing statements illustrate his contradictory feelings about "authentic" jazz and appropriation in the jazz industry. Potentially his opinion was relativist—that is, dependent on the particular individual, of Stan Getz versus Guy Lombardo, for example. His opinions may have also altered with time, his perspective being different in 1963 from what it would be twenty years later in his interviews with Ursula Broschke-Davis. Another explanation could be the difference in interviewers and a potential comfort level he may have felt with Broschke-Davis to be more blunt in his statements. Distance may have played a factor given that discussion about appropriation in an era of already universalized jazz (by the time of these 1980s interviews) would have little effect on the jazz industry.

Or Clarke's contradictory statements may illustrate tension between coexisting yet differing feelings about the acculturation of jazz into mainstream American culture and the deracializing effects that came with it. In *The African Diaspora: A Musical Perspective* Ingrid Monson keenly assesses these kinds of disparities, contradictions, and tensions as representative of the process of globalization:

> Examining that which is taken for authentic and legitimate in particular locations and at particular times, itself constructed against the backdrop of larger forces of globalization, also leaves space open for the inevitably contradictory and fallible aspects of human cultural practice. Indeed, points of contradiction in a particular genre, culture, or person may reveal most clearly the larger constellation of forces in which a culture is embedded. Imperfect attempt[s] to cope with these contradictions do not point to a lack of principle or character but to the ongoing difficulty of improving one's way through a minefield of global forces. (17)

Monson's insight leads me to think that Clarke's contradictory perspectives demonstrate both reconciliation to the globalization of jazz and mourning for the loss of ethnic distinction. When Kenny Clarke left the United States in 1956, he clung to the possibilities of maintaining a black aesthetic, of extending his financial opportunities and creative autonomy, and of securing universal human rights as a black man. He sought these possibilities in France. But years assimilating himself and the music in Paris would offer some progress in each of these areas while also presenting more challenges. In some ways his role disseminating jazz as "black music" and as "universal" music speaks to a survivalist approach—keeping him working despite French jazz quotas and greater competition. Clarke's further spreading and defining of the bebop genre in France gave it new life and potential for innovation. Perhaps the result is not too far afield of Keil's process of appropriation-revitalization. Keil's model, while more positive in outlook, is also focused on the potential productivity that comes out of appropriation.[12] Rather than seeing African American artists like Clarke as victims of a robbery or theft (per Baraka's perspective), Clarke has agency and choice in Keil's perspective.

I believe it is this agency that counteracts claims to appropriation (rather than other models of cultural exchange) in this case. Clarke made a choice to look beyond race with his musicians in the C-BBB. His time with the C-BBB, and Clare in particular, demonstrates his lack of attention to race in musical collaborations—many musicians have actually shared a similar sentiment, that good playing and skill rather than ethnic background was what they cared about. Instead of appropriation Clarke's relationship with

Clare was one of voluntarily "passing it on"—of teaching willingly and unselfishly—so that others could be included in a jazz diaspora. In *Thinking in Jazz: The Infinite Art of Improvisation* Paul Berliner describes this as the passing down of skills and knowledge from veterans to rookies; he states that passing it on (the modeling and teaching of good playing) is critical to the success and maturity of an aspiring jazz musician and is part of the jazz way of life (489).

Perhaps Clarke's voluntary mentoring was a testament of his kindness, his behind-the-scenes and peaceful personality, and his love of the music, for Clarke was generous with his cultural exchange. He did not distinguish by race, nationality, or gender those he chose to pass it on to. Instead, his pedagogy was widely shared. When Nathan Davis discussed his experiences of migration in Paris in *The Jazz Exiles,* many anecdotes featured Clarke at the center. For Davis, Kenny Clarke was welcoming host, bandmate, adviser, and ultimately "The Dean, my father" as he lovingly called him (Moody 126). In my interview with Nancy Holloway the African American vocalist described her first years residing in Paris and singing at places like the Mars Club in the 1950s: Kenny Clarke believed in her and supported her when others did not. She was almost blocked from playing when a drummer said she could not sing and refused to play with her; Kenny Clarke said he would do it, and he and African American bassist Ray Brown set up as her rhythm section (Holloway). We have seen the mentoring role that Clarke played for French pianist René Urtreger. In our interview Urtreger recalled similar support and backing that Clarke provided. He said, "When I was in trouble in an orchestra with a musician who said why did you take that young guy . . . he'd always take my defense" (Urtreger). Even years after Clarke's death, his role as a good teacher remains a key part of his legacy. In the 2003 radio series *Jazz à Paris, années 50* Alain Gerber labeled Clarke "un extraordinaire pédagogue" ("Jazz à Paris").

Clarke as a teacher and collaborator is just the side I see in the *Faces* documentary about the band. Produced in 1968 by a Swiss public television station, WDR, the documentary put a face to the band's eponymous album. With the scene of Clarke smiling as his drumming pupils practiced, the program portrays teaching as one of his key priorities. The very use of this scene indicates that the role of teacher was important to Clarke.

Band member Johnny Griffin said, "Those two drummers swung the band like crazy. . . . They complemented each other so well. One would concentrate on swinging the band and the other would handle the dynamics and fills" (quoted in Jewel). This was not an image of Clarke as a victim of appropriation. And Clare did not run off with Clarke's talent, as Byrd's quotation suggests. Clare was accepted in the band but always (in his own perception) as pupil and mentee. He never attempted to overtake Clarke's role or position. The relationship between Clare and Clarke actually seems to have been one of support, hard work, and rapport. In *Faces* the rapport between Clarke and Clare comes through. So writes critic John Legg: "Finally comes the finale with 'Kenny and Kenny,' the master and the pupil . . . a triumphant sforzando which had us standing and cheering night after night. The band has stopped playing and is dancing in groups around the two drummers" (Legg n.p.). Here Kenny Clare becomes a useful marketing conduit as well, in which the C-BBB highlights the unique sound of having two drummers in many of their songs, including "Kenny and Kenny." They were two drummers with distinctly different styles—one pounding and one subtle—yet both striving to create one complex sound and, at times, to work against each other. The complications came from this marriage between mentor and mentee. Clare could at times absorb his style by studying and playing with Clarke. But it was difficult for him to sustain it alone. When playing together, they worked toward that one unified and complex sound, but there were also times when their different styles were highlighted. The two complemented each other in these joint performances and made the C-BBB sound distinctive (with its two drummers) and rich (with its multiple accents).

I think the relationship between Clarke and Clare was not one of appropriation or the loss of "authentic" black music. Rather, Clarke musically made the case for integration in his career in France and with the C-BBB (which again demonstrates an interesting tension, given his espousal of racial segregation). He expanded who could be a part of that musical community, teaching the French about syncopation and creating a multinational jazz community in Germany. He helped change the way people thought about jazz and how they perceived their own relationship to it— from "black" to "universal" music, from racialized differentiation to integration of musical communities. By playing such a major role in moving jazz abroad, Kenny Clarke shared "universal" jazz with other people— other communities that were touched by its message; other people who performed it, hummed it, and connected it to their own lives.

Just as I do, as I jam to the hot, swinging tunes on *Jazz Is Universal*. Since its production the album continues to demonstrate good jazz that stands the test of time. The positioning of European jazz as good and "authentic" jazz happened under Clarke's watch. He once supported the album *Jazz Is Universal*, saying, "This album is proof positive that there are [just] as good musicians in Europe as there are in the States. . . . I've worked around the studios in the States, and I really think that music here in Europe is on a higher plane" (Hennessey, "Clarke-Boland" 24). From a man who'd been so fervent about the white appropriation of music in New York in the 1930s and 1940s, this change in discourse again demonstrates tension and contradiction.

In Europe Clarke worked alongside C-BBB cofounders Gigi Campi and Francy Boland and shared the power, reputation, and money. His use of qualifiers like *good* and *higher plane* to assess *Jazz Is Universal* performed several meanings: it gave credibility to his European colleagues; it also resituated the home of jazz, suggesting that "good" jazz could also be found in Europe. Clarke helped keep jazz alive abroad at a time when rock ruled and "jazz [was] dead" in the words of Miles Davis (Gilroy, *The Black Atlantic* 97). By including others in disseminating the music, Clarke ensured that the cultural history of African Americans traveled yet remained embedded in the sound. In this shift to universal jazz the idea of jazz as originating with African Americans—as synonymous with injustice and struggle—is forever attached to the music.

This all recalls Amiri Baraka's phrase "the changing same." In the 1966 essay "The Changing Same: R&B and New Black Music" Baraka ethnically stratifies jazz by distinguishing "jazz that is most European, popular or avant-garde" from "jazz that is Blackest, still makes reference to a central body of cultural experience" (Baraka 187). Baraka argues that all jazz genres share a blues impulse and are therefore "the changing same" (188). Paul Gilroy revises "the changing same" and contends that black cultural products change while simultaneously carrying some of their sameness so as to be recognizable (*The Black Atlantic* 101). He ultimately uses this reasoning to argue against the black particularism that Baraka espouses; Gilroy recognizes the inability to have pure black music because as it is exchanged, disseminated, critiqued, and shaped, black music resists sameness (80). Gilroy also connects his arguments against authenticity claims to appropriation debates: "It bears repetition that even where African American forms are borrowed and set to work in new locations they have often been deliberately reconstructed in novel patterns that do not respect their originators' proprietary claims or the boundaries of nation states and the supposedly natural political communities they express" (98).

This perspective recognizes the ability of non–African American musicians to absorb skills from African American musicians and to "reconstruct" the music—making it new. It allows them to take part in African American cultural expression while still acknowledging a debt owed to jazz's primarily African American founders. Kenny Clarke was the conduit for this reconstruction of jazz. Through his 1948 tour, subsequent mentoring, collaborations, and travels he contributed to the transformation of jazz from "black music" to a "universal" music accessible to—and playable by—those in France and beyond. Clarke's "universal" jazz is rife with tension, though. His journey to "universal" jazz illustrated voluntary collaboration and mentoring yet conflict over unequal power exchanges, recognition of good jazz in Europe and yet racialized critique of some jazz musicians, and enthusiastic participation in multinational jazz production yet mourning the loss of black power in the jazz industry. Despite these tensions, Kenny Clarke willingly passed on his skill to blacks and whites, Americans and Europeans, and men and women alike. He would continue to pass it on beyond Paris, disseminating jazz through the C-BBB to such places as Cologne and London.

KENNY CLARKE: BAD NATIONALIST, UNIVERSAL CITIZEN

When I am asked whether I don't feel like I lost my roots, I say, "What roots? The only roots I have are the roots that I have planted myself personally, and they will always be with me."

KENNY CLARKE

Kenny Clarke didn't see himself as American or French but rather as making a place for himself (and his African American culture) throughout the world. His one constant, wherever he was, was his race. His race would not change, and it would always differentiate him (Broschke-Davis 58). In France he found a way to sidestep racialized limitations to get what he wanted in life. Finally, at peace with his pipe and family home in Montreuil-sous-Bois, he still retained the life of the itinerant musician as he continually moved to the next opportunity and cultivated a "universal" identity for jazz.

Here my use of universalism is informed by, and is an extension of, the work of Brent Hayes Edwards and Robin D.G. Kelley. Edwards has termed this type of migrant a bad nationalist "who doesn't *perform* nationalism" but who remains the "unregistered, the undocumented, the untracked" (*The Practice* 239). Kelley investigates African American jazz musicians who turn outside the States to Africa for their roots and source of musical identity. The musicians in Kelley's study expanded their sense of national identity; "their family was global, universal, and it knew no boundaries of place or race—although it did privilege Africa" (*Africa Speaks* 4).

As a bad nationalist Clarke eschewed American identity while never technically claiming French citizenship. His laid-back demeanor and subtle silent activism kept him under the radar. Though he was popular, a well-loved and respected veteran of jazz in France, he did not challenge the system. He played along with it in silent dissent.

The epigraph of this section shares Clarke's emphasis on personal roots rather than national ones; it reveals that Clarke's identity was not shaped by the United States. His actions were not defined by loyalty, allegiance, or even continued participation while abroad. Clarke was a bad nationalist because he was a citizen of a jazz diaspora of his own making. He set his own roots, which were determined by where he could perform and how he could achieve his ideal lifestyle. His choices diametrically opposed Sidney Bechet's performance of multiple subjectivities in France. Bechet was more vocal about both his happiness at working in France and his desire to return home if possible; he actively played up different perspectives and subjectivities in order to be successful in France.

As for Kelley's discussion of a global family, Clarke built a global family for himself in Paris. His family drew on ethnic connections with African American musicians from home and newfound bonds with French mentees and bandmates. As he performed jazz outside of France, his family extended (e.g., with the C-BBB and its multinational group of musicians). His jazz diaspora pushed against national boundaries.

Clarke demonstrated that jazz is not a static American product but rather a migratory process that grew through international and interracial collaboration. In this transformation to universal jazz, authenticity claims, appropriation, and even loss of racial identity threatened. But his musical collaborations and assimilation into French culture eschewed these threats and instead generated a jazz diaspora that was universal in its consumption of black and global jazz.

The framing of Clarke's jazz as Gilroy's "changing same"—as both signifying black and global musical culture—speaks to a larger trend of universalist perspectives held by African American jazz musicians. Gillespie once remarked, "We never wished to be restricted to just an American context, for we were creators in an art form which grew from universal roots and which had proved it possessed universal appeal" (Gillespie and Fraser 287). Gillespie's comment exemplifies a prevalent mind-set among musicians that the more diversity and experimentation within jazz (in terms of cultures and musical elements), the better the music. Gillespie had collaborated with African and Caribbean musicians and applied new techniques, from the rapid-fire precision in bebop to the Latin rhythms he introduced in songs like "Manteca" (Von Eschen, *Race* 178–79).

Many jazz musicians refused to be limited by geography, notes Farah Jasmine Griffin: "But none of these musicians whom we talk about thought of themselves only as Americans. They knew that they were Americans, but they also thought of themselves as citizens of a global world. They were global citizens. Citizens who not just went and played music, but . . . who listened and changed the music of the places where they were, and consequently their music was changed as well" ("Jazz"). With this universalist perspective the wider path and signification of jazz was inevitable and would extend past the bounds of France and Germany. In *Northern Sun, Southern Moon: Europe's Reinvention of Jazz* Mike Heffley argues that European jazz, particularly from northern Europe, departs from American jazz and shows very few echoes of its roots; the music had decades to disseminate throughout Britain and Europe and develop its own styles (2). George McKay's *Circular Breathing: The Cultural Politics of Jazz in Britain* investigates the progress of jazz in Britain, focusing on the 1940s to the 1970s. Andrew Jones's *Yellow Music: Media Culture and Colonial Modernity in the Chinese Jazz Age* offers the first study of jazz in China. In *Blue Nippon: Authenticating Jazz in Japan* Taylor Atkins traces the entrance of jazz into Japan since the 1920s and the meanings of jazz to the Japanese. Naresh Fernandes's *Taj Mahal Foxtrot: The Story of Bombay's Jazz Age* introduces jazz fans to the entry of jazz in 1930s India, the American musicians who stayed there, the impact of jazz on Hindi film soundtracks, and the promotion of India's own version of Louis Armstrong. Taylor Atkins makes one of the first attempts to commence a dialogue between these different studies with the anthology *Jazz Planet*, which features essays about jazz in such places as Japan, Brazil, and Cuba.

This surge of transnational jazz texts from the new millennium makes quite a departure from the proliferation of texts with an Americancentric discourse published in the 1990s and the African American–centeredness at the core of essentialist discourse throughout the first half of the twentieth century. This discursive shift suggests that not only is jazz more than an American music, but it is also significant to more than just Americans. Mike Zwerin puts it well when he writes that "jazz is in the process of becoming the musica franca, the one language spoken everywhere, a glue in the global village, the musical common denominator, like English. It will not necessarily remain 'America's only native art form' forever. The music is changing and being changed by the music of the world around it" ("Global" n.p.). In jazz's travels, its history and people have expanded. I hope as the music travels it also grows in its capacity to represent universally human values rather than obscuring race, and that "universal" jazz can be a connective music—a "musica franca" above all.

Coda

Beyond Color-Blind Narratives: Reading behind the Scenes of Paris Blues

A legato piano-driven melody stumbles along in Ellingtonian fashion as two couples hug in parting at a train station. One couple, an African American man and woman, embrace multiple times as the woman steps onto a parting train. He just can't let her go and remains on the train step until the very last moment. Though he will reunite with her in just a couple of weeks in the United States, he still looks on sorrowfully. The other couple, a white American man and woman, dismisses a chance at embrace. He stares on in a blank, emotionless gaze. While his ladylove lashes out bitterly and mournfully at what he is throwing away by remaining in Paris. She walks away then without a second glance—out of his life, toward the train, and, ultimately, to the United States.

With both women safely on board, the train quickly sets off. The moody melody suddenly trips over itself to the cacophonous blaring of Murray McEachern's trombone. The trombone overpowers the now meek piano as the two men stroll away from the station and back into the bustling Parisian cityscape. Above their heads, amid the swelling horn, a billboard stands. Only minutes ago in love's last throws, African American jazz musician Wild Man Moore's grin overtook the billboard. The memory of his visit days before still hangs in the air. The platform had filled with a rush of young, waving jazz fans crowding the train, blocking the exits, as he commenced his Parisian jazz tour.

But now he has gone. Now, only bits of his black image remain as the white papering of a Larousse Book Store advertisement quickly replaces the vibrancy of his image. While the sound of jazz swells in my ears, the symbol of jazz is replaced by literature, vis-à-vis high culture. For now, both men will return to their prime spots as American jazz musicians in the heart of Paris, but only the white musician will remain. The train, too, will come again as it journeys to and from Paris, to and from the next jazz hot spot, always collecting jazz, always moving jazz forward.

So ends the film *Paris Blues*, at least in my mind's eye. Directed by native New Yorker Martin Ritt, the film is based on the eponymous book by fellow New Yorker, Harold Flender, which was published in 1957. The 1961 film received abysmal reviews after its release. *Down Beat* called it "dramatic nonsense" (Tynan 16), and *Variety* wrote that "within its snappy, flashy veneer [it] is an undernourished romantic drama" (*Variety* staff). So it is not the high caliber of the direction, acting, or plot that make *Paris Blues* memorable. Instead the movie lives on because of its soundtrack, which joins legends Duke Ellington and Billy Strayhorn (who composed the music) with Louis Armstrong (who performed two of the songs). Even without taking into account the high quality of the recording, the production of the film's soundtrack was a feat in itself for bringing together Armstrong and Ellington (who had never previously recorded together). Armstrong plays Wild Man Moore, a character much like himself, who draws swells of enthusiastic French fans.

Paris Blues tells the story of two American jazz musicians—one black and one white—thriving in a Parisian jazz community. When the musicians both meet schoolteachers and fall in love, they are forced to reevaluate staying in France. Played by Paul Newman, Ram Bowen is a lead trombonist who wants to be accepted as a classical musician. He presents his jazz-inspired work to a well-known classical composer and struggles with the feedback that he should get classical training and keep working at it. His affair with a visiting American teacher, Lillian Corning (played by Joanne Woodward), forces him to decide whether to pursue classical training or return with her to the United States and presumably continue with his career in jazz. Eddie Cook, played by Sidney Poitier, enjoys his life as the tenor saxophonist for Ram's band. As he falls in love with Connie Lampson (played by Diahann Carroll), he confronts "the race question" that he thought he had left behind.

Paris Blues exemplifies several of the major topics I have explored in *Jazz Diasporas*. The movie presents a Paris that is in love with jazz, is welcoming to African American musicians, and is a transformative space that expands jazz into a universal music. The film also unwittingly hints at what lies behind the scenes of this color-blind narrative: France's race consciousness and codependence on the United States. *Paris Blues* also features three different angles that parallel or highlight real-life issues revealed by jazz diasporas.

WHY PARIS?

Paris Blues portrays Paris as a city conducive to love affairs and ripe with its own love of jazz. Yet the film also constrains both romances. As young women flock to Wild Man Moore in one scene, he quells their raucous desires by engaging in call and response with the band that accompanied the throng of fans. So the scene portrays Paris as already having the audience, band, and even the accompaniment needed for a jazz star to succeed. On the eve of production, live bands also serenaded Armstrong and Ellington as they entered Parisian hotels (Edwards, "Rendez-vous" 182). The character of Wild Man Moore is reminiscent of Sidney Bechet. The scene of a throng of primarily white French women pushing up against the train as Moore arrives could be a reenactment of Bechet's celebration concert of his one-millionth recording. At the 1954 concert at Olympia Hall, a bevy of mostly white French fans broke windows and pushed over phone booths to get within striking distance of his jamming saxophone (Tournès 7). *Paris Blues* portrays this real French passion for jazz as it positions Paris as welcoming to jazz and African American jazz musicians.

Still, the departure of Wild Man Moore and the billboard papering that whites out his larger-than-life image suggests that Paris as a jazz hot spot can only be sustained periodically. Moore's exit parallels the movement that every African American jazz musician in France eventually undertakes: the touring circuit. Such a migrant life was true of Inez Cavanaugh and Kenny Clarke, especially, and it is just as true of African American musicians in France today. After World War II and through the 1960s a great jazz scene endured. But players always sustained that experience with travel. Paris was simply a spot on the itinerary for a global jazz musician.

Today this is truer than ever. I find this issue of transience comes up quite frequently in my interviews with modern-day African American jazz musicians. Tenor saxophonist Hal Singer still lives in a suburb of Paris, but he mostly plays abroad. (He particularly likes Japan, because the Japanese pay so well.) When I met John Betsch, he showed me his drum case, and I observed the stickers from locales all around the world. Pianist Bobby Few gave me a poster displaying his next concert; he was playing a two-day gig in Geneva right before Christmas. Interviewing vocalist Sylvia Howard, I learned that Thailand offered a steady stream of jobs, and Howard encouraged me to seek out a network of other female jazz musicians making their way to venues outside the United States—and outside France; from Janice Harrington in Germany to Sherry Roberson in Thailand, these women followed the music (Howard). And they kept moving with jazz. "We move; we don't stay," added Howard. This is the only way these musicians could survive the changing trends in jazz after the 1960s.

So why reside in Paris when the city offers diminishing job opportunities? One of the benefits is that the government recognizes music production on the same level as other professions. That's why guitarist Michael Felberbaum and trumpeter and singer Larry Browne remained in Paris: Felberbaum mentioned the French governmental social protection that legally offered support, while Browne liked the "paid vacations. The government supports music and other cultural forms because these are seen as indispensable to a good life" (Ake, *Jazz Matters* 130).

Another more obvious benefit of Paris is its physical location. It is a couple of hours (or less) by plane to most major cities: London, Amsterdam, Berlin, Munich, and Brussels. Though flights were not as common in the post–World War II era of this book, trains and ships also made the city very accessible. Major U.S. cities simply do not have the same degree of accessibility. Musician Jerome Harris elaborates on these benefits:

> It is clear that the relatively high cost of traversing the long distances between cities with developed jazz audiences forms a major barrier to touring in the United States; this is largely mitigated in Europe by the government-subsidized rail system. With regard to state-run broadcasting, it is presently quite common for one or two dates on a European tour (or major star-level Japanese tour) to be funded in part by the local state-run radio or television outlet. . . . Ongoing governmental support of the arts has helped foster sophistication and commitment in European jazz audiences. In my opinion, the effectiveness of such support for jazz in the United States pales in comparison to that in much of Europe. (115)

European governmental support keeps African American jazz musicians coming back for more. For many reasons Paris remains central for jazz musicians and attracts intermittent yet consistent interaction. It not only supports musicians on its own soil; it also offers the world to them. Therefore, it also offers jazz to the world.

With this dissemination of jazz alongside the teaching of jazz and mentoring of jazz musicians in Paris, the city has become essential to the genre. Yet opportunities for African American jazz musicians (and a historical understanding of jazz as born out of African American cultural expression) may have also been obscured, as France has shifted from positioning African American performers as the most "authentic." The Parisian jazz scene now hosts French, Italians, Americans, and even those who blur national and ethnic borders. For example, I remember the electric, impassioned interpretations of pianist Jackie Terrasson. At the 2013 Festival Pianissimo at Sunside, one of Paris's well-known jazz clubs in the first arrondissement, Terrasson energized the audience. He was born in Berlin, raised in Paris by a French father and African American mother, and now lives in New York yet remains a frequent visitor to Paris (Himes, "Jacky Terrasson"). Terrasson thus embodies one sense of "universal" jazz, in which the music has the potential to articulate multiple and diverse cultural experiences. Terrasson's heritage represents the ethnic and geographical diversity of jazz, as well as its African American roots. His journey resembles the negotiations between nations, races, and ethnicities that I have discussed in relation to Sidney Bechet's creolized heritage. For both musicians Paris is one stop among many on the journey that jazz takes. In this way Paris is a center of departure and return that supports continuous and interrupted interaction with it.

Paris Blues represents this movement to and fro in the beginning of the film, as the train pulls into the station, whistling and chugging to the beat of the zippy ensemble horn play in the Ellington Orchestra's performance of "Take the 'A' Train." But as the train departs, the billboard of Louis Armstrong is papered over. So, too, "universal" jazz has the potential to overwrite the contributions and history of African American jazz musicians as it opens up to the world.

BEHIND THE SCENES OF *PARIS BLUES:* THE SAME OLD RACISM FROM A DIFFERENT ANGLE

In one scene from *Paris Blues* the illusion of Paris as color-blind is given center stage, yet the film also unwittingly undermines the illusion:

FRENCH BOY: Merci Monsieur Noir. Merci Madame Noir.

CONNIE: So you don't mind being called Mr. Black Man?

EDDIE: Of course not. Why should I? That's what I am, a black man.

CONNIE: You don't mind because that's a French kid; if that were an American . . .

EDDIE: Hey, hey, you wanna have fun or you wanna discuss the race question?

CONNIE: I can't separate them, not with you; it's too important to me.

EDDIE: It's . . .

CONNIE: You . . .

> EDDIE: Look. Here nobody says Eddie Cook, Negro musician. They say Eddie Cook, musician. Period. And that's all I wanna be.
>
> CONNIE: And that's what you are here.
>
> EDDIE: And that's what I am here. Musician period. And I don't have to prove anything else.
>
> CONNIE: Like?
>
> EDDIE: Like because I'm Negro I'm different, because I'm Negro I'm not different. I'm different, I'm not different . . . who cares? Look, I don't have to prove either case. Can you understand that?
>
> CONNIE: There isn't a place on Earth that isn't hell for somebody, some race, some color, some sex.
>
> EDDIE: For me, Paris is just fine.

Here Eddie and Connie stroll romantically along the Seine. The two pause momentarily to return a lost bouncing ball to a French boy. The scene poignantly illustrates Eddie's innermost desire: to be perceived for what he contributes, not by how he looks. His perspective symbolizes the outlook of many African American artists who saw Paris as a land of liberty lacking in prejudice.

At the chance to migrate to Paris in 1928, Henry Crowder exclaimed: "No color bar there. No discriminations! Freedom!" (Shack 44). After World War II the love affair with Paris continued as writer Richard Wright said there was "more democracy in one square block of Paris than in the whole United States" (W. Smith, *A Return* 60).

Eddie similarly believes his race is not recognized or is ignored by the French. But a closer look at *Paris Blues* reveals a more complex race consciousness. The comment of the white French boy literally discounts a color-blind France, since his first impression of Eddie is that he is a black man. The boy's response also figuratively hints at the attention to racialized difference that pervades French society, too. Even Eddie's comment that he doesn't mind being called "Monsieur Noir" suggests his subconscious awareness that attention to his blackness will never disappear.

In *Paris Blues: African American Music and French Popular Culture, 1920–1960,* Andy Fry suggests that Eddie's color-blind dreams are not really about France but about his color-blind hopes for the United States. Fry writes, "In this sense, the film does not depict France as it actually was (or is), but rather as an idealized vision for the future of America. . . . [It uses]

France to shine a light on America, while ignoring or downplaying its own 'race problem'" (5). Fry's point foregrounds the importance of relation in this film. For the filmic representation of Paris for African Americans is not isolated from the United States. Being in Paris forces an obligation on Eddie to discuss why he is there and what he feels about race in the States. *Paris Blues* is really about American blues, in the sense of pains and sorrows suffered under American segregation and prejudice.

The film also unknowingly bears relation to the essays of James Baldwin, who also ponders "the race question," though at a much more complex level. The seemingly simple encounter that Eddie has on the Seine with the white French boy riffs on Baldwin's essay "Encounter on the Seine." Baldwin deconstructs several encounters that the African American in Paris faces: he sees other African Americans with a "wariness" and practices a "deliberate isolation" from the history of oppression and rage that the presence of other African Americans recalls; he is noticed by the visiting white American and responds almost in advance from "a lifetime of conditioning" against racialized prejudice; and he encounters French of African descent, noticing, above all, the differences between them that a "gulf of three hundred years" has rendered rather than their shared histories and experiences (*Notes* 85–90).

Eddie's encounter most significantly acts as a seemingly successful encounter of integration that counters the very violent xenophobia and racism that fueled the Paris Massacre. In the same year of the film, on October 17, 1961, two hundred Algerian protesters were massacred. Some of their bodies were thrown hastily and indifferently into the very Seine that the filmic characters Eddie and Connie casually strolled along. Rather than a simple dialogue about race, the scene alludes to the multiple angles of race relations both in the United States and in France. In these instances the narrative of a color-blind Paris was not solely about France but about the relationship between two countries, between multiple experiences of blackness, and between ways that performance (whether filmic or musical) served to obscure those complex relations.

Eddie's belief that racialized difference in Paris does not matter and that he is only perceived as a musician is actually founded on perceptions of exoticism and primitivism—part of the French conception of African and African-diasporic art and music. This exotic, primitive perception of race masked a very different relationship between the French and its residents of African descent. Connie foregrounds what Eddie hides or is blind to. Connie draws attention to the treatment of other peoples of African descent in the French metropoles and colonies when she states, "There isn't a place on Earth that isn't hell for somebody, some race, some color, some sex."

Several of the artists I have highlighted in this book shared Connie's realization. From saxophonist Sidney Bechet to pianist Art Simmons to writer James Baldwin, there was no getting around the disparate treatment of French of African descent. Even Bechet knew his success in Paris—as the city's "king of jazz"—was complex. He once called out the disrespectful way the French discussed their black colonists and immigrants (Ehrlich 95). Simmons recognized his own naiveté and observed how the French addressed African Americans with "a 'noble savage' attitude" (Hajdu 143). In the process of being jailed and eventually released for a crime he didn't commit, Baldwin learned that French policemen were not so different from U.S. officers; their disrespect and cruel laughter was representative of universal racial inequality (*Notes* 101–16). So Eddie's comment in *Paris Blues* paralleled the very real disparity in treatment between African Americans and French of African descent.

Yet the differences between these communities could also be superficial and potentially collapsible. In "Rendez-vous in Rhythm" Brent Hayes Edwards discusses the malleability of blackness in *Paris Blues*. For example, blacks from the Antilles were used to represent African American band members following Armstrong in the club (184). Edwards's discussion of the flatness, invisibility of distinction, and easy transferability of blackness reveals the illusion of racial equality and the particular privilege of African Americans (184–85). But the long-staying African American jazz musician risks misrecognition and conflation with French of African descent, particularly after mastering the French language and living in areas of Paris favored by populations of African descent.

Another point that speaks to the French color-blind narrative is that *Paris Blues* made a change to the book that featured Eddie Cook as an African American musician. Flender's book centered on Eddie's seeming success at escaping "the race question" by succeeding in the thick of the Parisian jazz scene and even having access to mixed relationships through his affair with a jazz cave owner, Marie Séoul. The film version diminished the role of the book's African American protagonist. The film also avoided reference to other black populations in France. In the book Eddie reads about the Algerian situation in the papers and hears curses against Algerians in the cab he takes: "But these North Africans, these Algerians, with them it's a different story," rails the cabbie; as the book's Eddie disavows such comments, he can no longer hold on to dreams of Paris as color-blind, the dreams his filmic persona clings to (Flender 165, 76). Additionally, the film deemphasizes race relations as the core struggle of the story, by foregrounding Ram Bowen's desire for his jazz compositions to be recognized by classical musicians.

Paris Blues also presents another important race-conscious plot change. With the aid of producer Sam Shaw and a team of writers (including Harold Flender), Martin Ritt originally planned to couple Ram Bowen with Connie Lampson; this performance choice is hinted at in the opening of the film with Newman's flirty attention to Connie (Hajdu 207; Gabbard, "Paris" 302). However, the United Artists film office forced Ritt and Shaw to back away from that idea (Hajdu 207). The film instead features one African American couple and one white American couple. Still, through the club scenes Ritt manages to encapsulate one of the freedoms African American musicians sought out and enjoyed in France—interracial relationships. The band and audience featured in the opening sequence of the film not only advertise integration in post–World War II Paris but also show the French as comfortable with mixed couples.

The scene commences with a close-up of Bowen's trombone, as it is poised to blow. The music begins and the camera cuts to a dancing couple. Behind them we see a painting. It is seemingly of a nineteenth-century party scene with a black man twirling a white woman at center canvas. The camera then shifts to a crowd with a black woman seated shoulder to shoulder with white fans. Later in the scene the camera zooms in on a white Frenchman sitting tucked in close to a black woman. All of these images are interspersed with dancing fans, audience members lounging at tables, and wide-angle shots of the band performing.

This scene, and the film's changes to the book, reflected Americans' discomfort with integration, onscreen and in real life. The film shies away from forcing a 1960s American audience—still influenced by Jim Crow—to focus on two interracial relationships. Yet this type of romantic integration was one of the freedoms African American musicians enjoyed and sought out in France: Miles Davis almost married Juliette Gréco. Sidney Bechet, Kenny Clarke, Hal Singer, Johnny Griffin, and a host of others married white Europeans and settled with them in France. My point in considering *Paris Blues* at length is that this film and the book on which it is based, both created by a New Yorker, reflected a race consciousness that was not actually absent in Paris but was experienced instead from a different angle.

"BATTLE ROYAL": AFRICAN AMERICANS AND FRENCH OF AFRICAN DESCENT

> Why did Ellington call his composition featuring Armstrong "Battle Royal"? The phrase still had a pointed connotation at the dawn of the civil rights era: in the Southern U.S., a battle royal was a sadistic ritual in a boxing ring. The "winner" was the last boy standing. . . . Is it possible that the subtle venom is intended not just to allude to this history, but to connect it to the context of the scene? To make the point, in other words, that there is a spectacular, racially tinged, element in the popularity of the so-called "cutting session" in jazz, where soloists attempt to outdo one another on the bandstand. Even in Paris, an Ellington-Armstrong encounter could only be viewed voyeuristically as a meeting in a ring: black behemoths grinning as they slice each other to shreds, to the delight of the crowd.
>
> BRENT HAYES EDWARDS, "Rendez-vous in Rhythm"

In a prominent scene in *Paris Blues,* Wild Man Moore tracks down his friends Ram and Eddie in Marie's Club. Along with a crowd of musicians following him, Moore musically challenges each band member, playing a measure and waiting for the response. It's classic call and response in a cutting session.[1] The brilliance of the "Battle Royal" composition and Armstrong's playing are definite standouts in the film.

In "Rendez-vous in Rhythm" Brent Hayes Edwards analyzes this penultimate meeting of the musical geniuses Duke Ellington and Louis Armstrong. Edwards's argument that the song title "Battle Royal" references both societal and musical battles recalls the significance of battle in a Parisian jazz setting. Particularly in this post–World War II setting, *Paris Blues* neglects to explicitly show the effects of the war on living in Paris and on seducing African American musicians to migrate. Missing entirely from this narrative, for example, is the Algerian War of Independence from France from 1954 to 1962 and the concurrent ill treatment and disrespect of North Africans living in Paris.

Tyler Stovall notes that with the Algerian War and the death of Richard Wright (a real cornerstone in this community), the mood in Paris changed to one of "antagonism and suspicions" (*Paris Noir* 189). African Americans would question their connections to the Algerian struggle and their fit in Paris. This change in mood was accompanied by a gradual decrease in the Paris Noir community, starting at the end of the 1960s.

The urgent struggle of the French of African descent did not stop there; actually, there have been waves of protest throughout the years. Bobby Few migrated to France in 1968 and witnessed student protests primarily in support of civil rights movements and in opposition to the Vietnam War. Protests actually broke out across Europe and the United States, but May 1968 stands out in French history as a zenith of political discontent. Few compared the 1968 protests to modern-day political discontent in France. In our interview, he said he noticed that the same economic needs were demanded today, especially improved schools and accommodation; he also pointed out some differences: "I see now more unrest, which is very evident since the demonstrations and the brutality against Algerians [. . . especially] North Africans has increased" (Few).

Few particularly identified a similar political outrage and uproar that occurred in the 2005 riots in Paris and echoed across France. In October and November of 2005 a group of teenagers consisting primarily of French of Arabic and North African descent protested by setting fire to cars and buildings. For a couple of months, each night yielded another report of violence in what Trica Keaton terms "'the other France'—the sprawling public housing projects on the outskirts of urban centers" ("Arrogant Assimilationism" 40). Tenants living in the "other France" have often felt marginalized not only geographically but also because of their ethnicity, religion, and class. Tensions have built over time because of this marginalization and treatment. Even though many have resided in Paris for multiple generations, they are still singled out as immigrants. Keaton argues that their acceptance into French society is ever challenged, since "arrogant assimilationism remains an expectation in French society" (40).

During that autumn I was sitting in my Parisian apartment and reading and writing about African American artists in post–World War II Paris. I remember writing about the incidents in my journal:

> 11.08.05: As I write amidst the flames of a burning and furious Paris, I am reminded of the differences asserted by the French and how that mentality was eventually recognized by visiting African Americans in times past. As each day of my present brings another even more tragic and disastrous spread of riots and burnings throughout France, the racial differences asserted between immigrants, especially those of Northern African and Sub-Saharan African descent, not only become apparent in the news, they positively seethe beneath the surface. It is day twelve of what is being called an insurrection by immigrant youth in the *banlieues* of Paris. What commenced with the deaths of two youths falling into an electrocution zone while reportedly running away from the police, has now embroiled youths around France and Germany. Each day the fires increase, illustrating astonishing ravages. Today, Paris no longer burns; it erupts.

Despite my awareness of the continuous injustices and repeated struggles by African residents, their lives seemed quite different from my own. I enjoyed the privileges of living in the Latin Quartier and the access of being a scholar. As an African American rather than African, I benefited from the remnants of negrophilia that still existed among jazz lovers and older French men and women who grew up in a golden age of African American jazz production in Paris. This all stood in direct contrast to the lifestyles of many Muslim residents featured in Trica Keaton's writings: "From the perspective of the children . . . their housing project is, in no uncertain terms, 'pourrie' [rotten, lousy]. It is a place known for varying degrees of poverty, overcrowded housing, violence, intergenerational disputes, and cultural clashes among its diverse residents. Coupled with this are the problems attributed to the euphemism of cultural differences to explain what is simply intense xenophobia between European French and other inhabitants of the projects" ("Muslim Girls" 53).

The place for the African American residing in Paris amid these struggles remains as complicated as ever. Distance and difference have been forged between African Americans and French of African descent. African American jazz musicians do not necessarily visit or live in the same areas inhabited by French of African descent.[2] But African Americans do cherish moments of connection and extend a sense of family to visiting Americans, what I have termed "the culture of catching up."

The legacy of the Paris Noir community came through in a 2005 performance by Bobby Few at Sept Lézards. Sitting in the front row, listening to him play smooth tones and unpredictable riffs, I was surprised to see trumpeter Rasul Siddik hop onto the stage. He pulled his trumpet out of his case, swayed to the beat, and prepped the mouthpiece. The next thing we knew, he was spurting out phrases at the end of the piece and totally in sync as he improvised with Few and his drummer. Few was so excited to have his pal on the stage that they embraced. Throughout the set, vocalist Sylvia Howard sat at the back of the club cheering Few on. She ran to the stage for a hug after he finished. They were all welcoming each other, full of hugs, old anecdotes, and ready for another moment to sustain their culture of catching up. They were also full of love for me: happy to put a face to a name, stay in touch, share their stories, include me in their circle, invite me to future gigs, and hear about the progress of my work.

With its primarily white, European audience and location in the heart of tourist Paris, this Parisian jazz club scene was seemingly a world away from the crowded projects of northern Paris suburbs and the lifestyles of the primarily French of African descent living there. Actually, the two ethnicities were often considered to be in a battle royal for the attention of the French political mainstream. African Americans benefited from their perceived exoticism and uniqueness, the cultural value placed on jazz, and the understanding of the prejudices they'd hoped to leave behind in the United States.

This weighted fight was most apparent to me after seeing the 2012 France 5 television documentary *Noirs de France: De 1889 à nos jours*. I was expecting to learn about the rich intellectual, political, and performative contributions of former colonists from Guadeloupe to Algeria. Prominent figures like Martiniquan writer and politician Aimé Césaire and Senegalese politician Blaise Diagne were certainly featured. But much of the series was overtaken by African American achievement, from boxer Jack Johnson and African American soldiers who fought in World War I to dancer Josephine Baker and jazz bandleader and composer Noble Sissle. Not until the late 1970s did political protests by French of African descent dominate the film's narrative. The unanswered question was how jazz became so influential on French culture that African Americans would be integral to a story of *Noirs de France*? (Or the keener question is why more of the stories of political articulation from French of African descent were not identified and featured prominently? And how did a history of African American artists in France perform politically in relation to French of African descent in this film? Perhaps a future scholar will continue the discussion and address these questions.)

For now, the concept of the jazz diaspora addresses this first question, because it presumes that the migratory experiences of African Americans and jazz cannot be analyzed as individualized or even as culturally singular. *Jazz Diasporas* rests on the premise that the migration of African Americans and jazz is about relationships (a significant point actually that distinguishes it from other texts). This is why I have explored the many ways that African American jazz musicians related their music and themselves to a recovering, war-torn, yet still jazz-hungry Paris.

French jazz critics like Charles Delaunay were so determined to increase their jazz production and the repute of France as a home for jazz that they had Sidney Bechet's ban reversed so that he could return. Apparently, serving jail time for shooting a person was not enough to keep him away (J. Chilton 83–84). Instead, adoration and opportunity in France enticed him to stay. Kenny Clarke was looking for peace. Civil rights conflicts and prejudiced business practices were all he could see in New York. His wartime tours and gigs in France seemed a world away from that pressure. James Baldwin fled the pressures of racism in the United States only to find that he would draw on the blues to articulate in France what he had fled in the United States. Inez Cavanaugh wanted security. Labor lockouts and the return of soldiers closed the door on job opportunities after World War II. She was able to create a jazz diaspora that offered jobs and socialization for a time in Paris.

Through their migrations to Paris these musicians left behind (but not so fully as they might imagine) their trials in the United States. An ocean away, white French fans, musicians, and critics seduced and absorbed jazz, attempting to meld it with French culture. Charles Delaunay seduced with jobs and recording contracts. Boris Vian defended jazz musicians, performed with them, and strove to possess their music. Claude Luter and René Urtreger learned from mentors like Sidney Bechet and Kenny Clarke. They passed jazz along, at times performing in places generally cordoned off by the Cold War.

Whether African American or white French, these jazzophiles were bound together in a relationship based on a love of jazz and dreams of a better life. They were also linked with the often silenced other, whether the French of African descent absented from the jazz scene or the white American still unforgotten in this French setting. These relationships were maintained through a mixture of realization, disillusionment, negotiation, collaboration, and exchanges of power. These jazzophiles often related to one another by reaching across sociocultural boundaries of race and nationality. And they were able to establish lifelong ties and make significant contributions to the global community via their production of jazz and jazz discourse—with all its passions, tensions, delusions, growth, and rupture of a people and culture in love with their music in post–World War II Paris. They were more than African Americans, white French, white Americans, or French of African descent; they were jazz people.

Notes

1. Throughout this book I use the word *jazzophile* to include not only jazz musicians but also non-musicians who in some way influence and represent jazz culture. One example is the writer James Baldwin, whose work and life I analyze in chapter 4. Baldwin was a fan, and he often employed blues and jazz in prominent ways throughout his writing.

2. This is a reference and addendum to jazz scholar Nicholas Evans's statement on jazz: "Its definitions and identity can be seen as determined by their definitions and identities (as in 'jazz is both white and black'), or its unique combination of their definitions and identities can make it something else altogether (for example, 'jazz *comes from* white and black but *is* neither')" (12).

INTRODUCTION

1. With the term *blood memories* I refer to the Alvin American Dance Theater. The troupe premiered the eponymous dance in 1960. The founder, Alvin Ailey, grew up in the South; though far removed from slavery historically, he described an absorption of the struggle, survival, and oppression of slavery through music, the church, and other activities. He once said, "I'm a black man whose roots are in the sun and the dirt of the South. I was born in Texas and stayed there until I was twelve. And the first dances that I ever made were what I like to call blood memories. My roots are also in the gospel churches of the South where I grew up: holy blues, peons to joy, anthems to the human spirit" ("Celebrating"). In sum, Ailey's dance was a form of blood memory and a way to express the truth and spirit of African American experience.

2. Here is the original quote from Stéphanie Singer, which I have translated in the body of my text: "De toute façon il a vécu, aux États-Unis à une période où il ne faisait pas bon être noir, ça l'a effectivement énormément marqué, je crois. Et par rapport à l'éducation donc qu'il nous a donnée, ç'a été un petit peu

une sorte de vengeance: 'j'ai pas pu faire ça, mais mes filles, elles, elles le feront'" (Felin).

3. In contrast to Singer, Miles Davis once said the French were easily impressed and didn't have the same standards as American musicians and fans; he believed it was harder to learn and innovate in France than at home (Davis and Troupe 218). The journalist and music historian James Lincoln Collier has also discounted this narrative that Europeans had greater intellectual knowledge, appreciation, and support for jazz. His perspective is particularly prominent in his response to Eric Hobsbawm's review of his book. See Hobsbawm "All That Jazz."

4. Some jazz scholars, such as James Lincoln Collier, strongly contest the assumption that jazz is "black music." For example, Collier writes, "How are we to deal with the fact that for decades the core audience for jazz has been middle-class white males? And finally, is it really possible to assign ethnicity to a cultural artifact like a poem, a dance, a musical performance? . . . Can Italian opera be performed only by Italians, English literature written only by the English, Chinese painting criticized only by the Chinese?" (185, 224). Jazz scholar Scott DeVeaux also has an instructive and thorough response in his review of Collier's book. For more information see Collier 183–224.

5. The unit was nicknamed "The Harlem Hellfighters," and it played a prominent role in introducing jazz to France between the world wars. For more information see Shack.

6. Here, Jeffrey Jackson summarizes Delaunay's report captured by Bill Gottlieb in *Down Beat* (Gottlieb 12).

7. As a gypsy musician Django Reinhardt should have been one of the most reviled and harshly oppressed in the Nazi Occupation, explains Gerard Régnier. He adds that Reinhardt played up the Frenchness of his sound and performances, as a core member of the Quintette of the Hot Club of France; plus, his German-sounding surname, *Reinhardt*, did not hurt. He also kept moving and therefore escaped rules that impeded the residence of foreign professionals. Officials didn't follow the letter of the law, enamored as they were by his unique sound; so Reinhardt was able to tour throughout France without danger (Régnier 180–81). For more on Django Reinhardt and jazz in France during the occupation see Régnier; Tournès; and Zwerin, *La tristesse*.

8. But there were exceptions. Trumpeter Arthur Briggs and singer Valaida Snow, having relinquished their chances to return to the United States before the war, were later caught and interned in prisoner camps—though Snow's story has been challenged (Shack 113–14). Mario A. Charles explains: "The facts surrounding Valaida's life for 1940 and the two succeeding years are incomplete. She may have been incarcerated, under the 'Racial Infamy Law to Protect Blood' for being non-Aryan. . . . Or she may have been accused of theft and drug possession which may have ended in her deportation to Germany where she may have spent the next two years in the Wester-Faengle concentration camp. Both of these scenarios are possible" (5). For more information see M. Charles.

9. Musicologist Andy Fry is keen to note that Panassié was stringent, authoritarian, and purist in his identification of "real jazz"; however, he was at times supportive of French musicians, avoiding comparison with American musicians and believing that not *all* white musicians were inferior to African American musicians (Fry 106).

10. Mary Lewis writes that the prompt for the universalist policy in the creation of the French republic came out after the Great War and in attempts to support increased immigration. So it seems ironic that the application of the policy would challenge assimilation and acculturation of immigrants in France. See Lewis.

11. With lyrics by Géo Koger and Henri Varna and music by Vincent Scotto, the song was originally performed in the 1930 Casino de Paris revue, *Paris qui remue*, and Columbia recorded it in the fall of that year (Jules-Rosette, *Josephine Baker* 62–63). Occurring at the same time as the Colonial exposition, Baker's performance emphasized an exotic persona and gratitude for colonial ties to France; she later changed the lyrics from "J'ai deux amours, mon pays et Paris" (I have two loves, my country and Paris) to "J'ai deux amours, mon pays c'est Paris" (I have two loves, my country is Paris) (63). The shift from *et* to *c'est* firmly announced France as her permanent home. The song would become her signature song; its repeated performance critiqued her earlier life and the continued civil rights inequities in the United States. For more information on Baker's political actions and performances during the Cold War see Dudziak, "Josephine."

12. In "Black France: Myth or Reality? Problems of Identity and Identification," Elisabeth Mudimbe-Boyi parses out significations, challenges, and opportunities that come from the use of the term *black*. She explores discourse on race from the era of the Harlem Renaissance to its political uses in present-day France.

1. PERFORMING JAZZ DIASPORA WITH SIDNEY BECHET

1. In 1941 Bechet used the new technology of overdubbing to create a multitrack rendition of "Sheik of Araby." He played six instruments and explained his process to George Hoeffer: "I started by playing The Sheik on piano, and played the drums while listening to the piano. I meant to play all the rhythm instruments, but got all mixed up and grabbed my soprano, then the bass, then the tenor saxophone, and finally finished up with the clarinet" (quoted in Hoeffer).

2. Though many works have recounted Bechet's temperament and could support this claim, I refer here primarily to Bechet's autobiography and my interviews with Claude Luter. See Bechet, *Treat*; and Luter (personal interviews).

3. Though Bechet was among the first musicians to spread jazz to Europe, the Original Dixieland Band had toured earlier in England in 1917, and James Reese Europe's Hellfighters band introduced jazz to France in 1918.

4. In his first trip to England, in 1919, Bechet experienced his highest and lowest moments. He played for the Prince of Wales and was arrested by the British police. He was subsequently tried and sentenced to fourteen days in prison for sexual assault against a British dancer; he was deported thereafter. So his trouble, jail time, and deportation in France was not a new occurrence but emblematic of Bechet's tempestuous nature, as well as the potentially violent underground culture of shady dealings that could accompany jazz whether in New Orleans, London, or Paris.

5. The body text includes my translation of the following passage: "Il ne manquait jamais une occasion de rappeler ses origines françaises, ni de parler créole avec Albert Nicholas. Et il insistait sur la prononciation de son nom 'à la française'" (Delaunay, *Delaunay's* 188).

6. Jazz historian Ted Gioia clarifies that *Storyville* was not a term used by jazz musicians in New Orleans, nor did early jazz musicians play in brothels as jazz lore and histories proclaim; instead, most musicians like Pops Foster simply called the area "The District" (29). For more information about jazz in The District see Barker; Charters; and Hersch.

7. The original text reads: "Noirs et blancs, vedettes chevronnées et amateurs boutonneux, se relaient une semaine durant sur scène de bonne réputation."

8. For more about the French jazz debates between New Orleans–style jazz and bebop see chapter 2.

9. Hodeir's original quote follows: "Le grand triomphateur du Festival fut sans nul doute Sidney Bechet, dont chaque apparition sur scène a suscité une énorme vague l'enthousiasme" (7).

10. Gilroy claims Amiri Baraka's phrase "the changing same" and redefines it as representative of black cultural products that change while simultaneously carrying some of their sameness in order to be recognizable (Gilroy 101). Baraka first coined "changing same" in an eponymous essay in 1966, arguing that while different popular music genres originated by African Americans may have differed in sound and form, they shared some inherent characteristics, such as the blues impulse ("The Changing" 188). For continued consideration of the "changing same" see chapter 5.

11. Underground clubs, called *caves* in French, took the form of small, narrow, and arched rooms and were habitually filled with floor-to-ceiling smoke, vibrant music, and bouts of dancing and debates on life and war.

12. It is important to note that *-ette* is the feminine version of *-et*. Thus, this pronunciation may also promote a diminution or feminization of Bechet's persona.

13. "J'appréciais sa simplicité. Il avait un côté homme de la terre, à la fois rude et madré." Delaunay attributes several things to Bechet's success, from his youthful and energized performance to his gift at musical interpretation.

14. Though I discuss only Césaire here, Léopold Sédar Senghor, from Senegal, and Léon Gontran Damas, from French Guyana, helped shape *négritude* and have different variations on its meaning. The three studied together in

Paris and cofounded the literary journal *L'étudiant noir* in 1935, which became a critical site for articulating ideas of global black consciousness and unity.

15. Bryan Wagner introduces an insightful analysis of *Bras coupé* in his book, *Disturbing the Peace: Black Culture and the Police Power after Slavery*.

16. Sidney Bechet's All-Star Band included Sidney Bechet, Kenny Clarke, Bill Coleman, Charlie Lewis, Frank "Big Boy" Goodie, and Pierre Michelot.

2. JAZZ AT HOME IN FRANCE

1. The title and epigraph of this chapter are my translation of the following text: "Le jazz est-il chez lui en France? En tout cas, il ya toujours été à l'aise, comme si notre pays constituait sa seconde patrie, ou il venait se refugier parfois, mais aussi se développer et s'épanouir. La France est l'un des lieux du jazz à part entière où se sont produits de nombreux événements marquants pour l'histoire de cette musique: pendant l'entre-deux guerres, autour de Pigalle, après la Libération a Saint-Germain-des-Prés . . ." (Amar).

2. TSF JAZZ does not have live shows with DJs for twenty-four hours a day. The station often features taped shows that are replayed on different days.

3. Even before *Jazz Hot, Jazz-tango-dancing* was first published in 1928 and *La revue du jazz* soon followed in 1929. Both were among the earliest jazz-centered magazines in the world.

4. Django Reinhardt, though readily claimed by the French, was actually born in Belgium but really lived a gypsy lifestyle; he lived and traveled in a caravan and laid no claim to a particular home.

5. For extensive studies of Panassié's criticism see Lane, "Jazz as Habitus"; Perchard, "Tradition"; Perchard, "Hugues"; and Perchard, *After Django*.

6. "Mr. LEONARD FEATHER s'est toujours étonné de ce que les revues de Jazz européennes—notamment Jazz-Hot—consacrent la presque totalité de leur pages aux musiciens noirs. C'est pourquoi il a entrepris de nous défaire de ce 'préjugé' en un article bien caractéristique de la critique américaine" (Derens 8).

7. An excerpt from Delaunay's letter to his HCF secretary, Daidy Davis-Boyer, follows: "Ma vieille branche, ne dis plus que tu t'occupes du HCF, ne parle plus du HCF: le HCF n'existe plus (souligné deux fois), pas plus que Jazz Hot et le reste. Il suffit d'une mauvaise langue ou d'une imprudence de quelque personne pour qu'on te coffre et qu'on bazarde tout ce qu'il y a rue Chaptal. Il ne faut absolument pas qu'il y ait un seul disque, en dehors des quelques disques Swing à toi, car à cette époque, je veux dire à l'heure actuelle, nous sommes gouvernés par des vendus et par des traitres (souligné), des types que rien n'embarrasse pour s'attribuer des places. . . . Je te répète encore des recommandations au sujet des voisins, concierge et relations diverses: méfie-toi!" (Régnier 7).

8. Jeffrey Jackson notes that in revising his *Hot Discography* Delaunay drew on a community of European jazz fans that had extended itself greatly during the war, from Sweden, Switzerland, and even a German officer, all trying to document and keep the history of European jazz recording alive (194).

9. "De 1945 à 1950 naît un nouveau monde, dans les caves de Saint-Germain, où se mêlent avec bonheur la doctrine existentialiste de Sartre et les musiques révolutionnaires venues d'Amérique.... Figure emblématique de Saint-Germain-des-Prés, le clarinettiste de jazz Claude Luter lance le style Nouvelle-Orleans en France dès l'après-guerre, et il est resté l'âme de cette musique" (Zammarchi, *Claude* 18, jacket cover).

10. Note that Lorientais was actually in the neighboring fifth arrondissement, the Latin Quarter, housed at 5 Rue des Carmes.

11. "Le jazz de la Libération était plutôt symphonique. Celui de Claude Luter superclassique. Les cultes des origines. Plus New Orleans que les claques de la Nouvelle-Orléans eux-mêmes" (Ténot, *Frankly* 48).

12. For more details about this concert and Sidney Bechet see chapter 1.

13. In his book on jazz in Japan, Taylor Atkins discusses how the authenticity debates among critics and the journey to a unique Japanese sound traveled similar territory. He locates a hierarchy in the relationship between Japanese and American jazzophiles that is pertinent to this case and others of musical assimilation:

> There is much cultural capital, racial pride, and national prestige invested in jazz: the music has been an integral part of the image that the United States projects of itself abroad, and of the image that African Americans in particular promote among themselves and others in their legitimate efforts to redress erasure of their contributions from history.... Jazz has thus become an integral element in a self-aggrandizing narrative of American ingenuity, dynamism, and creativity. This means that throughout its history Japan's jazz community has had to locate itself in an aesthetic hierarchy that explicitly reflects and reinforces asymmetries of power and cultural prestige in the Japan-U.S. relationship by placing American jazz artists at the apex as "innovators" and non-Americans at the bottom as "imitators." (Atkins, *Blue Nippon* 11)

Atkins deftly identifies the national and racial stakes for the United States over the globalization of jazz. Though discussing jazz in Japan, his insights about the perceived threats of globalized jazz to the United States are representative beyond Japan's shores. Holding close to jazz as American, and specifically African American, helps retain some nativist power in the global image of jazz.

14. After the 1947 schism between him and Hugues Panassié, Delaunay had limited financial backing and official support. Panassié would continue as president of the official Hot Club of France, while Delaunay remained in charge of the magazine *Jazz Hot* and gained support from multiple Hot Clubs across France. However, the negotiations and knowledge of gigs and musicians would put Delaunay over the top.

15. "Les anciens musiciens qui avaient été célèbres pendant la guerre nous détestaient. Ils se figuraient qu'ils seraient toujours les rois, et nous les jeunes, nous étions des dérangeurs. Ils trouvaient que nous faisions de la mauvaise

musique alors que nous nous inspirions des orchestres de la Nouvelle-Orléans comme celui de King Oliver" (Luter, *Jazz Hot* 7).

16. For more accounts and photos on the impact of Armstrong and the festival on the Lorientais see Zammarchi, *Claude* 66–68.

17. "L'orchestre de Luter fut tel que nous le connaissons: brutal, primitive, 'chauffant' plus qu'il ne 'swingue.' . . . Mais quand donc les Lorientais se décideront-ils à travailler leur justesse?" (Hodeir, *Jazz Hot* 7–9).

18. Below is the actual French text: "La 'bebop' provoque à la Salle Pleyel une nouvelle bataille d'Hernani" (Schiller 3). In *Le Figaro* the following appears: "La guerre des jazz . . . avec Dizzy Gillespie offensive de 'bebop'" ("La guerre des jazz").

19. "Cette musique, comme chacun sait, est la 'musique des noirs' parce que ceux-ci non seulement l'ont créée, mais de tous temps s'en sont montrés les maîtres incontestés. . . . On peut dire en toute impartialité, je crois, que parmi ces groups de musiciens qui dans tous les pays ont recueilli le message des noirs, les Français, dès l'avant-guerre, avaient pris une place plus qu'honorable avec des individualités comme Django Reinhardt, Stéphane Grappelly, André Ekyan, Philippe Brun ou Alix Combelle" (Delaunay, "Faut" 18).

20. For more details on this seminal festival see chapter 1.

21. Note that though much of the same personnel recorded *Au chat qui pêche* (1958) at the eponymous venue, Urtreger did not appear on Byrd's standout live album.

22. The sessions were remastered and sold under the title *Sidney Bechet and Martial Solal Featuring Kenny Clarke* by Vogue in 2005. In addition to Bechet, Clarke, and Solal, Lloyd Thompson on bass, Al Levitt on drums, and Pierre Michelot contribute to the sessions.

3. INEZ CAVANAUGH

1. Valerie Mercer explains that there weren't many African American artists in Paris after the war, as they were not eligible for the G.I. Bill, and the trip to Paris was expensive (41). Mercer's statement applies more to artists than musicians though, because there were several women who performed and lived in Paris after World War II, including Hazel Scott, Mary Lou Williams, and Eartha Kitt. However, most did not stay long. For more details see Mercer 41.

2. In 2010 Karen Chilton wrote a thorough biography of Hazel Scott: *The Pioneering Journey of a Jazz Pianist, from Café Society to Hollywood to HUAC.* Chilton follows Scott's early success in film and song, her lifetime of political activism and its contribution to her decline, her prompt for migration to Europe in 1956, and her return to the United States more than a decade later.

3. At the beginning of U.S. involvement in World War II all Americans were requested to return to the States. Several African American jazz musicians were among those who stayed in Paris, including trumpeters Arthur Briggs and

Harry Cooper and composer Maceo Jefferson. Soon after the Nazi occupation of Paris, Hitler forbade African American performers to play in mixed establishments. What had been mixed clubs were taken over by all-white crowds, and jazz soon disappeared from the playlists. For more on this development see Shack 113–14.

4. Bill Moody and Larry Ross have written extensive accounts documenting a range of African American musicians who settled in Paris, as well as throughout Europe. For more information see Moody; and Ross.

5. Robeson's biographer Martin Duberman (341–42) makes the strong case that this was a life-changing misquote.

6. For detailed accounts on the AFM and Musician's Union bans see "The Music Union" in Frith; and DeVeaux, "Bebop."

7. For more details on the 1949 concert see chapter 1.

8. For more information on his experiences in Paris see Hughes and Rampersad 140–205.

9. Paris is divided by the River Seine. Most residents make distinctions between the Left Bank (below the river) and the Right Bank (above). After World War I, Montmartre (on the Right Bank) became the new reigning cultural hot spot. Saint-Germain-des-Prés and the Latin Quarter are located on the Left Bank, and they became the hot spots of jazz and African American activity after World War II.

10. Donald Clarke has noted that Timmes Club did not have an apostrophe on the signage and was actually advertised with the typo. See D. Clarke, *Donald Clarke*.

11. Donald Clarke and Fradley Garner's work on the life of Timme Rosenkrantz has undergirded my research on Inez Cavanaugh; for more on her known recordings see Rosenkrantz, *Harlem* 111n6.

4. BORIS VIAN AND JAMES BALDWIN IN PARIS

1. Ralph Ellison recognized the influence of African American culture in the United States, claiming that without African American contributions American culture "would be lacking in the sudden turns, shocks and swift changes of pace (all jazz-shaped) that serve to remind us that the world is ever unexplored" (Ellison, *Living* ix).

2. The original text from *Jazz Hot*, June 1952, follows: "Je précise que les trois grands moments de mon existence furent les concerts d'Ellington en 1938, les concerts de Dizzy en 1948 (c'est bien 48?) et Ella en 1952" (Vian, "Revue" 17).

3. Vian's reviews and radio broadcasts have been collected in a number of works. For more information see Vian, *Jazz*; Vian and Rameil, *Chroniques*; Vian and Rameil, *Autres*; and Vian and Zwerin.

4. The Prix Goncourt is one of the highest French literary awards for up-and-coming writers.

5. There is some great scholarship on the import of music on Baldwin's work; see, e.g., Kun; Borshuk; Sherard; and Werner.

6. Notably, Murray wrote the passage quoted here in a critique of Baldwin's "Everybody's Protest Novel."

7. *Zazou* was a term given to young existentialists who engaged in music and philosophical debate on the Left Bank. They were often characterized as young, excitable nonconformists. The zazous were also heavily linked with the antiwar populace—especially those against World War II and the conflict with Algeria (Shack xviii, 119–23).

5. KENNY CLARKE'S JOURNEY BETWEEN "BLACK" AND "UNIVERSAL" MUSIC

1. For more on African American soldiers returning to Paris after the war see chapter 3.

2. For more information on the postwar rise in lynching see Appel; and Robinson 131–34.

3. The following is the original French passage that Monson translates: "Il peut jouer du jazz formidablement s'il le veut, mais il n'aime pas ça. Ce qu'il aime c'est Bach et Chopin. C'est fou ce que j'ai pu m'ennuyer dans le M.J.Q. Je voulais jouer du jazz et il n'y avait moyen avec ces maudits arrangements. Alors je suis parti" (Monson, *Freedom Sounds* 349n80).

4. See chapter 2 for details about the schism between Hot Club of France fans who supported New Orleans–style jazz and those who advocated modern bebop, as well as for an account of the overall French reaction to the 1948 concert and its impact.

5. The participants of Gillespie's seventeen-piece big band were Benny Bailey, Dave Burns, Elmon Wright, Lammar Wright (tp), Dizzy Gillespie (tp, vo), Ted Kelly, Bill Shepherd (tb), John Brown, Howard Johnson (as), Joe Gales, Big Nick Nicholas (ts), Cecil Payne (bars), John Lewis (p), Al McKibbon (b), Kenny Clarke (d), Chano Pozo (cga), and Kenny Pancho Hagood (vo). For the full discography see "Dizzy Gillespie Discography."

6. For more about primitivism see Lemke; and Martin. For primitivism in relation to France see Blake; and Archer-Straw.

7. For more on the interaction between these key African American figures and African intellectuals see Kesteloot; Edwards, *The Practice*; Fabre, *From Harlem*; V.Y. Mudimbe; and Jules-Rosette, *Black Paris*.

8. The body text is my translation of the following quotation: "En France, il contribua à élever le niveau de nos musiciens. Mieux, on peut affirmer qu'on ne savait pas jouer de la batterie avant son arrivé. Qui écoute le jazz français d'autrefois est frappé par la gentille médiocrité des sections rythmiques" (Ténot, "Frankly" 35).

9. Though biographer Mike Hennessey lists the trio as including Clarke, Powell, and Michelot, I've run across multiple accounts that replace Michelot with Oscar Pettiford as the third member. So it is possible that Pettiford also participated in the trio. Additionally René Urtreger often switched on the piano with Bud Powell in Clarke's house band.

10. For more details on this collaboration with Sidney Bechet see chapter 1.

11. In *Making Jazz French* Jeffrey Jackson discusses the first institution of the quota in 1930s Paris as an attempt by French musicians to benefit from the economic boom that jazz prompted:

> When many of the most famous American musicians visited Paris, they were treated with great fanfare by a growing number of jazz aficionados. But at a moment of economic crisis, foreigners were often as much a threat to French musicians' material interests as they were a boon to their musical fascination. [Stéphane] Mougin and others did propose schemes to restrict and exclude American musicians, and their words did sometimes sound like those of the more xenophobic nationalists of the era who stirred up feelings against foreigners. . . . But they did not hope to exclude jazz from France altogether. Instead, they continued to welcome this music so that they could perform it themselves and reap the financial rewards of its popularity. (152)

12. Appropriation debates such as those between Keil and Baraka were not new in the 1960s. I discuss these figures particularly because of the focus on the mid-1960s era in the chapter. However, there are earlier examples that are relevant and specific to Paris: in French writer and activist Nancy Cunard's 1934 book *Negro: An Anthology*, the American-born composer George Antheil described the musical racial integration and the threat it first posed according to his observations from living and performing among white American poets, artists, and musicians residing in interwar Paris: "The American Negroes advanced upon musical Paris, took command, reigned for a time, and then disappeared leaving everywhere gigantic mulatto patches; musicians particularly seemed to have turned at least to octoroons. . . . Every time a white composer was caught consorting with Negro music he was promptly run off and musically lynched; after a vigorous year of campaigning Europe sat back and told itself that Negro music was no more" (Antheil 216).

Antheil describes the early fascination and horror concerning jazz, but he also notes the progression in dissemination and opinion. By the interwar period, he argues that many of the successful European compositions became racially hybrid under the influence of jazz on their work. Antheil attempts to give agency and power back to African American musicians by presenting jazz as a music that makes hybrid all that comes into its frame rather than white Europeans absorbing and making jazz their own: "The Negro is *not* absorbed, but absorbs. . . . Music will no longer be all the white keys of the piano, but will have keys of ebony as well" (217). His perspective forwarded assimilation as inevitable. In the end, Antheil advocated African American artistry and saw assimilation as a commendation that would much more signify their musical contributions rather than hide them. Note that the interwar period of publication is important here since, as I've argued, French jazz musicianship had not yet threatened to compete with or overtake opportunities for African Americans in Paris. The French level of play did not yet meet the French jazz public's expectations of authentic jazz.

CODA

1. "Call and response" is a technique characteristic of many musical forms originating in African American performance; in this technique, a musical phrase is rendered and space is left afterward for a response. A prime example is the song "Salt Peanuts," wherein the band plays the motif and quickly follows by shouting out, "Salt Peanuts, Salt Peanuts." The cutting session is also a tried-and-true component of learning and performing for jazz musicians. Cutting sessions are challenges, in which performers are given quick moments to perform and show their chops, often with a brief moment to solo. If they can't hold their weight, they are literally cut down or cut out of participation and their reputation takes a hit.

2. Perhaps the distance between these different ethnic communities and experiences shifts depending on age and generation. Many of the musicians I interviewed were middle-aged or elderly and had lived in Paris for ten years or more. More recently, I have met musicians in their twenties and thirties who live in communities with French of African descent and who commingle more. One example is Toli Nameless, a Jamaican/African American jazz bassist who has lived in Paris since 2008. Her founding of the Black Girls Rock! program in Paris bridges the distance between African Americans, white French, French of African descent, and other ethnicities.

Works Cited

Ake, David. *Jazz Cultures*. Berkeley: U of California P, 2002.

———. *Jazz Matters: Sound, Place, and Time Since Bebop*. Berkeley: U of California P, 2010.

Alsop, Kenneth. "Obituary." *Daily Mail* May 15, 1959: n.p.

"Along the Rue Bechet." *Time* Sept. 20, 1954: 83–84.

Amar, Yvan, narr. "Le jazz en France." *Euphonia*. Radio France. July 7, 1997. Radio.

Angelou, Maya. *Singin' and Swingin' and Gettin' Merry like Christmas*. New York: Random House, 1976.

Ansermet, Ernest. "Sur un orchestra nègre." 1919. *Écrits sur la musique*. Ed. Ernest Ansermet. Neuchâtel: Baconnière, 1971. 171–78.

Antheil, George. "The Negro on the Spiral, or a Method of Negro Music." 1934. *Negro: An Anthology*. Ed. Nancy Cunard and Hugh Ford. New York: Ungar, 1970. 214–19.

Appel, Dora. *Imagery of Lynching: Black Men, White Women, and the Mob*. New Brunswick, NJ: Rutgers UP, 2004.

Appiah, Anthony. *Cosmopolitanism: Ethics in a World of Strangers*. New York: Norton, 2006.

"Après la congrès." *Présence Africaine* Dec. 11, 1956: 3–4.

Archer-Straw, Petrine. *Negrophilia: Avant-Garde Paris and Black Culture in the 1920s*. New York: Thames, 2000.

Armstrong, Louis. "La vie en rose." *All-Time Greatest Hits*. MCA, 1994. CD.

Arnaud, Noël. *Les vies parallèles de Boris Vian*. Paris: Le livre de poche, 1998.

Atkins, Taylor. *Blue Nippon: Authenticating Jazz in Japan*. Durham, NC: Duke UP, 2001.

———, ed. *Jazz Planet*. Jackson: UP of Mississippi, 2003.

Badger, Reid. *A Life in Ragtime: A Biography of James Reese Europe*. New York: Oxford UP, 1995.

Baker, Josephine, and Jo Bouillon. *Josephine*. Trans. Mariana Fitzpatrick. New York: Harper, 1976.

Baldwin, James. *Amen Corner: A Play*. 1954. New York: Vintage, 1998.

———. *Another Country*. 1962. New York: Penguin, 2011.

———. *Collected Essays*. New York: Penguin, 1998.

———. *Conversations with James Baldwin*. Ed. Fred L. Standley and Louis H. Pratt. Jackson: UP of Mississippi, 1989.

———. *The Devil Finds Work*. Baldwin, *Collected Essays* 477–576.

———. *Go Tell It on the Mountain*. 1953. New York: Vintage, 2013.

———. *Nobody Knows My Name*. Baldwin, *Collected Essays* 137–290.

———. *No Name in the Street*. Baldwin, *Collected Essays* 349–476.

———. *Notes of a Native Son*. Baldwin, *Collected Essays* 5–136.

———. "Sonny's Blues." *James Baldwin: Early Novels and Stories*. New York: Library of America, 1998. 831–64.

Balliet, Whitney. *American Musicians II: Seventy-One Portraits in Jazz*. New York: Oxford UP, 1986.

Baraka, Amiri. *Blues People: Negro Music in White America*. 1963. New York: Harper, 1999.

———. "The Changing Same: R&B and New Black Music." *The Leroi Jones / Amiri Baraka Reader*. Ed. William J. Harris. Berkeley, CA: Thunder's Mouth, 1991. 186–209.

———. *Digging: The Afro-American Soul of American Classical Music*. Berkeley: U of California P, 2009.

Baraka, Amiri, and Amina Baraka. "The Great Music Robbery." *The Music: Reflections on Jazz and Blues*. New York: Morrow, 1987. 328–33.

Barker, Danny. *Buddy Bolden and the Last Days of Storyville*. 1998. Ed. Alyn Shipton. New York: Continuum, 2001.

Bechet, Sidney. "American Rhythm: Klook Klux Klan." *Sidney Bechet and His All-Star Band*. Vogue, 1949. LP.

———. "As-tu le cafard?" *Sidney Bechet et L'Orchestre de Claude Luter*. Vogue, 1952. LP.

———. "Les oignons." *Sidney Bechet et L'Orchestre de Claude Luter*. Vogue, 1949. LP.

———. "Preface." *La musique, c'est ma vie*. Paris: Table ronde, 1977. 1–2.

———. "Sheik of Araby." *Bechet of New Orleans*. RCA Victor, 1965. LP.

———. *Sidney Bechet Intégrale, 1949–1959*. Vogue, n.d. LP.

———. *Treat It Gentle: An Autobiography*. New York: Hill and Wang, 1960.

Bechet, Sidney, and Ferdinand Bonifay. *Petite fleur*. Paris: Editions Warner Chappell, 1958. LP.

Bergmeier, Horst J.P., and Rainer E. Lotz. *Hitler's Airwaves: The Inside Story of Nazi Radio Broadcasting and Propaganda Swing*. New Haven, CT: Yale UP, 1997.

Berliner, Brett. *Ambivalent Desire: The Exotic Black Other in Jazz-Age France*. Amherst: U of Massachusetts P, 2002.

Berliner, Paul. *Thinking in Jazz: The Infinite Art of Improvisation*. Chicago: U of Chicago P, 1994.

Bernard, Catherine. "Confluence: Harlem Renaissance, Modernism, and Negritude: Paris in the 1920s–1930s." Buffalo, *Explorations in the City of Light* 21–27.

Béthune, Christian. *Sidney Bechet.* Marseille: Edition Parenthèses, 1997.

Bhabha, Homi. *The Location of Culture.* New York: Routledge, 1994.

Blake, Jody. *Le tumulte noir: Modernist Art and Popular Entertainment in Jazz-Age Paris, 1900–1930.* University Park: Pennsylvania State UP, 1999.

Blesh, Rudi. *Shining Trumpets.* 2nd ed. New York: Knopf, 1958.

Braggs, Rashida. "Between African American and European: Kenny Clarke's Musical Migrations." *African and Black Diaspora: An International Journal* 4.2 (July 2011): 201–11.

———. "Sidney Bechet: The Hybrid Ambassador." Jazz & Anthropology Seminar. École des hautes études en sciences sociales, Paris, France, Dec. 8, 2005. Lecture.

Broschke-Davis, Ursula. *Paris without Regret: James Baldwin, Kenny Clarke, Chester Himes, and Donald Byrd.* Iowa City: U of Iowa P, 1986.

Brown, Tony. "Where It All Began." 1968. *National Jazz Archive.* National Jazz Archive, n.d. Web. Jan. 12, 2014.

Buerkle, Jack V., and Danny Barker. *Bourbon Street Black: The New Orleans Black Jazzmen.* London: Oxford UP, 1973.

Buffalo, Audreen, ed. *Explorations in the City of Light: African-American Artists in Paris, 1945–1965.* New York: Studio Museum in Harlem, 1996.

Büttner, Armin, et al. *Don Redman's 1946 European Tour.* WordPress.com, n.d. Web. Jan. 14, 2014.

Cahn, Ashley. "After Hours: New York's Jazz Joints through the Ages." *Jazz Times* Sept. 2006: n.p. Web. Feb. 27, 2014.

Campbell, James. *Exiled in Paris: Richard Wright, James Baldwin, Samuel Beckett, and Others on the Left Bank.* New York: Scribner, 1995.

Carson, Lee. "Penny-Wise Paris." *Flair* April 1950: 106–7.

Cavanaugh, Inez. Letter to Mary Lou Williams. Feb. 10, 1947. Box 7, Folders 17–19. Ms. Mary Lou Williams Collection. Series 3. Subsection 3B, Institute of Jazz Studies, Rutgers University, Newark, NJ. July 26, 2004.

———. Letter to Timme Rosenkrantz. May 1949. Personal collection of Bente Arendup, Klampenborg/Copenhagen, Denmark. Nov. 19, 2005.

———. Letter to Timme Rosenkrantz. June 2, 1949. Personal collection of Bente Arendup, Klampenborg/Copenhagen, Denmark. Nov. 19, 2005.

———. Notebook Cover. February 10, 1947. Series 5. Box 1, Folders 12. Ms. Mary Lou Williams Collection. Institute of Jazz Studies, Rutgers University, Newark, NJ. July 26, 2004.

"Celebrating 'Revelations' at 50." Alvin Ailey American Dance Theater. Dir. Judy Kinberg. YouTube, Dec. 8, 2010. Web. March 16, 2015.

Césaire, Aimé. *Le cahier d'un retour aux pays natal / Return to My Native Land.* 1947. Paris: Présence Africaine, 1971.

Chernoff, John Miller. *African Rhythm and African Sensibility.* Chicago: U of Chicago P, 1979.

Charters, Samuel. *A Trumpet around the Corner: The Story of New Orleans Jazz.* Jackson: UP of Mississippi, 2008.

Charles, Mario A. "The Age of a Jazzwoman: Valaida Snow, 1900–1956." *Journal of Negro History* 80.4 (1995): 183–91.

Charles, Ray. "Georgia on My Mind." *The Genius Hits the Road.* New York: ABC-Paramount, 1960. LP.

Charles, Ray, and David Ritz. *Brother Ray: Ray Charles' Own Story.* Cambridge: Da Capo, 2004.

Chilton, John. *Sidney Bechet: The Wizard of Jazz.* New York: Oxford UP, 1987.

Chilton, Karen. *Hazel Scott: The Pioneering Journey of a Jazz Pianist, from Cafe Society to Hollywood to HUAC.* Ann Arbor: U of Michigan P, 2010.

Clarke, Donald. *Billie Holiday: Wishing on the Moon.* Cambridge: Da Capo, 2002.

———. "Cavanaugh, Inez, and Timme Rosenkrantz." *MusicWeb Encyclopaedia of Popular Music.* Music Web, 2005. Web. Oct. 22, 2005.

———. *Donald Clarke's Music Box.* Donald Clarke, n.d. Web. Jan. 14, 2014.

Clarke, Kenny. "Kenny Clarke and His 52nd Street Boys." *Rue Chaptal / 52nd Street Theme.* 1946. Swing, 1947. LP.

Clarke-Boland Big Band. *Faces.* MPS, 1968. LP.

———. *Jazz Is Universal.* Atlantic, 1961. LP.

Collier, James Lincoln. *Jazz: The American Theme Song.* New York: Oxford UP, 1995.

Conquergood, Dwight. "Performance Studies: Interventions and Radical Research." *Drama Review* 46.2 (2002): 145–56.

———. "Rethinking Ethnography: Cultural Politics and Rhetorical Strategies." *Communication Monographs* 58 (1991): 179–94.

Costigliola, Frank. *France and the United States: The Cold Alliance since World War II.* New York: Twayne, 1992.

Crouch, Stanley. "Dancer in the Drum Forest." *Village Voice* Feb. 12, 1985: n.p.

Cruz, Jon. *Culture on the Margins: The Black Spiritual and the Rise of American Cultural Interpretation.* Princeton, NJ: Princeton UP, 1999.

Cugny, Laurent. *Une histoire du jazz en France: Du milieu du XIXe siècle a 1929.* Vol. 1. Paris: Outre mesure, 2014.

Culshaw, Peter. "Martial Solal—The Veteran Jazzman Still Going Strong." *Toronto Telegraph* Nov. 15, 2010. Web. Jan. 14, 2015.

Dahl, Bill. "Artist Biography." *All Music.* All Music, n.d. Web. Nov. 26, 2005.

Dahl, Linda. *Morning Glory: A Biography of Mary Lou Williams.* Berkeley: U of California P, 1999.

Daubresse, J.P. *Claude Luter et les Lorientais: Intégrale, 1947–1949.* Liner Notes. Memories—MECD, 2003. CD-ROM.

Davis, Miles, comp. *Ascenseur pour l'échafaud.* Dir. Louis Malle. Nouvelles éditions de films, 1957. Film.

Davis, Miles, and Quincy Troupe. *Miles: The Autobiography.* New York: Miles Davis, 1989.

Dayal, Samir. "Blackness as Symptom." *Blackening Europe: The African American Presence.* Ed. Heike Raphael-Hernandez. New York: Routledge, 2004. 35–52.

de Crèvecœur, J. Hector St. John. *Letters from an American Farmer.* London: Davies, 1782.

Delaunay, Charles. *Delaunay's Dilemma: De la peinture au jazz.* Mâcon: Editions W, 1985.

———. "Delaunay in Trenches, Writes 'Jazz Not American.'" Trans. Walter E. Schapp. *Down Beat* May 1, 1940: 6, 19.

———. "Faut-il Enterrer le Jazz Français?" *Jazz Hot* (May 1949): 18–19.

———. "Preliminary Rough Draft Outline." April 15, 1984. Interview with Charles Delaunay. Trans. Phil Nurenburg. Box 12. Fonds Delaunay. Bibliothèque nationale de France, François Mitterand, Paris. May 17, 2005.

Derens, Pierre. "Critiques Américains." *Jazz Hot* (Feb. 1952): 8–9.

de Romanet, Jerome. "A Conversation with Melvin Dixon." *Callaloo* 23.1 (2000): 84–109. *Project Muse.* Web. Oct. 23, 2005.

de Toledano, Ralph, ed. *Frontiers of Jazz.* 3rd ed. Gretna, LA: Pelican, 1994.

DeVeaux, Scott. "Bebop and the Recording Industry: The 1942 AFM Recording Ban Reconsidered." Journal of the American Musicological Society 41.1 (Spring 1988): 126–65.

———. *The Birth of Bebop: A Social and Musical History.* Berkeley: U of California P, 1997.

"Dizzy Gillespie Discography." *Jazz Disco.* Jazz Disco, 2001. Web. July 7, 2012.

Drouin, Pierre. "De Sydney à Charlie Parker: Un panorama du jazz concerts en huits concerts." *Le monde* May 8–9, 1949: Les spectacles section.

Duberman, Martin. *Paul Robeson.* New York: New Press, 1989.

Du Bois, W. E. B. *The Souls of Black Folk.* New York: Library of America, 1986.

Dudziak, Mary. *Cold War Civil Rights: Race and the Image of American Democracy.* Princeton, NJ: Princeton UP, 2002.

———. "Josephine Baker, Racial Protest and the Cold War." *Journal of American History* 81.2 (1994): 543–70.

Edwards, Brent Hayes. *The Practice of Diaspora: Literature, Translation, and the Rise of Black Internationalism.* Cambridge, MA: Harvard UP, 2003.

———. "Rendez-vous in Rhythm." *Connect* 1 (Fall 2000): 182–90.

Ehrlich, Blake. "Old Man with a Horn: Sidney Bechet, at Sixty-One, Is America's Most Renowned Expatriate Musician." *Esquire* July 1958: 93–98.

Ellington, Edward Kennedy. *Music Is My Mistress.* New York: Da Capo, 1973.

Ellington, Edward Kennedy, and Stanley Dance. "The Art Is in the Cooking." *Down Beat* June 7, 1962: 13–15.

Ellison, Ralph. "The Blues." *New York Review of Books* Feb. 6, 1964. Web. Dec. 30, 2014.

———. *The Collected Essays of Ralph Ellison.* Ed. John F. Callahan. New York: Random House, 1995.

———. *Invisible Son.* New York: Random House, 1952.

———. *Living with Music: Ralph Ellison's Jazz Writings.* Ed. Robert O'Meally. New York: Modern Library, 2001.

———. *Shadow and Act.* New York: Random House, 1964.

Emerson, Ken. *Doo-dah! Stephen Foster and the Rise of American Popular Culture.* Cambridge, MA: Da Capo, 1998.

"Etymology of Jazz." *A Passion for Jazz.* 2006. Web. May 7, 2006.

"Europe and Travels in the 50s." *Mary Lou Williams: Soul on Soul.* Online Exhibit. Institute of Jazz Studies. Rutgers U, n.d. Web. August 14, 2004.

Evans, Nicholas. *Writing Jazz: Race, Nationalism and Modern Culture in the 1920s.* New York: Garland, 2000.

Fabre, Michel. "The Cultural Milieu in Postwar Paris." Buffalo, *Explorations in the City of Light* 33–37.

———. *From Harlem to Paris: Black American Writers in France, 1840–1980.* Urbana: U of Illinois P, 1991.

Fabre, Michel, and John A. Williams. *Way B(l)ack Then and Now: A Street Guide to African Americans in Paris.* Paris: Cercle d'études Afro-Américaines, 1992.

Fanon, Frantz. *Black Skin, White Masks.* Trans. Charles Lam Markmann. New York: Grove, 1967.

———. *Theories of Race and Racism: A Reader.* Ed. Les Back and John Solomos. Trans. Charles Lam Markmann. New York: Routledge, 2000.

———. *The Wretched of the Earth.* 1961. Trans. Richard Philcox. New York: Grove, 2005.

Feather, Leonard. *Inside Jazz.* 1949. New York: Da Capo, 1977.

Feld, Steven. *Jazz Cosmopolitanism in Accra: Five Musical Years in Ghana.* Durham, NC: Duke UP, 2012.

Felin, Guetty, dir. *Hal Singer: Keep the Music Going.* Perf. Hal Singer, Arlette Singer, Stéphanie and Lina Singer, Steve Potts, Phyl Shapp, and Jessica Care Moore. Yenta Production and Muzzik, France, 1999. Film.

Fernandes, Naresh. *Taj Mahal Foxtrot: The Story of Bombay's Jazz Age.* New Delhi: Roli Books, 2012.

"Festivals Abroad: Europe Will Offer Rich Fare This Summer." *New York Times* May 8, 1949: X7.

Finkelstein, Sidney. *Jazz: A People's Music.* New York: Citadel, 1948.

Flender, Harold. *Paris Blues.* New York: Ballantine, 1957.

Floyd, Samuel. "African Roots of Jazz." Kirchner, *Oxford Companion to Jazz* 7–16.

Foster, Stephen. "Old Folks at Home." New York: Firth, Pond, 1851.

Francis, Terri. "Embodied Fictions, Melancholy Migrations: Josephine Baker's Cinematic Celebrity." *Modern Fiction Studies* 51.4 (2005): 824–45.

Friedman, Susan Stanford. "Migrations, Diasporas, and Borders." *Introduction to Scholarship in Modern Languages and Literatures.* Ed. David Nicholls. New York: MLA, 2007. 260–93.

Frith, Simon, et al. *The History of Live Music in Britain.* Vol. 1. Surrey: Ashgate, 2013.

Fry, Andy. *Paris Blues: African American Music and French Popular Culture, 1920–1960*. Chicago: U of Chicago P, 2014.

———. "Remembrance of Jazz Past: Sidney Bechet in France." *Oxford Handbook of the New Cultural History of Music*. Ed. Jane Fulcher. New York: Oxford UP, 2011. 307–34.

Gabbard, Krin. *Jazz among the Discourses*. Durham, NC: Duke UP, 1995.

———. "Paris Blues: Ellington, Armstrong, and Saying It with Music." *Uptown Conversation: The New Jazz Studies*. Ed. Robert G. O'Meally, Brent Hayes Edwards, and Farah Jasmine Griffin. New York: Columbia UP, 2004. 297–311.

Gac, Scott. "Jazz Strategy: Dizzy, Foreign Policy and Government in 1956." *Americana: The Journal of American Popular Culture* 4.1 (2005): n.p. Web. May 4, 2006.

Gebhardt, Nicholas. *Going for Jazz: Musical Practices and American Ideology*. Chicago: U of Chicago P, 2001.

Gelly, Dave. *Stan Getz: Nobody Else but Me*. San Francisco: Backbeat, 2002.

Gennari, John. *Blowin' Hot and Cool: Jazz and Its Critics*. Chicago: U of Chicago P, 2006.

Gentry, Herbert. "Artful Lives: Travelling in the Tradition." Buffalo, *Explorations in the City of Light* 9.

Gillespie, Dizzy, and Al Fraser. *To Be, or Not—To Bop*. Garden City, NY: Doubleday, 1979.

Gillett, Rachel. "Crossing the Pond: Jazz, Race and Gender in Interwar Paris." Diss. Northeastern University, 2010.

Gilroy, Paul. *The Black Atlantic: Modernity and Double Consciousness*. Cambridge, MA: Harvard UP, 1993.

———. "'. . . To Be Real: The Dissident Forms of Black Expressive Culture." *Let's Get It On: The Politics of Black Performance*. Ed. Catherine Ugwu. Seattle: Bay, 1995. 20–33.

Gioia, Ted. *The History of Jazz*. New York: Oxford UP, 1997.

Glissant, Édouard. *Le discours Antillais*. Paris: Éditions du Seuil, 1981.

———. *Poetics of Relation*. Trans. Betsy Wing. Ann Arbor: U of Michigan P, 1997.

Goffin, Robert. *Aux frontières du jazz*. Paris: Le Sagittaire, 1932.

Goffin, Robert, and Charles Delaunay, eds. *Jazz 47*. Spec. issue of *America: Cahiers France-Amérique-Latinité* 5 (July 1947).

Gondola, Didier. "But I Ain't African, I'm American!" *Blackening Europe: The African American Presence*. Ed. Heike Raphael-Hernandez. New York: Routledge, 2004. 201–15.

Gottlieb, Bill. "Delaunay Escapades with Gestapo Related." *Down Beat* Sept. 9, 1946: 12.

Grandt, Jürgen E. *Kinds of Blue: The Jazz Aesthetic in African American Narrative*. Columbus: Ohio State UP, 2004.

Grier, William, and Price Cobbs. *Black Rage*. Toronto: Bantam, 1968.

Griffin, Farrah Jasmine. *If You Can't Be Free, Be a Mystery: In Search of Billie Holiday*. New York: One World, 2002.

———. "Jazz and American Democracy: A Symposium." *Jazz at Lincoln Center.* Lincoln Center, Dec. 10, 2003. Web. March 12, 2004.

Haggerty, Michael. "Under Paris Skies." *Black Perspective in Music* 13.2 (1985): 195–221.

Hajdu, David. *Lush Life: A Biography of Billy Strayhorn.* New York: Farrar, Straus, Giroux, 1996.

Hamilton, Kimberly, Patrick Simon, and Clara Veniard. "The Challenge of French Diversity." *Migration Policy Institute.* Migration Policy Institute, Nov. 1, 2004. Web. Jan. 14, 2015.

"Harlem in Montmartre." *Thirteen.* Dir. Dante James. WNET.org, New York. August 26, 2009. Television.

Harper, Douglas. *Online Etymology Dictionary.* Online Etymology Dictionary, Nov. 2001. Web. May 4, 2006.

Harris, Jerome. "Jazz on the Global Stage." *The African Diaspora: A Musical Perspective.* Ed. Ingrid Monson. New York: Routledge, 2003. 101–36.

Harsløf, Olav. "For Europeans Only." *Tango del Norte: Festschrift für Walter Baumgartner.* Ed. Cornelia Krueger and Frithjof Strauß. Greifswald: Universität Greifswald, 2006. 255–71.

Hayman, Ronald. *Sartre: A Life.* New York: Simon and Schuster, 1987.

Healy, Jim. "What's on in London." TamTam Books, July 26, 2001. Web. Sept. 23, 2004.

Heffley, Mike. *Northern Sun, Southern Moon: Europe's Reinvention of Jazz.* New Haven, CT: Yale UP, 2005.

Henderson, Mae. "Josephine Baker and *La Revue Nègre:* From Ethnography to Performance." *Text and Performance Quarterly* 23.2 (2003): 107–33.

Hennessey, Michael. "The Clarke-Boland Big Band. Jazz Internationale." *Down Beat* April 20, 1967: 22–24.

———. *Klook: The Story of Kenny Clarke.* Pittsburgh: U of Pittsburgh P, 1994.

———. *Melody Maker* March 8, 1969: 22.

Hergé. "Basin Street à Paris." Goffin and Delaunay, *Jazz 47* 70–71.

Hersch, Charles. *Subversive Sounds: Race and the Birth of Jazz in New Orleans.* Chicago: U of Chicago P, 2008.

Himes, Geoffrey. "Jacky Terrasson: Souirire [sic] de Français." *Jazz Times.* Jazz Times, May 2003. Web. Jan. 28, 2014.

———. *The Jazz Scene.* New York: Pantheon, 1989.

Hobsbawm, Eric. "All That Jazz: James Lincoln Collier." *New York Review of Books.* The New York Review of Books, March 26, 1987. Web. Nov. 11, 2014.

Hodeir, André. *Jazz: Its Evolution and Essence.* Trans. David Noakes. New York: Grove, 1956.

———. "Le festival 1949." *Jazz Hot* (June 1949): 7–9.

Hoeffer, George. "Sheik of Araby." Liner Notes. Sidney Bechet. *Bechet of New Orleans.* RCA Victor, 1965. LP.

hooks, bell. "Performance Practice as a Site of Opposition." *Let's Get It On: The Politics of Black Performance.* Ed. Catherine Ugwu. Seattle: Bay, 1995. 210–21.

Horricks, Raymond. "Sidney Bechet." *Profiles on Jazz: From Sidney Bechet to John Coltrane.* New Brunswick, NJ: Transaction, 1991. 1–9.

Hughes, Langston. *The Weary Blues.* New York: Knopf, 1926.

Hughes, Langston, and Arnold Rampersad. *The Big Sea: An Autobiography.* 1940. New York: Hill and Wang, 1993.

Hughes, Marveline H. "Soul, Black Women and Food." *Food and Culture: A Reader.* Ed. Carole Counihan and Penny Van Esterik. New York: Psychology, 1997. 272–79.

Irele, Abiola. *The African Experience in Literature and Ideology.* London: Heinemann, 1981.

Jackson, Edgar. "Jazz and Swing." *Gramophone* (July 1950): 29. Web. Feb. 10, 2011.

Jackson, Jeffrey. "Making Jazz French: The Reception of Jazz Music in Paris, 1927–1934." *French Historical Studies* 25.1 (2002): 149–70.

———. *Making Jazz French: Music and Modern Life in Interwar Paris.* Durham, NC: Duke UP, 2003.

Jackson, Shannon. *Lines of Activity: Performance, Historiography, Hull-House Domesticity.* Ann Arbor: U of Michigan P, 2001.

"Jazz à Paris, années 50: La batteur Kenny Clarke." *Black and Blue.* Narr. Alain Gerber. France Culture. Nov. 28, 2003. Radio.

Jewel, Derek. Liner Notes. Clarke-Boland Big Band. *Two Originals.* Verve, 1969. LP.

Johnson, Bruce. "The Jazz Diaspora." *The Cambridge Companion to Jazz.* Ed. Mervyn Cooke and David Horn. New York: Cambridge UP, 2002. 33–54.

Johnson, E. Patrick. *Appropriating Blackness: The Performance and Politics of Authenticity.* Durham, NC: Duke UP, 2003.

Johnson, Jerah. "New Orleans's Congo Square: An Urban Setting for Early Afro-American Culture Formation." *Louisiana History: The Journal of the Louisiana Historical Association* 32.2 (1991): 117–57.

Jones, Andrew. *Yellow Music: Media Culture and Colonial Modernity in the Chinese Jazz Age.* Durham, NC: Duke UP, 2001.

Jones, Max. Interview with Kenny Clarke. *Melody Maker* March 15, 1968: n.p.

Jones, Omi Osun Joni L., and Sharon Bridgforth. *Experiments in a Jazz Aesthetic: Art, Activism, Academia, and the Austin Project.* Austin: U of Texas P, 2010.

Jordan, Matthew F. *Le jazz: Jazz and French Cultural Identity.* Urbana: U of Illinois P, 2010.

Jules-Rosette, Bennetta. *Black Paris: The African Writers' Landscape.* Urbana: U of Illinois P, 2000.

———. *Josephine Baker in Art and Life: The Icon and the Image.* Urbana: U of Illinois P, 2007.

Keaton, Trica. "Arrogant Assimilationism: National Identity Politics and African-Origin Muslim Girls in the Other France." *Anthropology and Education Quarterly* 36.4 (2005): 405–23.

———. "The Muslim Girls and the 'Other France': An Examination of Identity Construction." *Social Identities* 5.1 (1999): 47–64.

Keaton, Trica, T. Denean Sharpley-Whiting, and Tyler Stovall. *Black France / France Noire: The History and Politics of Blackness.* Durham, NC: Duke UP, 2012.

Keil, Charles. *Urban Blues.* 1966. Chicago: U of Chicago P, 2014.

Kelley, Robin D.G. *Africa Speaks, America Answers: Modern Jazz in Revolutionary Times.* Cambridge, MA: Harvard UP, 2012.

———. *Freedom Dreams: The Black Radical Imagination.* Boston: Beacon, 2002.

Kenney, William H., III. "The Assimilation of American Jazz in France, 1917–1940." *American Studies* 25.1 (1984): 5–23.

"Kenny Clarke." *Opus.* France Culture. Sept. 25, 1993. Radio.

Kesteloot, Lilyan. *Black Writers in French: A Literary History of Negritude.* Trans. Ellen Conroy Kennedy. Philadelphia: Temple University Press, 1974.

Kirchner, Bill, ed. *The Oxford Companion to Jazz.* Oxford UP, 2000.

Korall, Burt. "View from the Seine." *Down Beat* Dec. 5, 1963: 16–17.

Kuisel, Richard. *Seducing the French: The Dilemma of Americanization.* Berkeley: U of California P, 1997.

Kun, Josh. "Life According to the Beat." *Audiotopia: Music, Race and America.* Berkeley: U of California P, 2005. 86–112.

"La guerre des jazz." *Figaro* Feb. 22, 1948: n.p.

"La guerre des jazz éclate en France." *Liberation* Feb. 18, 1948: n.p.

Lane, Jeremy. *Jazz and Machine-Age Imperialism: Music, "Race" and Intellectuals in France.* Ann Arbor: U of Michigan P, 2013.

———. "Jazz as Habitus: Discourses of Class and Ethnicity in Hugues Panassié's *Le Jazz Hot* (1934)." *Nottingham French Studies* 44.3 (2005): 40–53.

Lebovics, Herman. *True France: The Wars over Cultural Identity, 1900–1945.* Ithaca, NY: Cornell UP, 1992.

Lee, Susanna. "The Jazz Harmonies of Connection and Disconnection in 'Sonny's Blues.'" *Genre* 37.2 (2004): 285–99.

Leeming, David. *James Baldwin: A Biography.* New York: Knopf, 1994.

Legg, John. Liner Notes. Clarke-Boland Big Band. *Faces.* MPS, 1968. LP.

"Le jazz en Europe." Goffin and Delaunay, *Jazz 47* 54–55.

"Le jazz en France." *Euphonia.* Narr. Yvan Amar. Radio France. July 7, 1997. Radio.

Lemke, Sieglinde. *Primitivist Modernism: Black Culture and the Origins of Transatlantic Modernism.* New York: Oxford UP, 1998.

Lewis, Mary. *The Boundaries of the Republic: Migrant Rights and the Limits of Universalism in France, 1918–1940.* Stanford, CA: Stanford UP, 2007.

Lott, Eric. "Double V, Double-Time: Bebop's Politics of Style." O'Meally, *The Jazz Cadence* 457–68.

Luter, Claude. Interview with Philippe Adler. Radio 83.5 (1985). Radio.

———. "Jazz et parti-pris." *Jazz Hot* (Feb. 1949): 7.

Macey, David. "Adieu foulard. Adieu madras." *Frantz Fanon's "Black Skin, White Masks": New Interdisciplinary Essays.* Ed. Max Silverman. Manchester, UK: Manchester UP, 2005. 12–32.

Major, Clarence. *Juba to Jive: A Dictionary of African American Slang*. New York: Penguin, 1994.

Martin, Wendy. *Prehistories of the Future: The Primitivist Project and the Culture of Modernism*. Ed. Elazar Barkan and Ronald Bush. Stanford, CA: Stanford UP, 1995.

McEnnerney, Dennis. "Frantz Fanon, the Resistance, and the Emergence of Identity Politics." *The Color of Liberty: Histories of Race in France*. Durham, NC: Duke UP, 2003. 259–81.

McKay, George. *Circular Breathing: The Cultural Politics of Jazz in Britain*. Durham, NC: Duke UP, 2005.

McPartland, Marian. "Crowds Jam Paris Jazz Festival." *Down Beat* July 1, 1949: 3.

Mercer, Valerie. "Explorations in the City of Light: African-American Artists in Paris, 1945–1965." Buffalo, *Explorations in the City of Light* 38–44.

Merriam, Alan, and Fradley Garner. "Jazz and American Culture." O'Meally, *The Jazz Cadence* 7–31.

Michelot, Pierre. Liner Notes. Miles Davis. *Ascenseur pour l'échafaud*. Verve, 1958. LP.

Miller, Paul Eduard. "At the Edge of the Clef." 1945. IJS Clippings File 1926–46. II 44. Institute of Jazz Studies, Rutgers University, Newark, NJ. July 27, 2004.

Monson, Ingrid. Introduction to *The African Diaspora: A Musical Perspective*. Ed. Ingrid Monson. New York: Routledge, 2003. 1–19.

———. *Freedom Sounds: Civil Rights Call Out to Jazz and Africa*. New York: Oxford UP, 2007.

———. "Jazz." *African American Music: An Introduction*. New York: Routledge, 2006. 163–89.

———. *Say Something: Jazz Improvisation and Interaction*. Chicago: U of Chicago P, 1996.

Moody, Bill. *The Jazz Exiles*. Reno: U of Nevada P, 1993.

Moore, Celeste Day. "Black like Boris: Boris Vian's Fictions of Identity in Post–World War II Paris." Thesis. Haverford College, 2003. Web. Dec. 13, 2003.

Mudimbe-Boyi, Elisabeth. "Black France: Myth or Reality? Problems of Identity and Identification." *Black France/France Noire: The History and Politics of Blackness*. Durham, NC: Duke UP, 2012. 17–31.

Mudimbe, V.Y., ed., *The Surreptitious Speech: Presence Africaine and the Politics of Otherness, 1947–1987*. Chicago: University of Chicago Press, 1992.

Murray, Albert. *The Omni-Americans: Some Alternatives to the Folklore of White Supremacy*. 1970. New York: Da Capo, 1990.

"Musique nègre." *Circulaire du Hot Club de France* (Jan. 1944): cols. 1–4.

Nettelbeck, Colin. *Dancing with DeBeauvoir: Jazz and the French*. Carlton: Melbourne UP, 2004.

Neupert, Richard. "Introduction." *A History of the French New Wave Cinema*. Madison: U of Wisconsin P, 2002. vi–xxix.

"New Orleans Musician Europe's Top Jazzman." *Toronto Telegraph* Jan. 31, 1958: n.p.

Newton, Francis. *The Jazz Scene.* London: Macgibbon, 1959.

Noirs de France: De 1889 à nos jours. France 5. Wri. Pascal Blanchard. Dir. Juan Gelas. 2012. Film.

"Old Folks at Home." *Center for American Music.* U of Pittsburgh, n.d. Web. August 5, 2010.

O'Meally, Robert. "Introduction: Blues for Huckleberry." *Adventures of Huckleberry Finn.* By Mark Twain. New York: Barnes and Noble Classics, 2008. 1–24. *Jazz Studies Online.* Web. March 23, 2008.

———, ed. *The Jazz Cadence of American Culture.* New York: Columbia UP, 1998.

Owens, Thomas. *Bebop: The Music and Its Players.* New York: Oxford UP, 1995.

Panassié, Hugues. *Le jazz hot.* Paris: Editions R. A. Correa, 1934.

———. *The Real Jazz.* Trans. Anne Sorelle Williams. Westport, CT: Greenwood, 1942.

"Paris Night Life." *Ebony* Nov. 1949: 71–75.

Peabody, Sue, and Tyler Stovall. *The Color of Liberty: Histories of Race in France.* Durham, NC: Duke UP, 2003.

Pells, Richard. *Not like Us: How Europeans Have Loved, Hated, and Transformed American Culture Since World War II.* New York: Basic, 1997.

Perchard, Tom. *After Django: Making Jazz in Postwar France.* Ann Arbor: U of Michigan P, 2015.

———. "Hugues Panassié's Supernatural Swing: Criticism, Politics and the Iconic Jazz Recording." *After Django: Making Jazz in Postwar France.* Ann Arbor: U of Michigan P, 2015. 20–53.

———. "Tradition, Modernity, and the Supernatural Swing: Rereading 'Primitivism' in Hugues Panassié's Writing on Jazz." *Popular Music* 30.1 (2011): 25–45.

Peretti, Burton. *Jazz in American Culture.* Chicago: Dee, 1998.

Piaf, Edith. *La vie en rose.* Columbia Records, 1947. LP.

Playback. n.d. Bechet Artist Profile Folder. 4. Institute of Jazz Studies, Rutgers University, Newark, NJ. July 28, 2004.

Pochonet, Gérard. "Les disques: Vogue, Bechet-Luter." *Jazz Hot* (Jan. 1950): 16.

Porter, Eric. *What Is This Thing Called Jazz? African American Musicians as Artists, Critics, and Activists.* Berkeley: U of California P, 2002.

Prévost, Xavier. "Martial Solal." *Académie du jazz.* Académie du jazz, 2014. Web. Jan. 14, 2015.

The Price of the Ticket. Dir. Karen Thorsen. Perf. James Baldwin. American Masters. PBS Home Video, 1989. DVD.

Proyect, Louis. "Jazz and the Left." *Unrepentant Marxist.* Unrepentant Marxist, Nov. 30, 2005. Web. Feb. 12, 2006.

Ramsey, Guthrie, Jr. *The Amazing Bud Powell: Black Genius, Jazz History, and the Challenge of Bebop.* Berkeley: U of California P, 2013.

————. *Race Music: Black Cultures from Bebop to Hip-Hop.* Berkeley: U of California P, 2003.

Régnier, Gérard. *Jazz et société sous l'Occupation.* Paris: L'Harmattan, 2009.

Robeson, Paul. Speech Made at Paris Peace Conference. April 25, 1949. Trans. W.W. Smith. Box 19. Folder: 1949 Paris Peace Conference. Paul Robeson Collection. Manuscript Division, Moorland-Spingarn Research Center. Howard University, Washington, DC.

Robinson, Cedric. *Black Movements in America.* New York: Psychology, 1997.

Rosenkrantz, Timme. *Harlem Jazz Adventures: A European Baron's Memoir, 1934–1969.* Ed. and trans. Fradley Garner. New York: Scarecrow, 2012.

————. Liner Notes. Inez Cavanaugh with Teddy Wilson. *An Evening at Timme's Club.* Storyville, 1968. LP.

Rosenthal, David. *Hard Bop: Jazz and Black Music, 1955–1965.* New York: Oxford UP, 1993.

Ross, Larry. *African-American Jazz Musicians in the Diaspora.* Lewiston, NY: Mellon, 2003.

Sartre, Jean-Paul. "I Discovered Jazz in America." Trans. Ralph de Toledano. *Saturday Review of Literature* Nov. 29, 1947: 48–49.

————. "Jazz in America." Toledano, *Frontiers of Jazz* 64–66.

Saul, Scott. *Freedom Is, Freedom Ain't: Jazz and the Making of the Sixties.* Cambridge, MA: Harvard UP, 2003.

Saury, Maxime. "Sidney Bechet: Grand homme de jazz." *Jazz Hot* (May 1949): 7, 22.

Schiller, Willy. "La guerre des jazz gagne la France." *France Soir* Feb. 22, 1948: 3.

Shack, William. *Harlem in Montmartre: A Paris Jazz Story between the Great Wars.* Berkeley: U of California P, 2001.

Sherard, Tracy. "Sonny's Bebop: Baldwin's 'Blues Text' as Intracultural Critique." *African American Review* 32.4 (1998): 691–705.

Shipton, Alyn. *Groovin' High: The Life of Dizzy Gillespie.* New York: Oxford UP, 1999.

"Sidney Bechet." *Black and Blue.* Narr. Alain Gerber. France Culture. Sept. 5, 1997. Radio.

The Sidney Bechet Society. "The Recordings of Sidney Bechet." *The Sidney Bechet Society.* Sidney Bechet Society, n.d. Web. July 1, 2010.

Smith, Bessie, and James P. Johnson. *Backwater Blues.* Columbia, 1927. LP.

Smith, William Gardner. "It's Six Years Ago." *Pittsburgh Courier* Sept. 20, 1952: n.p.

————. *A Return to Black America.* Englewood Cliffs, NJ: Prentice-Hall, 1970.

Solal, Martial, and Frank Médioni. *Ma vie sur un tabouret: Autobiographie.* Arles: Actes sud, 2008.

Stanton, John. "The New Expatriates." *Life* August 22, 1949: 75–87.

Stearns, Marshall. *The Story of Jazz.* New York: Oxford UP, 1958.

Stovall, Tyler. *France since the Second World War.* Harlow: Pearson Education, 2002.

———. "Harlem-sur-Seine: Building an African American Diasporic Community in Paris." *Stanford Electronic Humanities Review* 5.2 (1997): n.p. Web. Jan. 14, 2015.

———. *Paris Noir: African Americans in the City of Light.* Boston: Houghton Mifflin, 1996.

———. "Preface to *The Stone Face.*" *Contemporary French and Francophone Studies* 8.3 (2004): 305–27.

Sullivan, Vernon. *J'irai cracher sur vos tombes.* Paris: Éditions du scorpion, 1946.

Taylor, Art. *Musician to Musician Interviews.* New York: Da Capo, 1993.

Taylor, Jeff. "The Early Origins of Jazz." Kirchner, *Oxford Companion to Jazz* 39–52.

Teachout, Terry. "Top Brass." *New York Times* August 3, 1997: n.p. Web. March 15, 2004.

Ténot, Frank. *Frankly Speaking: Chroniques de jazz, 1944–2004.* Paris: Editions Du Layeur, 1999.

———. "Frankly Speaking," *Jazz Magazine* Dec. 1999: 34–35.

Thigpen, Ed. "Kenny Clarke: Jazz Pioneer." *Modern Drummer* 8.2 (Feb. 1984): 16–21.

Thomas, Damion L. "The Showcase African-American: Paul Robeson, Jackie Robinson, and the Politics of Cold War Prosperity and Repression." *Globetrotting: African American Athletes and Cold War Politics.* Champaign: U of Illinois P, 2012. 13–40.

Tournès, Ludovic. *New Orleans sur Seine: Histoire du jazz en France.* Paris: Fayard, 1999.

Turner, Elizabeth Hutton. *Jacob Lawrence: The Migration Series.* Washington, DC: Phillips Collection, 1993.

Tynan, John. "Paris Blues." *Down Beat* Nov. 23,1961: 16.

Vail, Ken. *Bird's Diary: The Life of Charlie Parker, 1945–1955.* Castle Communications, 1996. LP.

Variety staff. "Review: *Paris Blues.*" *Variety* Dec. 31, 1960. Web. Jan. 14, 2015.

Vian, Boris. "50 Years of Jazz." *Reading Jazz.* Ed. David Meltzer. Trans. Christopher Winks. San Francisco: Mercury, 1993.

———. *Chroniques de jazz.* Paris: La Jeune Parque, 1967.

———. *I Spit on Your Graves.* 1946. Trans. Boris Vian. Los Angeles: Tam Tam, 1998.

———. *Jazz in Paris.* Paris: Fayard, 1996.

———. *L'écume des jours: Romans, nouvelles, oeuvres diverses.* Ed. Gilbert Pestureau. Paris: Compofac, 1991.

———. *Le manuel de Saint-Germain-des-Prés.* Paris: Chêne, 1974.

———. "Orgueil et préjuges." May 14–15, 1949. *Autres écrits sur le jazz.* Vol. 1, *Jazz-Hot / Combat.* Ed. Claude Rameil. Paris: Christian Bourgois, 1981.

———. "Revue de press." *Jazz Hot* (June 1952): 17, 20.

Vian, Boris, and Claude Rameil. *Autres écrits sur le jazz.* Paris: Librairie générale française, 1999.

———. *Chroniques de jazz*. Paris: La Jeune Parque, 1967.

Vian, Boris, and Mike Zwerin. *Round about Midnight: The Jazz Writings of Boris Vian*. Trans. Boris Vian. New York: Quartet, 1998.

Vihlen, Elizabeth. "Sounding French: Jazz in Postwar France." Diss. State University of New York at Stony Brook, 2000.

Von Eschen, Penny. *Race against Empire: Black Americans and Anticolonialism, 1937–1957*. Ithaca, NY: Cornell UP, 1997.

———. *Satchmo Blows Up the World: Jazz Ambassadors Play the Cold War*. Cambridge, MA: Harvard UP, 2006.

Wagner, Bryan. *Disturbing the Peace: Black Culture and the Police Power after Slavery*. Cambridge, MA: Harvard UP, 2009.

WALL-E. Dir. Andrew Stanton. Walt Disney Motion Pictures and Pixar Animation Studios, 2008. Film.

Ward, Geoffrey, and Ken Burns. *Jazz: A History of America's Music*. New York: Knopf, 2002.

Werner, Craig. "James Baldwin: Politics and the Gospel Impulse." *Playing the Changes: From Afro-Modernism to the Jazz Impulse*. Champaign: U of Illinois P, 1997. 212–40.

White, Charles. *The Return of the Soldier*. 1946. Pen and ink. Heritage Gallery, Los Angeles.

Wilber, Bob. *Music Was Not Enough*. New York: Oxford UP, 1988.

Wilder, Gary. "Panafricanism and the Republican Political Sphere." *The Color of Liberty: Histories of Race in France*. Durham, NC: Duke UP, 2003. 237–58.

Willett, Ralph. "Boris, Bebop and Blackness." *International Jazz Archives Journal* 1.4 (1996): 75–84.

Winock, Michel. "The Cold War." *The Rise and Fall of Anti-Americanism: A Century of French Perception*. Ed. Denis Lacorne, Jacques Rupnik, and Marie-France Toinet. Trans. Gerald Turner. London: Macmillan, 1990. 67–78.

"'With an Even Hand': Brown v. Board at Fifty." *Library of Congress—Exhibitions*. Library of Congress, Feb. 12, 2006. Web. April 9, 2006.

Wright, Michelle M. "'Alas, Poor Richard!': Transatlantic Baldwin, the Politics of Forgetting, and the Project of Modernity." *James Baldwin Now*. Ed. Dwight A. McBride. New York: New York UP, 1999. 208–32.

Wright, Richard. "I Choose Exile." n.d. MS. 1–3. Box 6, Folder 110. Richard Wright Papers. Yale Collection of American Literature. Beinecke Rare Book and Manuscript Library, Yale University, New Haven, CT. May 11, 2009.

———. Personal letter to Mrs. Shelton. Oct. 9, 1951. TS. Box 10. The Michel Fabre Archive of African American Letters. Special Collections and Archives Division of the Woodruff Library, Emory University, Atlanta, GA. May 4, 2006.

Zammarchi, Fabrice. "An African American in Paris: Sidney Bechet as Classical Composer." *CBMR National Conference for Black Music Research*. New Orleans, Center for Black Music Research: Oct. 1, 1993.

———. *Claude Luter: Saint Germain Dance*. Lausanne: Favre, 2009.

Zwerin, Mike. "Global Jazz: Everything Is Fusing with Everything." *International Herald Tribune.* International Herald Tribune, April 14, 2001: n.p. Web. Nov. 1, 2005.

———. "Jazz in Europe: The Real World Music . . . or the Full Circle." Kirchner, *Oxford Companion to Jazz* 528–57.

———. "Kenny Clarke: Dropping Bombs on Paris." *Culture Kiosque: Jazz Net.* Culture Kiosque, July 2, 1998. Web. May 8, 2009.

———. *La tristesse de Saint Louis: Jazz under the Nazis.* New York: Beech Tree Books, 1987.

———. *Swing under the Nazis: Jazz as a Metaphor for Freedom.* New York: Cooper Square, 2000.

PERSONAL INTERVIEWS

Betsch, John. Nov. 23, 2005.

Chautemps, Jean-Louis. April 3, 2008.

Clarke, Laurent. Dec. 7, 2005.

Few, Bobby. Dec. 6, 2005.

Himidi, Salim. Oct. 23, 2014.

Holloway, Nancy. August 9, 2010.

Howard, Sylvia. April 13, 2008.

Luter, Claude. April 17, 2005; May 3, 2005.

Shepp, Archie. Dec. 3, 2005.

Singer, Hal. Dec. 5, 2005.

Speaks, Almeta. Sept. 24, 2014.

Urtreger, René. March 27, 2008.

Vasseur, Benny. May 3, 2005.

Zwerin, Mike. Nov. 16, 2005.

Index

Page numbers in italics refer to illustrations.